THE BEDFORD SERIES IN HISTORY AND CULTURE

A Traveler from Altruria

by William Dean Howells

Edited with an Introduction by

David W. Levy

University of Oklahoma

D0221987

BEDFORD BOOKS *of* ST. MARTIN'S PRESS

Boston   New York

To Philippa Strum and Melvin Urofsky,
thereby completing — with affection and
admiration — the circle of dedications

For Bedford Books
President and Publisher: Charles H. Christensen
General Manager and Associate Publisher: Joan E. Feinberg
Developmental Editor: Jane Betz
Managing Editor: Elizabeth M. Schaaf
Production Editor: Maureen Murray
Copyeditor: Barbara Sutton
Indexer: Steve Csipke
Text Design: Claire Seng-Niemoeller
Cover Design: Richard Emery Design, Inc.
Cover Art: Courtesy of the BALSAMS Grand Resort Hotel, Dixville Notch, N.H.

Library of Congress Catalog Card Number: 95–83515
Copyright © 1996 by BEDFORD BOOKS *of* St. Martin's Press

Manufactured in the United States of America.

0   9   8   7   6
f   e   d   c   b   a

For information, write: St. Martin's Press, Inc., 175 Fifth Avenue, New York, NY 10010
Editorial Offices: Bedford Books *of* St. Martin's Press, 75 Arlington Street, Boston, MA 02116

ISBN: 0 – 312–11799 – X

Foreword

The Bedford Series in History and Culture is designed so that readers can study the past as historians do.

The historian's first task is finding the evidence. Documents, letters, memoirs, interviews, pictures, movies, novels, or poems can provide facts and clues. Then the historian questions and compares the sources. There is more to do than in a courtroom, for hearsay evidence is welcome, and the historian is usually looking for answers beyond act and motive. Different views of an event may be as important as a single verdict. How a story is told may yield as much information as what it says.

Along the way the historian seeks help from other historians and perhaps from specialists in other disciplines. Finally, it is time to write, to decide on an interpretation and how to arrange the evidence for readers.

Each book in this series contains an important historical document or group of documents, each document a witness from the past and open to interpretation in different ways. The documents are combined with some element of historical narrative — an introduction or a biographical essay, for example — that provides students with an analysis of the primary source material and important background information about the world in which it was produced.

Each book in the series focuses on a specific topic within a specific historical period. Each provides a basis for lively thought and discussion about several aspects of the topic and the historian's role. Each is short enough (and inexpensive enough) to be a reasonable one-week assignment in a college course. Whether as classroom or personal reading, each book in the series provides firsthand experience of the challenge — and fun — of discovering, re-creating, and interpreting the past.

Natalie Zemon Davis
Ernest R. May

Preface

The story told in William Dean Howells's *A Traveler from Altruria* is disarmingly simple. It opens with the arrival of a visitor from a country called Altruria. He enters the closed, middle-class world of a New England resort hotel. From the beginning, he impresses all who encounter him with his openness, likability, honesty, and innocence. But his frank questions and his well-intentioned actions (helping the porter hoist the luggage or leaping up to assist the waitress with her heavy tray) force the hotel guests to explain and, with increasing discomfort, to justify various American beliefs and practices. The stranger lays his penetrating questions before them unrelentingly — but always with obvious sincerity and good will. Patiently at first, but with growing exasperation, the patriotic Americans attempt to interpret and defend a way of life they have always assumed to be the most perfect and enlightened of any ever invented. At one point, the Altrurian is taken from the hotel into the surrounding countryside where he encounters severe poverty, deserted farms, and considerable bitterness on the part of the area's "natives," whom the pampered hotel dwellers had supposed to be perfectly contented. Finally, much against his will, the modest traveler is persuaded to give a lecture on the features of life in his country. He describes a society with very different social and economic arrangements, one built on mutual respect, kindness, and unselfish devotion to the community. The hotel guests, who interrupt the lecture with whispered sarcasm and disbelief, remain unconvinced; but the humble common people, deeply moved by the Altrurian's talk, leave inspired and ennobled.

Among the large number of utopian novels written at the end of the nineteenth century, only this one by Howells and Edward Bellamy's *Looking Backward* attract much notice today. Between these two, Howells's tale should probably be awarded higher marks for characterization, subtlety, puckish irony, and pure literary elegance — though Howells could never match Bellamy's book for sheer popularity or national influence. For students of history, however, Howells's undoubted skill as a novelist — a skill that by 1894 had already made him one of the most widely acclaimed writers in the United States — is less important in considering this remarkable novel than the message that he wished to convey.

Howells wanted his readers to confront some very difficult and troubling questions about their country. This document enables us, as students of the American past, to see how one particularly sensitive and intelligent observer assessed the values and the obsessions and probed, like a surgeon, the inconsistencies, the imperfections, and the injustices of his society. It is inviting to consider, however, whether this book also speaks to us apart from our roles as students of the American past. At a time when so many of our own practices and attitudes seem to bear a striking resemblance to those of the Gilded Age, the traveler from Altruria might once again provoke us to reflect on things we have always taken for granted. No doubt William Dean Howells would be gratified to know that, a full century after his book was published, it still has something to say to thoughtful Americans.

ACKNOWLEDGMENTS

I have accumulated many debts in connection with this project, and it is a great pleasure to acknowledge some of them here. I must begin with my colleague, Norman L. Crockett, who, more than two decades ago, first called Howells's novel to my attention. The Introduction that precedes the text profited enormously from sensitive and intelligent readings by some good friends: Henry McDonald, H. Wayne Morgan, Ronald Schleifer, Robert Shalhope, and Melvin I. Urofsky. Each noticeably improved the final product. In addition, four readers for Bedford Books also made extremely thorough and helpful comments on the introductory essay. They are John W. Crowley, Jackson Lears, David J. Nordloh, and Timothy B. Spears. If these scholars, none of whom I have ever met, happen to read again the pages that follow, they will surely notice many places where I have benefited from their expert suggestions. In addition to their locating such able critics, the highly professional staff at Bedford Books has been a pleasure to work with in every other way as well. I would like to single out especially Niels Aaboe, Jane Betz, and Richard Keaveny, who have been models of support, patience, efficiency, and unfailing good advice. And in the final stages of preparing the manuscript for production, Barbara Sutton and Maureen Murray rendered invaluable service.

David W. Levy

Contents

PART ONE

Introduction:
William Dean Howells
and His America

A NATION TRANSFORMED

When William Dean Howells was born, in March 1837, all of the railroads of the United States combined operated less than fifteen hundred miles of track. By the time he published *A Traveler from Altruria,* only fifty-seven years later, there were more than a thousand railroad *companies,* and together they operated 230,000 miles of track. Howells was born into a rural America whose 15.8 million people averaged nine souls to the square mile; in the year of his birth there were only thirty-seven places in the entire nation that could boast a population of more than ten thousand. Fifty-seven years later, the population had skyrocketed to 68.2 million, averaging around twenty-three to the square mile. Suddenly there were more than 350 places with populations over ten thousand, and thirty of those places claimed more than one hundred thousand residents.[1]

This explosion of rail transport, cities, and population fueled an era of industrial productivity that was unlike anything in the history of the world. The railroads made the nation into one vast marketplace: Raw materials could now be gathered from long distances and converted by

[1] Bureau of the Census, *Historical Statistics of the United States, Colonial Times to 1970* (Washington, D.C.: U.S. Government Printing Office, 1975), 8, 11–12, 731.

new processes into finished products; the finished products could now be loaded onto boxcars and carried cheaply for sale across the continent. The new cities, where these miracles of productivity took place, erupted in energy and size (during the 1880s, more than a hundred American cities had to cope with at least a doubling of their populations). Ambitious men and women flocked to the burgeoning enterprises, many coming from the countryside, many others pouring in from abroad. During the ten years before Howells's birth, around 420,000 immigrants arrived in the United States; well over ten times that number came during the decade preceding the publication of *A Traveler from Altruria.*[2]

These breathtaking changes were only the beginning. Between 1860, when Howells was a twenty-three-year-old Ohio newspaperman hard at work on a campaign biography of Abraham Lincoln, and 1890, when he was a famous novelist, editor, and literary critic, many Americans must have felt that they had witnessed the creation of an entirely different country. The billion dollars that was invested in manufacturing in 1860 had become, by 1890, $6.5 billion. In 1860 the country produced 821,000 tons of pig iron; in 1890, 9.5 million tons. In 1860 the U.S. Patent Office issued 4,778 patents for new inventions; in 1890, more than 26,200. In 1860 the United States was fourth in the world in the value of its manufactures. By 1893 New England alone had a per capita output higher than any nation in the world, and by 1894 America led the world in the value of its manufactured products. Andrew Carnegie, the powerful iron and steel maker who no doubt watched the whole process with special satisfaction, chose a particularly appropriate symbol when he wanted to describe what it looked like: "The old nations of the earth creep on at a snail's pace," he wrote. "The Republic thunders past with the rush of the express."[3] One of the country's leading economists, Edward Atkinson, was unable to mask his enthusiasm: "There has never been in the history of civilization," he proclaimed in 1891, "a period, or a place, or a section of the earth in which science and invention have worked such progress or have created such opportunity for material welfare as in these United States in the period since the end of the Civil War."[4]

[2] Ibid., 105–06.

[3] Andrew Carnegie, *Triumphant Democracy: Fifty Years' March of the Republic* (New York: Scribner, 1886), 1–2.

[4] Quoted in Arthur M. Schlesinger, *The Political and Social Growth of the American People, 1865–1940* (New York: Macmillan, 1941), 42. For the story of the growth of American industry after the Civil War, see Victor S. Clark, *History of Manufactures in the United States* (Washington, D.C.: Carnegie Institute of Washington, 1916–28), vol. 2; Edward C. Kirkland, *Industry Comes of Age: Business, Labor and Public Policy, 1860–1897* (New York: Holt, Rinehart & Winston, 1961); or Thomas C. Cochran and William Miller, *The Age of Enterprise: A Social History of Industrial America* (New York: Macmillan, 1942).

Carnegie and Atkinson were scarcely alone in noticing the country's transformation from an agricultural society to one characterized by an energetic industrial capitalism centered in cities. Americans everywhere — sophisticated intellectuals and owners of small businesses, farm boys who yearned for the excitement of the city and their sisters who dreamt of careers as shop attendants or stenographers, ministers and novelists, inventors and newspaper editors, moral philosophers and former slaves, lawyers, real estate salesmen, eager immigrants — all sensed that some momentous and invigorating change was afoot. Two months after the final installment of *A Traveler from Altruria* appeared in *Cosmopolitan* magazine, the historian Frederick Jackson Turner read a paper at a meeting of fellow historians in Chicago and announced the close of "the first period of American history." His explanation for the great transformation of the nation was the disappearance of the frontier after nearly three centuries when readily available land lured pioneering Americans westward. Other observers offered other reasons, but no one doubted that one sort of America was dying and another was being born. In a little book of 1910 aptly titled *The Old Order Changeth,* the Kansas progressive William Allen White invited his readers to compare the America of the 1830s, the America of William Dean Howells's birth, with the nation as it now stood: "The two — politically, economically, and socially — are almost utterly dissimilar," he noted. "Something has intervened."[5]

MAJORITY REACTION TO ECONOMIC CHANGE

In the closing years of the nineteenth century, the great majority of Americans were convinced that whatever *had* "intervened" was decidedly beneficial. They tended to applaud the changes they saw taking place all around them. In the first place, the country's leading experts in many fields enthusiastically celebrated the tremendous alterations of American life. These prestigious authorities endorsed a set of related economic, social, and political doctrines that they insistently called "progressive" and "natural" — doctrines that tended to promote the growth of business and industry. They included a faith in unrestrained free enterprise, a belief that the struggle between unfettered individuals was desirable even

[5] Frederick Jackson Turner, "The Significance of the Frontier in American History," *Annual Report of the American Historical Association for 1893,* 227; William Allen White, *The Old Order Changeth: A View of American Democracy* (New York: Macmillan, 1910), 3.

if that struggle should result in serious divisions within American society, an assumption that the free marketplace could efficiently correct injustices and bring prosperity, and an abhorrence of government interference with the laws of supply and demand.

The most prominent and highly regarded economists in the United States, for example, reached a remarkable consensus that lasted at least through the mid-1880s. Whether they were connected to well-known colleges and universities or employed in business or government service, these economists agreed, in general, on some important basic precepts. They accepted as natural the premise that human beings were essentially selfish, that they were intent on private gain and the storing up of wealth, and that this trait in them was a part of "human nature." But rather than wringing their hands over human greed, these authorities saw in it the great mechanism of progress: Because each selfish individual wanted money, each sought to perform some needed economic service. The unintended result of this panorama of grasping and scurrying acquisitiveness would be a steadily rising standard of living as energetic citizens went to work in factories or on farms, started businesses or became doctors, lawyers, engineers, schoolteachers, or garbage collectors.

The greatest danger to the steady growth of prosperity, these economists believed, was the well-meaning but inevitably disastrous attempts by the government to "regulate" the free functioning of the economic machinery. There would naturally be many failures and disappointments in the scramble for wealth, but the system of supply and demand, if left entirely alone, was capable of infinitely minute fine-tuning, infinitely delicate adjustments to the needs of society. If a woman could not find work as a teacher in a town that already had enough teachers, it merely indicated that she should either pursue teaching in a place where teachers were scarce or find work in a factory or a shop where society actually needed her labor. When workers in the textile mill or the coal mine were laid off because the market for cloth or coal was sluggish, it merely indicated that society did not need them there at the moment and was therefore unwilling to give them money to stay. Their desire for money would (and should) send them to the bicycle factory, the lumberyard, the countryside, or the wharves — places where their strength and skill were required. Such dislocations did cause genuine hardship for the individual, but the effects of some bureaucrat's trying to soften the harshness of the marketplace by imposing regulations on it would have been even more damaging. Similarly, unscrupulous businessmen who enjoyed monopolies and raised their prices unfairly would quickly and automatically attract into the field honest and energetic competitors who would cut the giants down to size by charging lower prices for the same product.

These orthodox economists — with their confident advocacy of continued industrial expansion through individualism, competitive struggle, and no government interference — controlled economic thought in the years immediately after the Civil War. Richard T. Ely, an economist who later opposed their doctrines, recalled in his autobiography more than half a century later that "if you were held to be unorthodox, it was a terrible indictment." Francis A. Walker, another economist who eventually developed doubts about the prevailing dogmas, remembered that believing in the standard set of economic ideas "was not made the test of economic orthodoxy merely. It was used to decide whether a man were an economist at all."[6]

If the army of economists constituted one important group of defenders of unregulated industrial productivity, a band of social thinkers, sociologists, and political scientists, led by the distinguished professor of sociology at Yale, William Graham Sumner, composed another. Deeply influenced by the teachings of the English thinker Herbert Spencer (who first coined the phrase "survival of the fittest"), they set out to apply to American society the social implications of the theory of evolution presented to the world by the English biologist Charles Darwin in 1859. To Darwin, the history of life was the history of ceaseless struggle and adaptation to the ceaselessly changing environment; those organisms able to adapt successfully triumphed over their unfit competitors and, in the process, moved life in a progressive and beneficial direction. Animals with the largest brains, the keenest eyes, the strongest hind legs, the most acute hearing, the sharpest beaks tended, over the long ages, to win out over those whose biological equipment was inferior; plants that could adapt successfully to changing soil, climate, and terrain crowded out and conquered their unadaptable rivals.

To Spencer and his American followers, the history of *social* life was also a history of ceaseless struggle and adaptation. In that pitiless contest, successful individuals were those who, by intelligence, strength, or skill, bested their less able, less adaptable adversaries. There should be no blinking at the fact that the competition was brutal and ugly, or that many, unable to satisfy the remorseless demands of the environment, fell along the way. But humanity's advance was guaranteed by the vicious compet-

[6] Both quotations are cited in Sidney Fine, *Laissez Faire and the General-Welfare State: A Study of Conflict in American Thought* (Ann Arbor: University of Michigan Press, 1956), 47–48. In general, Fine's book is an excellent place to study the extent to which these ideas dominated American economic thought between 1865 and 1885.

itive struggle; gradually the favorable traits would be engrafted on the human species and the unfavorable ones would disappear as those who carried them went down in life's battle. Here, as in the prevailing economic theory, governmental interference in the contest for survival would be fatal to the hope of progress. Some people, wrote Sumner, "seem to be terrified that distress and misery still remain on earth and promise to remain as long as the vices of human nature remain." These people are frightened of competition because "they think it bears harshly on the weak." What they don't understand is that " 'the strong' and 'the weak' are terms which . . . are equivalent to the industrious and the idle, the frugal and the extravagant." Furthermore, "if we do not like the survival of the fittest, we have only one possible alternative, and that is the survival of the unfittest. The former is the law of civilization; the latter is the law of anti-civilization."[7] By this interpretation, of course, those who had grown wealthy in late-nineteenth-century America could be regarded as the highest type the species had to offer — those who had made the most successful adaptation to the new industrial environment. Not many business leaders were on record as rejecting out of hand this view of things.

The belief that the leaders in the expansion of American commerce and industry were among the noblest and best of the nation's citizens was also furthered by many of the country's most eminent Protestant ministers. To a surprising extent, mainline American religion endorsed the economic holiday after the Civil War and praised the work of those responsible for it. The commonest religious defense of free competition was the traditional notion that success came only to those who labored in accord with God's will — those who worked diligently in their callings, who were honest in their dealings with others, frugal and upright, and who shunned sloth, lust, drunkenness, sinful luxury, and corrupt practices. Episcopal Bishop William Lawrence of Massachusetts thought that "in the long run, it is only to the man of morality that wealth comes. We believe in the harmony of God's Universe. We know that it is only by working along His laws natural and spiritual that we can work with efficiency. Only by working along the lines of right thinking and right living can the secrets and wealth of Nature be revealed. . . . Godliness is in league with riches."[8] Russell Conwell, minister of the largest Baptist church in the country, delivered his famous lecture "Acres of Diamonds"

---

[7] "The Influence of Commercial Crises on Opinions about Economic Doctrines," in Albert G. Keller and Maurice R. Davie, eds., *The Essays of William Graham Sumner* (New Haven: Yale University Press, 1934), 2:56.

[8] William Lawrence, "The Relation of Wealth to Morals," *World's Work* 1 (January 1901): 286–92.

more than six thousand times: "To secure wealth is an honorable ambition, and is one great test of a person's usefulness to others," Conwell told his hearers. "For a man to say 'I do not want money' is to say, 'I do not wish to do any good to my fellowmen.' "[9]

In the last analysis, however, the American public did not prize the new factories, machines, cities, and railroads simply because some economists, professors of sociology, and ministers told them to. The industrial eruption commanded the enthusiasm of most citizens because its pulsating energy was so hypnotizing, its intrinsic excitement and vitality so alluring, its opportunities so seductive. Americans were also persuaded of the truth of two pervasive myths that accompanied the process of industrialization: first, that the new inventions and processes were making the lives of countless men and women better and easier; second, applicable only to males, that any lad with enough ambition, brains, imagination, and character could earn fabulous wealth. There were just enough examples behind these two beliefs to sustain their plausibility. Who could resist the miracle of the electric light bulb, the telephone, the typewriter, store-baked bread, the tin can, and the hundreds of other new things that penetrated common life and promised release from drudgery? And who did not know the thrilling stories of Andrew Carnegie, John D. Rockefeller, Thomas Edison — poor boys who did not remain poor for long in this golden land of opportunity? And if them, why not others?

Taken together, this was a powerful array of arguments and attitudes. Those caught up in the swirling economic activity must have felt little reason for moral hesitancy. The work of their hands, after all, was endorsed by an economic theory that commanded almost universal assent; it was sanctioned by a social science that based itself on the latest revelations of Darwinian biology; it was approved by countless ministers from countless pulpits every Sunday morning. Everywhere one looked one saw impressive evidence of material prosperity and a rising standard of living — at least for the middle classes. Everywhere one looked one saw growth, expansion, energy, ambition. It would later be the mistake of some of the disgruntled to suppose that the leaders of American commerce and industry — the hard factory owner who drove his men, the crafty businessman who indulged in sharp practices, the pitiless banker who foreclosed on people's homes and farms — were every day torn by guilt and shame at what they were doing, every night kept awake by their nagging consciences. Probably the exact opposite was true.

---

[9] Conwell's "Acres of Diamonds" has been reprinted in many versions. See Daniel W. Bjork, *The Victorian Flight: Russell Conwell and the Crisis of American Individualism* (Washington, D.C.: University Press of America, 1978), 41 n. 39.

Morally certain that their efforts were as beneficial to the nation as they were profitable to themselves, they every day plunged boldly ahead and every night slept like babies.

Perhaps no historian captured the mood of late-nineteenth-century America, the America in which William Dean Howells grew to middle age, better than Vernon L. Parrington, who wrote during the 1920s. It was, Parrington declared, "a generation that underneath its crudities and vulgarities was boldly adventurous and creative — a generation in which the democratic freedoms of America, as those freedoms had taken shape during a drab frontier experience, came at last to spontaneous and vivid expression." America was suddenly "a society that for the first time found its opportunities equal to its desires, a youthful society that accounted the world its oyster and wanted no restrictions laid on its will. . . . If it ran to a grotesque individualism — if in its self-confidence it was heedless of the smiles of older societies — it was nevertheless by reason of its uncouthness the most picturesque generation in our history; and for those who love to watch human nature disporting itself with naive abandon, running amuck through all the conventions, no other age provides so fascinating a spectacle."[10]

THE GILDED AGE: MINORITY DOUBTS

And yet amid all of this enthusiasm, some voices of doubt and dissent could be heard by 1890. The reservations sprang from three powerful misgivings: the suspicion (mostly intellectual) that the system was not functioning as smoothly and fairly as the theoretical experts had thought it would; the discomfort (mostly emotional) caused by the enormous and growing gulf between the rich and the poor and by the wretched conditions under which the poor suffered; and the dismay (mostly aesthetic) at the vulgarity and tawdriness of a civilization devoted so wholeheartedly to exalting dog-eat-dog competition and the mindless multiplication of material possessions.

Perhaps the most graphic indication that the system was not functioning as smoothly as the economists promised was the series of economic downturns that punctuated the last three decades of the nineteenth

[10] Vernon L. Parrington, *Main Currents in American Thought: The Beginnings of Critical Realism in America, 1860–1920* (New York: Harcourt Brace, 1930), 10–11.

century. In the mid-1870s and the mid-1880s the nation suffered dramatic drops in production, massive unemployment, and enormous suffering. But those slumps, dreadful as they were, were eclipsed by the depression that started in 1893 and lasted through mid-decade, bringing indescribable hardship to every American community, large and small.[11] From the 1870s through the 1890s, therefore, there were almost as many months of depression as there were of prosperity. The explanations of the orthodox economists — that these things were natural and inevitable, the market's way of solving the problems of overproduction and surplus accumulation, and that nothing could or should be done collectively about it — began to sound a little hollow.

Other things seemed wrong with the confident assurances of the economic experts. As the start-up costs for entering a field that was already dominated by giant corporations rose, the faith that powerful wrongdoers could be brought to heel by ambitious young competitors seemed less realistic. How could a youngster, however ambitious, enter into competition, for example, against an established but unscrupulous railroad corporation that employed a thousand people; owned depots in every city, ten thousand miles of track, dozens of locomotives, and hundreds of boxcars; and had established a solid reputation and political influence? Or how could some potential competitor, discontented with the behavior of a big metropolitan newspaper, raise the capital needed to hire reporters, columnists, proofreaders, photographers, and advertising salesmen or buy the huge presses, establish the distribution system and the billing department, and pay the wire services? As gigantic concerns came to dominate one industry after another, the dream of easy access by any American to meaningful competition receded like a mirage. But what also disappeared was the confidence that powerful evildoers could be brought to bay, their high prices reduced and their immoral practices corrected, by more scrupulous and efficient competitors.

As industry consolidated and depressions struck, moreover, the economists' faith in the ability of workers to glide smoothly from overcrowded industries to ones where they were needed — from the sluggish coal mines to the booming bicycle factories — seemed naive. That faith

[11] For the cold details of the worst economic catastrophe in American history until the 1930s, see Charles Hoffmann, *The Depression of the Nineties: An Economic History* (Westport, Conn.: Greenwood Publishing, 1970). A more human face of the situation is given in Gerald T. White, *The United States and the Problem of Recovery after 1893* (University: University of Alabama Press, 1982).

did not envision large-scale general unemployment and the prospect of hungry men and women crowding desperately at the bicycle plant gates. Nor did the notion that workers could move easily from one sort of labor to another weigh fully enough the kinds of specialized training required for particular kinds of work in a sophisticated industrial society. And with the reduced ability of laborers to drift effortlessly from one calling to another went a reduction of faith in the ability of an unregulated system of free enterprise to perform the delicate tasks of fine-tuning and adjustment — or at least to perform them without causing an unacceptable level of suffering on the part of those who did the work.

Even these assaults on the theories of the orthodox economists did not exhaust the growing list of doubts. How could the system manage the potential for mischief by the great trusts and monopolies? How could the nation protect and conserve its priceless natural resources in an arena where it was everyone for himself and the government powerless to act? In an unregulated economy, who protected the town from the manufacturer who poured poisons into the stream or smoke into the air or chemicals into the meat simply because those were the cheapest ways to "do business"? What happened to a rural economy that produced larger and larger surpluses, driving farm prices down to the point where farmers could not earn enough to meet their costs? Who was responsible for maintaining the safety of workers in the big factories? What defense did a democratic society have against the ability of millionaire businessmen to corrupt the legislative process — buying the laws they wanted, killing the ones they didn't?

In short, by the time Howells began to write *A Traveler from Altruria* a number of heretical economists, social scientists, and other intellectuals were raising challenges to the theoretical underpinnings of the industrial system. But even those who never read the debates of the academics could be deeply touched, and deeply angered, by their own observations of obvious injustice. Up to a point, discrepancies in wealth could be justified by defenders of the new America. They were the natural product, they insisted, of differences in individual ability, imagination, and willingness to toil. Moreover, the differences could serve a useful social purpose if their existence coaxed greater effort from those below. On the other hand, some social critics believed that the huge chasm separating the rich from the poor in late-nineteenth-century America was likelier to be demoralizing than stimulating. They also contended that in a society that prided itself on a rough equality among citizens, the vast divisions in money and power endangered the basic principles of democracy itself.

The rich — often men and women into whose hands legendary sums of money had been suddenly thrust — carried on their sport oblivious to appearances. Stories of the gay masquerade parties that featured costumes worth thousands of dollars, the extravagant banquets and fancy dress balls, the huge mansions and dazzling equipages, the trips to Europe and the art collections were well publicized by journalists and eagerly devoured by the middle and lower classes. Meanwhile, in any big city in the country, one could observe ghastly tenements with ten or twelve people to the room, four- and five-year-old children literally starving to death, wretched immigrant families living in disease spread by filth, lack of fresh water and air, and a meager diet. The stench of garbage that the city rarely collected filled the air, and ragged beggars slept in the doorways. Even before the newspaperman Jacob Riis described the New York City slums in all their unforgettable horror, some sensitive Americans had reason to suspect that there was truth in the socialist slogan that under the American economic system the rich man's dog got the poor child's milk.[12] At some visceral level — and despite all of the abstract theories and the logical rationalizations of the experts — it didn't seem quite right.

Finally, by 1890 there were serious complaints about the quality of the civilization that the new commercial and industrial elites were creating. As early as 1873, the writers Mark Twain and Charles Dudley Warner gave the era a name that has stuck for more than a century now. They called it "the Gilded Age" to denote that its thin coating of cheap glitter could never quite cover the reality of crudity and greed. Once again, it was Vernon Parrington who left the most caustic description of that "picturesque and uncouth generation." The Gilded Age, Parrington thought, was "a world of triumphant and unabashed vulgarity without its like in our history, it was not aware of its plight, but accounted its manners genteel and boasted of ways that were a parody on sober good sense."[13] Parrington's view is no doubt too extreme, for it ignores some notable late-nineteenth-century achievements in art and architecture. Nevertheless, he accurately echoes the complaints of many of the period's upper-middle-class, college-educated professionals — sophisticates who fled to Europe when in need of "real" culture and who shook their heads knowingly but sadly at American barbarism, materialism, and garish ostentation. One of those who looked at American civilization in dismay was William Dean Howells, by 1894 one of the foremost novelists and most influential critics in the country.

---

[12] Jacob Riis, *How the Other Half Lives* (New York: Charles Scribner's Sons, 1890).
[13] Parrington, *Main Currents,* 10.

WILLIAM DEAN HOWELLS:
FROM VILLAGE LIFE TO DISSENT

At one point in *A Traveler from Altruria,* Howells tackles the question of what kind of place is best to live in. While visiting the Camp family in the countryside, Mr. Homos breaks his long silence about his native land. He smiles and says, "I do not think you will find anything so remarkable in our civilization, if you will conceive of it as the outgrowth of the neighborly instinct. In fact, neighborliness is the essence of Altrurianism" (p. 109). By this standard, both the city and the country depicted in the novel are found wanting. The urban socialite, Mrs. Makely, admits that she doesn't even know the people next door. "We live in a large apartment house, some forty families, and I assure you I do not know a soul among them. . . . One day the people on the same landing with us lost one of their children, and I should not have been a whit the wiser if my cook hadn't happened to mention it" (p. 109). When the astonished Altrurian says, "But surely . . . you have friends in the city whom you think of as your neighbors?" the socialite makes a shocking disclosure: "No, I can't say that I have. . . . I have my visiting-list, but I shouldn't think of anybody on *that* as a neighbor" (p. 109). But Reuben Camp, the young farmer, thinks the city might not be so bad: "Well, I thought it was better than living as we do in the country, so far apart that we never see each other, hardly. And it seems to me better than not having any neighbors at all. . . . Folks rust out, living alone. It's human nature to want to get together" (p. 110). The Altrurian has the final word. In the perfect society of Altruria, he tells them, "we have neither city nor country in your sense, and so we are neither so isolated nor so crowded together" (p. 110). Later, in his lecture, he says that Altrurians live mostly in "villages."

Howells knew about villages. He was born on March 1, 1837, in one called Martinsville (now known as Martin's Ferry) in Belmont County, Ohio, across the Ohio river from Wheeling, Virginia (now West Virginia).[14] His father, William Cooper Howells, was a self-educated itinerant printer and editor and a man of decidedly unconventional views — stridently anti-Jacksonian in politics, abolitionist in social philosophy, and a follower of the eighteenth-century mystic Emanuel Swedenborg in religion. He had wandered the Ohio countryside for years before his son's

---

[14] The standard biographies are the two-volume work by Edwin H. Cady, *The Road to Realism: The Early Years, 1837–1885, of William Dean Howells* and *The Realist at War: The Mature Years, 1885–1920, of William Dean Howells* (Syracuse: Syracuse University Press, 1956, 1958), and Kenneth S. Lynn, *William Dean Howells: An American Life* (New York: Harcourt Brace Jovanovich, 1971).

birth, working as a farmer or a house painter whenever his own journalistic enterprises failed and he could find no work on some small-town newspaper. When luck ran out in Martinsville, in the spring of 1840, William Cooper and his wife, Mary Dean Howells, took their two boys to Hamilton, Ohio, a village with a population of fewer than twelve hundred.

Howells's boyhood was far from idyllic. There were times when the family (which eventually grew to ten) suffered severe privation. The future author spent a few years in grammar school but had no chance to go to high school or college. He worked long hours in the family print shop, setting type and folding papers, before he was ten years old. Howells was also frequently haunted by profound and debilitating psychological fears and doubts — grotesque images of ghosts and demons, self-accusations and visions of violent death, vague sexual longings that bordered on neuroses.[15] Despite the afflictions of poverty and the anguish of living in his private mental world, Howells nevertheless looked back on his village life fondly. "I can recur to the time only as a dream of love and loving," he wrote when he was nearly eighty, "and though I came out of it no longer a little child, but a boy struggling tooth and nail for my place among other boys, I must still recur to the ten or eleven years passed in Hamilton as the gladdest of all my years." He could certainly recall "some occasions of grief and shame in that far past" but insisted that they merely interrupted "the long spaces of blissful living."[16] For him the village was a place of boyish companionship, sports, and informal neighborliness. It was also a place for unpretentious, democratic equality. In the little northeastern Ohio town of Jefferson, to which the Howells family moved in the mid-1850s, the popular congressman and famous abolitionist Joshua Giddings could be observed during the summers strolling the dusty streets barefooted or playing baseball with the locals.[17]

From the start Will Howells, like so many other boys who grew up in print shops, longed to be a writer. In an extraordinary display of self-discipline and self-education, he made himself a little "study" at home — a curtain hung from the staircase with a table inside — and spent much of his free time reading voraciously, writing poetry and then prose, learning the rudiments of five foreign languages.[18] His parents recog-

[15] Edwin H. Cady, "The Neuroticism of William Dean Howells," *Publication of the Modern Language Association* 61 (1946): 229–38; John W. Crowley, *The Black Heart's Truth: The Early Career of W. D. Howells* (Chapel Hill: University of North Carolina Press, 1985); and Rodney D. Olsen, *Dancing in Chains: The Youth of William Dean Howells* (New York: New York University Press, 1991).

[16] William Dean Howells, *Years of My Youth* (1916; Bloomington: University of Indiana Press, 1975), 14–15.

[17] Cady, *Road to Realism,* 42.

[18] William Dean Howells, *My Literary Passions* (New York: Harper & Brothers, 1895).

nized a talent in him and encouraged his early efforts; his father secretly sent an early poem to a newspaper in 1852, and from that point onward Howells's vocation was fixed. At nineteen he became a reporter for the *Ohio State Journal;* at twenty-two he published, with a friend, his first book — a collection of poems. In the summer of 1860, Howells wrote a campaign biography of Abraham Lincoln and, as a reward, was named American consul to Venice. While in Italy he married Elinor Mead, an American woman from a prominent New England family whom he had met in Cincinnati — the two remained together affectionately until her death forty-seven years later. At the end of the American Civil War, Howells returned to the United States and went hopefully to work as a writer. His first position was with the prestigious *Nation* in New York City. Then, from 1866 to 1881, he was an assistant editor and then the editor of the *Atlantic Monthly* in Boston, the center of genteel American literary culture. After resigning from the *Atlantic,* he worked for *Century Magazine,* briefly edited the socialistically inclined magazine *Cosmopolitan* in 1891–92, and wrote for *Harper's Monthly* from 1886 almost without interruption until his death in 1920. He moved from Boston to New York City in 1891. And throughout his long and prolific career he poured out novels, poetry, editorials, and literary criticism at a prodigious pace.

During the 1890s, for example, the decade in which he wrote *A Traveler from Altruria,* Howells also produced ten other novels, three novellas, two children's books, four autobiographical volumes, a book of poetry, one of literary sketches and one of literary criticism, twelve plays, some short stories, essays on social topics, and introductions. While doing that, he wrote twenty-seven columns for *Harper's Monthly,* edited *Cosmopolitan* for a year, and for eighteen months composed an "American Letter" for publication in an English periodical. As Kenneth Lynn observes, "Clearly, Howells was not an author who suffered from writing blocks, but a remorselessly efficient literary machine — whose output, furthermore, was highly profitable."[19]

Howells earned a reputation as a practitioner of a style of writing known as "realism." He thought it was important for novelists to tell the truth, to embrace the ordinary and the everyday, to shun the preposterous, the wildly romantic, and implausible. His novels were centered on the social lives of middle-class families, and no American writer was better at portraying social ambitions, family tensions, decorous amusements, and urbane dinnertable banter. He specialized in deflating vulgarity and snobbery and in vindicating the traditional moral principles of late Victor-

[19] Lynn, *William Dean Howells,* 4. For an exhaustive listing of Howells's published works, see William M. Gibson and George W. Arms, *A Bibliography of William Dean Howells* (New York: New York Public Library, 1948).

ian America. As might be expected, therefore, he drew criticism both from remnant romanticists, who found his work pedestrian and trivial, and from the young naturalist writers and their supporters, who found it timid. That he was the foremost literary authority in the United States was widely acknowledged; it was also understood that he was a man of broad tolerance and had a keen eye for young writers of talent, whose careers he encouraged and whose critical acceptance he furthered with wonderful generosity.

By the mid-1880s, the genial Howells was expressing more strenuous doubts about some of his country's social developments, economic arrangements, and cultural standards. Part of this can be attributed, no doubt, to the insistent Quaker-Swedenborgian idealism of his upbringing.[20] Partly it was, by his own acknowledgment, due to his discovery in the mid-1880s of the work of Leo Tolstoy. Tolstoy's novels, thought Howells, were "worth all the other novels ever written."[21] He was also intensely touched by the trial of the Chicago anarchists in the aftermath of the Haymarket riot of 1886. A bomb thrown at an anarchist rally resulted in the deaths of seven policemen; four leaders of the movement were executed in November 1887, despite the absence of the slightest evidence that they had played any role in the actual commission of the crime. Howells was one of the leaders in the fight to save them, circulating a petition, publishing an eloquent plea in the press, assuming a public role with unaccustomed passion and boldness. The tragic conclusion of the affair left him devastated at what he considered "the civic murder" of innocent men.[22]

It was, of course, the dramatic intrusion of the jarring features of urban and industrial life that most bothered Howells. In the end it was American conditions that made him receptive to the reformist influences of his father's and Tolstoy's religion; it was his reading of the new American situation that made him feel social and political injustices with such particular force. By the time he was ready to speak his doubts in *A Traveler from Altruria,* Howells, in his search for a better society, had

[20] See Edwin H. Cady, *Young Howells & John Brown: Episodes in a Radical Education* (Columbus: Ohio State University Press, 1985).

[21] Quoted in Clara M. and Rudolf Kirk, *William Dean Howells* (New York: Twayne Publishers, 1962), 112.

[22] Sender Garlin, *William Dean Howells and the Haymarket Era* (New York: American Institute for Marxist Studies, 1979). For lucid accounts of his steady march toward radicalism in the years before 1894, see Robert L. Hough, *Quiet Rebel: William Dean Howells as Social Commentator* (Lincoln: University of Nebraska Press, 1959); Clara M. Kirk, *W. D. Howells, Traveler from Altruria, 1889–1894* (New Brunswick: Rutgers University Press, 1962); or William R. H. Alexander, *William Dean Howells: The Realist as Humanist* (New York: B. Franklin, 1981).

joined hands with others. He lent his name to the Church of the Carpenter, a Boston mission of the Episcopal church that was founded in 1890 by the reformist minister W. D. P. Bliss in an effort to implement the social teachings of the New Testament. He enlisted in one of the Nationalist Clubs that had been established to discuss the implications and possibilities of the ideas expressed in Edward Bellamy's *Looking Backward.* He considered himself a Christian socialist and was sympathetic to the goals of the Populist party in the early 1890s. In a letter to his friend and fellow novelist Henry James in 1888, Howells acknowledged his turn toward radical solutions to his country's problems: "After fifty years of optimistic content with 'civilization' and its ability to come out all right in the end, I now abhor it, and feel that it is coming out all wrong in the end, unless it bases itself anew on a real equality."[23]

A Traveler from Altruria, the novel in which Howells registered his criticisms of American society and presented his idea for a social order based "on a real equality," began to appear in *Cosmopolitan* in November 1892; the twelfth and final installment was printed in October 1893. Harper and Brothers published the book in May 1894.[24] Edward Bellamy, whose own *Looking Backward* had created such widespread excitement and sympathy for utopian speculation only three years earlier, noticed Howells's book immediately on the publication of the final *Cosmopolitan* installment. "It is surely a most significant sign of the present trend of thought in this country," he wrote, "… that the leading novelist of the times should have turned aside from the conventional types of polite fiction to give his countrymen this drastic arraignment of the way we live now, and this glowing exposition of a nobler, higher, better life which beckons us on."[25]

LITERARY ASPECTS OF
A TRAVELER FROM ALTRURIA

A Traveler from Altruria borrows some of its literary attributes from two well-established categories of fiction. The first is, of course, the utopian novel, a work in which an author presents a conception of what an ideal society would be like. A utopian novel offers its special vision of the perfect society, however, in order to call attention to the social evils and

---

[23] Howells to Henry James, October 10, 1888, in George W. Arms et al., eds., *W. D. Howells, Selected Letters,* vol. 3, *1882–1891* (Boston: Twayne, 1980), 231.

[24] For the publishing history of this work and its sequels, see the splendid Introduction by Clara and Rudolf Kirk to the scholarly edition, *The Altrurian Romances* (Bloomington: Indiana University Press, 1968).

[25] Quoted in Clara M. Kirk, *W. D. Howells,* 35.

economic injustices that bedevil existing arrangements. Utopian novels, therefore, are always combinations of social criticism and the imagination of a better way, and these two sides of the work are inevitably related. Alert readers should be able to predict some of the features of the better society by noting what especially bothers the author in his or her description of the existing one. Thoughtful and perceptive readers will also be able to deduce from the writer's vision of the ideal world what he or she found so annoying in the present. For reasons that must be obvious in view of the enormous social upheavals of the period, during the last thirty-five years of the nineteenth century many American novelists and social thinkers were attracted to this literary form. One scholar has been able to locate close to a hundred utopian works written between 1865 and 1900, the great majority of them produced after Edward Bellamy's enormous success with *Looking Backward*.[26]

The second type of fiction that *A Traveler from Altruria* exemplifies is the so-called mysterious-stranger story. These stories are characterized by the dramatic entrance into an isolated and stable environment of some outsider, usually a male. This outsider, who is often enigmatic and whose origins and background are typically shrouded in mystery, unsettles the stability of the place and changes things forever. The inhabitants, the insiders, don't know precisely what to make of this outsider's intrusion, but they do understand that nothing can ever be quite the same. After the stranger dies, disappears, or moves on, they are left to ponder the experience. Perhaps the American story of this type that is most familiar to modern readers is Ken Kesey's *One Flew over the Cuckoo's Nest* (1962), but there are dozens of other examples by authors ranging from Hawthorne, Melville, Twain, James, and Crane in the nineteenth century to Hemingway, Steinbeck, Faulkner, Albee, Malamud, Oates, Flannery O'Connor, and Robert Penn Warren in the twentieth.[27] Films in which dangerous (or likable) aliens from space intrude on peaceful farmhouses and disrupt all the appliances, or some murderous lunatic bursts in on the secluded but unsuspecting campsite, or a gunslinger rides into town and walks boldly into the saloon are other examples of the mysterious-

[26] Robert L. Shurter, *The Utopian Novel in America, 1865–1900* (New York: AMS Press, 1973). See also Kenneth M. Roemer, *The Obsolete Necessity: America in Utopian Writings, 1888–1900* (Kent, Ohio: Kent State University Press, 1976), and Jean Pfaelzer, *The Utopian Novel in America, 1886–1896: The Politics of Form* (Pittsburgh: University of Pittsburgh Press, 1984). For an intelligent and illuminating discussion of Bellamy's work, see Daniel Borus's Introduction to the newest edition of *Looking Backward* (Boston: Bedford Books of St. Martin's Press, 1995).

[27] Roy R. Male, *Enter, Mysterious Stranger: American Cloistral Fiction* (Norman: University of Oklahoma Press, 1979). The author lists more than four dozen examples of this kind of story (pp. 119–21), including Howells's *A Traveler from Altruria*.

stranger story. This form is particularly appropriate, obviously, when an author wishes to emphasize an assault on the safety, but also, as in *A Traveler from Altruria,* on the complacency and self-satisfaction of some community of insiders.

From a literary point of view, therefore, William Dean Howells's artistry can be judged, at least in part, by how well he combines and manipulates the requirements of these two venerable forms of storytelling. But Howells, who was widely regarded as the most accomplished American novelist of his era, and who had already published a great many novels before writing this one, was too inventive and original to be content with working entirely in already established forms. His novel is also notable for some of its other literary ingredients. One of the most interesting is the way in which Howells uses his first-person narrator, Mr. Twelvemough. Most writers use their narrators to convey to the reader the picture of the "reality" they want the reader to accept, and usually we readers are able to "believe" in the truth of the narrator's account. Some writers, however, have experimented with narrators whose accounts we are meant to suspect, whose judgments we are meant to doubt.[28] In this novel we soon learn to distrust Mr. Twelvemough's view of things. He is so obviously bound by a culture that we come to feel is seriously flawed in ways he cannot see; he is so protective of his reputation and so terrified of losing his standing with the other vacationers; and he is so hopelessly confused in his answers to the Altrurian's honest inquiries. While everything we know about the Altrurian's visit we learn from the narrator who is telling us the story, it is a measure of Howells's considerable skill that we end by distrusting and even by mocking our only source of information.

Another mark of Howells's skill as a writer is his talent for characterization. The inhabitants of the hotel, whose composure and complacency the mysterious Mr. Homos is destined to challenge, are much more than the wooden figures that less talented authors might have presented. Howells gives each of them a distinct personality, a distinct set of traits and attitudes. Thus we learn to expect unblinking honesty and brutal frankness from the banker, empty-headed sociability from Mrs. Makely, pathetic weakness and timidity from the minister, doctrinaire and snide heartlessness from the professor, and so on. Howells intertwines the

---

[28] The well-known literary critic Wayne C. Booth has written illuminatingly about "the unreliable narrator"; see his *The Rhetoric of Fiction* (Chicago: University of Chicago Press, 1961), chap. 6. Once again, Ken Kesey's *Cuckoo's Nest* provides a good modern example — the story comes to us through Chief Bromden, an inmate in a mental hospital, who is a highly unreliable narrator.

dialogue and the cast of characters so smoothly that the particular sentiments each expresses could come only from him or her. Finally, we should notice the ironic twists that Howells applies to the business and professional men whom the Altrurian engages in conversation. In a novel whose central purpose is to point out the weaknesses of the American system of business, industry, and finance, Howells cleverly makes the banker and the manufacturer the most attractive and admirable of the guests. The professionals — those occupational brothers of William Dean Howells himself — are despicable: The lawyer and the minister are helpless and ineffective, the professor is contemptible, and the novelist that novelist Howells creates is a pretentious and priggish egotist.

MR. HOMOS'S CRITIQUE OF AMERICAN LIFE

Howells divided his novel into two parts. In the first ten chapters he presents, by means of Mr. Homos's searching questions and the hotel guests' inept attempts to answer them, his penetrating critique of American society. These chapters also contain both the excursion into the countryside, where Mr. Homos sees with his own eyes the hardships faced by rural Americans, and the story of the little conspiracy by which Mrs. Makely gets Mr. Homos to give his talk. The novel's last two chapters consist of the traveler's open-air lecture, his description of the glories of Altrurian civilization, interrupted here and there by the sarcastic and skeptical remarks of the hotel guests.

The central thrust of Howells's critique will be obvious to most readers. American civilization, he suggests, has abandoned two of its most praiseworthy founding principles. The first of these principles was the commitment to human equality. "Ah, you have read our Declaration of Independence then?" Mr. Twelvemough asks proudly. "Every Altrurian has read that," replies the traveler. But it quickly emerges that Americans no longer believe in that document's proud proclamation of equality; nor is the falling away to be smoothly glossed over with Mr. Twelvemough's "Well . . . we don't take that in its closest literality" (p. 36). As the conversations between Mr. Homos and his American acquaintances proceed it becomes obvious that modern Americans don't believe in equality at all. None of the hotel guests can recall ever having invited a manual worker to dinner at their homes, the minister is forced to admit that not a single workingman's family worships at his middle-class church, and the socialites regard the notion of the farmers' sons actually dancing with their daughters as abhorrent. The Americans try to explain that all citizens are equal in *political* status, but the Altrurian makes short work of that: "I don't mean that," he says. "I suppose that in America you have learned, as we have in Altruria, that equal political rights are only means to an end, and as an end have no value or reality. I meant the economic status of the workingman, and his social status." No one answers, the narrator suspects, because the truth would appear "uncomfortable or discreditable" (p. 54).

And if modern Americans have rejected the ideal of equality, they have also turned their backs on Christianity, the second of Howells's basic principles. The teachings of Christ, the Altrurian makes clear in many places, are crucial to his own society. "Our civilization is strictly Christian," he tells the lawyer, "and dates back to no earlier period than that of the first Christian commune after Christ" (p. 51). Indeed, Altruria was founded by an evangelist on his way to Britain. The very first words of his lecture are couched in the unmistakable words and imagery of Christian belief. Imagine the traveler's dismay, therefore, when the manufacturer informs him that the first principle of American business is "the good of Number One first, last, and all the time" (p. 63) or the novelist lets him know that "America is a republic where every man is for himself, and you cannot help others as you do at home; it is dangerous — it is ridiculous" (p. 83) or the plain-speaking banker admits that "we are a purely commercial people; money is absolutely to the fore; and business, which is the means of getting the most money, is the American ideal" (p. 122). In the privacy of his room, the narrator entertains bitter thoughts about the Altrurian because "it ought to have been self-evident to him that when a commonwealth of sixty million Americans based itself upon the great principle of self-seeking, self-seeking was the best thing, . . . whatever hardship it seemed to work" (p. 81). Instead of a society grounded on Christian love, mutual help, and solicitude for the poor, Howells shows readers an America based on ruthless competition, a frenzied desire to rise above one's neighbors, and a callous disregard for everything except money.

In 1955 the American historian Richard Hofstadter offered a provocative explanation for the rise of progressive reform at the turn of the century. The traditional, middle-class leaders of American life, Hofstadter contended, were finding themselves elbowed roughly aside by the masters of the new industrial wealth: "The newly rich, the grandiosely or corruptly rich, the masters of great corporations, were bypassing the men of the Mugwump type — the old gentry, the merchants of long standing, the small manufacturers, the established professional men, the civic leaders of an earlier era." Hofstadter emphasized that this displacement was not merely a question of money; it was also a question of prestige and status, of whom other Americans respected and trusted and honored: "They were less important and they knew it."[29] From the realization that they were less important, that they had suffered a loss of status — and that they had lost their standing to a set of men whom they regarded as greedy, corrupt, uneducated, and crude — it was but a small step to the conviction that there was something terribly, terribly wrong with America. From that conviction many members of this old but threatened elite turned to social reform causes. Hofstadter's status-revolution theory has been subjected to spirited criticism by more recent American historians,[30] and few of them now believe that the status displacement suffered by middle-class intellectuals, professionals, and old gentry explains all, or even the most important part, of the rise of progressivism. Nonetheless, many historians think that Hofstadter isolated a real component in the explosion of social reform activity during this period.

In any case, Hofstadter's analysis (although he never mentions Howells's novel) helps to clarify several aspects of *A Traveler from Altruria* and its powerful indictment of American society. Mr. Twelvemough, for example, laments the loss of status by the members of his (and Howells's) class in terms that Hofstadter would understand: "I wish you would explain to Mr. Homos," he begs the banker,

"why, in every public exigency, we instinctively appeal to the business sense of the community, as if it were the fountain of wisdom, probity, and equity. Suppose there were some question of vital interest — I won't say financial, but political, or moral, or social — on which it was necessary to rouse public opinion, what would be the first thing to do? To call a meeting over the signatures of the leading business men; because no other names appeal with such force to the public. You might get up a call signed by all the novelists, artists, ministers, lawyers, and doctors in the state, and it would not have a tithe of the effect, with the people at large, that a call signed by a few leading merchants, bank presidents, railroad men, and trust officers would have. What is the reason?" (pp. 121–22)

[29] Richard Hofstadter, *The Age of Reform: From Bryan to F.D.R.* (New York: Alfred A. Knopf, 1955), chap. 4.

[30] For an intelligent review, see Alan Brinkley, "Richard Hofstadter's *The Age of Reform: A Reconsideration*," *Reviews in American History* 13 (1985): 462–80.

Another indication that Howells might have been speaking largely on behalf of his own class, one that felt itself being superseded by the rich, is in the nature of the social problems that the book emphasizes. There are certainly nodding acknowledgments of the plight of factory workers, coal miners, street beggars, and struggling urban immigrants — and even chance references to African Americans, particularly to their former conditions as slaves. Howells was not blind to the situation of America's most oppressed citizens. But it is not the problems of urban workers or black sharecroppers or homeless immigrant children that engage Howells most directly; it is instead a set of quandaries that touch with special force the lives of the traditional elite. How many coal miners, one wonders, were deeply troubled about whether it was suitable for college students to wait tables or for farm boys to dance with the hotel girls? Howells gives most attention, in other words, to matters that America's professionals and intellectuals found troubling: the absurd wastefulness and emptiness of lives caught up in high society; the extent to which women of leisure dominated American culture, especially influencing tastes in literature; the abysmal ignorance of books on the part of businessmen; the ways in which city dwellers overworked themselves so terribly at the office that they needed some time at a summer resort; whether a college education unfitted a young man for a life in business; how artists and writers were trapped, in America, between their need for money and their desire to create lasting works of art. These matters are not trivial, of course (although coal miners and sharecroppers worried about their next meal might have thought them so), but they are issues peculiar to a sinking old elite.

There are some other indications that the novel was written from the perspective of an upper-middle-class professional. Howells made the decision, for example, to have Mr. Homos's outing take him into the countryside, not to the slums of an industrial city or the killing floor of a slaughterhouse or the back room of a garment sweatshop. In the early 1890s rural poverty and dislocation were widespread and awful enough, but they probably could not compare with the horrifying conditions of disease, stench, filth, and starvation that Mr. Homos would have found in an industrial city had Howells chosen to let him visit one. Is it unfair to speculate that Howells may have shrunk from describing the lives of the urban poor partly because, like other middle-class professionals, he did not "know" them as well as he knew country and village people? Perhaps Howells, like others in his social set, may have felt greater sympathy with native-born Protestant agrarians like Mrs. Camp (whose late husband had fought so bravely in the Civil War) than he felt for the Roman Catholic and Jewish immigrants from southern and eastern Europe who suffered unspeakable tortures in the tenement houses.

Another trait of the group of Americans for whom Howells chiefly spoke was their fear of social chaos of any sort. This is why the great, bloody strikes of the period sent such shivers of fear through them. As members of a class that prided itself on its gentility, learning, and culture, they were without either the physical resources of the upper classes or the capacity for breathtaking violence that they saw in the lower. We should not be surprised, therefore, that one of the Altrurian's strongest assurances was that the barbarous conditions of the present can be transformed into happy ones in the future "without a drop of bloodshed." Even better, within five years after being voted peacefully out of authority, Altruria's old aristocracy appeared to be not only reconciled but actually grateful for the revolution that had stripped away their power. In general, revolutionaries from orders of society lower than that of Howells and his friends were neither so frightened of violence nor so certain that real changes could be brought about without employing some of it.

ALTRURIA:
PREINDUSTRIAL AMERICA

The second part of *A Traveler from Altruria,* the final two chapters wherein Mr. Homos describes his own society's turbulent history and present perfection, also contains important meanings for the historian. To approach them, however, it is critical to understand something about literary utopian schemes in general: No matter how far in the future authors might place their perfect societies or how remote geographically or even how much miraculous new technology they might imagine, these exemplary societies embody at least in part an author's vision, often idealized, of the past.[31] Utopian schemes are brought into being, after all, because an author is dissatisfied with aspects of the present. The troubling aspects of the writer's society can easily be seen as impositions on some happier past, and the writer, with that happier past in mind, constructs (in the twenty-fifth century, on the planet Zondor-14, or on some long-hidden island in the Aegean Sea) a make-believe place where the annoyances are erased. By studying the features of the utopian society, we can begin to see what was bothering the writer about his or her own

[31] This idea is hinted at in Lewis Mumford, "Utopia, the City and the Machine," *Daedalus* 94 (Spring 1965): 271–92.

time and what vision of the past, before these bothersome intrusions appeared, the writer held.

Mr. Homos begins his lecture with a description of the history of Altruria, a history of hardships and injustices so like those belaboring modern America that even the rough and uneducated farmers in the audience see the point: "I wouldn't give a copper to know all you went through beforehand," one of them shouts. "It's too dumn like what we have been through ourselves" (p. 147). In the portrayal of the rise of the Accumulation and its many wrongdoings, therefore, Howells reveals a great deal about his view of America. But even when the lecturer gets finished with the history and starts to outline the principal characteristics of the Altrurian way of life, it is also possible to detect, and perhaps at an even deeper level, what aspects of modern America William Dean Howells found so irritating. "I will tell you, as well as I can, what Altruria is like," the traveler says. But then he adds the significant remark, "But . . . you will have to cast out of your minds all images of civilization with which your experience has filled them" (p. 147).

In many ways, Altruria is America with the products of industrialization — both physical and spiritual — removed. What happens to the railroads (which had developed with such stunning rapidity during Howells's lifetime) is symptomatic: "One of the earliest effects of the Evolution was the disuse of the swift trains which had traversed the continent, night and day, that one man might overreach another, or make haste to undersell his rival, or seize some advantage of him, or plot some profit to his loss" (p. 149). The traveler assures his hearers that nine-tenths of the railroads were abandoned, that the Commonwealth operated the few that were necessary, and that "the rails were stripped from the landscape, which they had bound as with shackles, and the road-beds became highways for the use of kindly neighborhoods, or nature recovered them wholly and hid the memory of their former abuse in grass and flowers and wild vines" (p. 149). The ugly towns that had been called into existence by the railroads ("as Frankenstein was fashioned, from the materials of the charnel" [pp. 149–50]) were allowed to deteriorate. What could be salvaged from them went into the construction of villages.

As with railroads, so also with cities — that other intrusive growth upon a once natural nation: "We had, of course, a great many large cities under the old egoistic conditions, which increased and fattened upon the country, and fed their cancerous life with fresh infusions of its blood" (p. 150). The Altrurians realized that these cities were centers of injustice and that neither the palaces of the millionaires nor the tenements of the "swarming poor" were fit to survive in any enlightened social order. Thus the Altrurians "let them fall to ruin as quickly as they would" (p. 150). The language Howells uses to describe the cities, moreover, is so violent, passionate, and loaded with disgust that one senses, in the village boy from Ohio, a special hatred for these places: "Ravening beasts and poisonous reptiles lurk in those abodes of the riches and the poverty that are no longer known to our life." One of the "less malarial" urban sites is preserved as a cautionary museum and is studied by historians and moralists: "A section of a street is exposed, and you see the foundations of the houses; you see the filthy drains that belched into the common sewers, trapped and retrapped to keep the poison gases down; you see the sewers that rolled their loathsome tides under the streets, amidst a tangle of gas pipes, steam pipes, water pipes, telegraph wires, electric lighting wires, electric motor wires, and grip-cables; all without a plan, but make-shifts, expedients, devices, to repair and evade the fundamental mistake of having any such cities at all" (pp. 150–151).

Howells was no less certain that other unpleasant features of industrial life could be removed with the same decisive speed as railroads and cities. Altrurians, Mr. Homos tells his listeners, no longer feel the need to rush about; such hectic scurrying was the product of the insane obsessions with getting ahead and making money. Altrurians, he says, have stopped producing shoddy, vulgar, cheap, inferior goods and now make only honest, durable, and beautiful ones. They have abolished money. They take pride in their work again. Instead of trying to defeat one another, they now devote themselves to acts of neighborly assistance and civic duty. The debilitating division of labor that condemned men and women to repetitive and mentally crippling tasks, some of them dangerous and difficult, has given way to a general sharing of physical labor, the lessening of narrow specialization, and plenty of leisure for the pursuit of relaxation, sociability, and the arts. Altruria, in short, is the imagined (and romanticized) country of Howells's youth — rural villages, unhurried leisure, unspecialized labor, neighborliness, and pride in workmanship. Whether that America ever really existed is, of course, quite another question, but we may be sure that William Dean Howells was not the only American of the troubled 1890s who looked back with nostalgia at a simpler society and wished for the return of some of its features.[32]

A Traveler from Altruria is, finally, susceptible to another sort of analysis, a psychological reading that by no means contradicts the more obvious political and economic one but that readers may want to have in

---

[32] On the general phenomenon and its various manifestations, see T. J. Jackson Lears, *No Place of Grace: Antimodernism and the Transformation of American Culture, 1880–1920* (New York: Pantheon, 1981).

mind as they begin. Is it possible to see the novel, at least in part, as a thoughtful conversation between two sides of Howells's own personality? On the one hand, Mr. Twelvemough, the popular novelist whose work everyone knows and loves, is presented as the comfortable and quite successful writer of pleasant fiction — a man very like Howells himself, after all. He writes what he thinks will sell and is not overscrupulous about it. Can Mr. Homos, on the other hand, be seen as the nagging voice of conscience, giving expression to the high ideals that Mr. Twelvemough has ignored for so long or even forgotten entirely? This conscience will not be satisfied by the glib rationalizations that excuse lax practice, and that is why Homos makes Twelvemough so nervous. It is the job of consciences, after all, to make their hosts nervous about what they are doing.

One often quoted passage in the novel seems to substantiate the view that Howells, the successful novelist who had done what needed to be done to succeed in the literary world of the gilded age, was confronting in this work the insistent inner voice that called him back to former beliefs and ideals: "I glanced at the Altrurian, sitting attentive and silent, and a sudden misgiving crossed my mind concerning him. Was he really a man, a human entity, a personality like ourselves, or was he merely a sort of spiritual solvent, sent for the moment to precipitate whatever sincerity there was in us, and show us what the truth was concerning our relations to each other? It was a fantastic conception" (p. 104). Whatever one thinks about this way of looking at the novel, this much is true: Just as William Dean Howells was not the only American of his generation who longed for the simpler and better America of his youth, he was probably not the only one either who was deeply troubled and torn personally by the ways that the values and requirements of the new age seemed to rub up against those traditional ideals and more generous impulses that seemed suddenly to have gone out of fashion.

THE FATE AND CONTINUING RELEVANCE OF MR. HOMOS

The hardest part about writing a mysterious-stranger story is to determine what to do with the stranger once you are finished with him. Some authors kill their strangers off; others have them disappear as mysteriously as they originally entered. Howells, of course, causes Mr. Homos to wander off with the hard-working farmers of the countryside, men and women whose simple habits and loving concern for one another he finds so appealing. In this case, however, the stranger keeps reappearing, a clear sign that Howells had considerable trouble letting him go.

Thus as soon as the author finished publishing the twelfth and final installment of *A Traveler from Altruria* in *Cosmopolitan* (October 1893), he embarked on a series of "Letters of an Altrurian Traveler," which ran in the same magazine from November 1893 through September 1894. The format of the later installments is a series of letters written from New York and Chicago by Mr. Homos to his friend Cyril, back in Altruria. In these letters Mr. Homos continues his withering critique of American society — its barbaric economics, its selfish egoism, its tawdry ugliness. While visiting the World's Fair in Chicago, Mr. Homos runs into his old friend the banker from the hotel, and the two carry on their conversation.

In 1907 Howells was ready to publish another Altrurian romance. Called *Through the Eye of the Needle,* this book makes use of some of the Altrurian "Letters" but also involves a love story. While visiting Mrs. Makely and the others in New York City, Mr. Homos meets a generous-hearted and enlightened widow named Eleveth Strange. The two fall in love, but she is at first unwilling to give up her fortune and follow him to Altruria. In the end, love wins out, and she gives up all to become Mrs. Homos. The second part of *Through the Eye of the Needle* consists of Eleveth's enraptured letters back to Mrs. Makely — letters that contrast her happy life in Altruria with conditions in her native America.

Howells died in May 1920, thirteen years after the final appearance of the curious visitor from Altruria. It is natural to ask if his traveler has anything to say to us, three-quarters of a century after his creator's death, exactly a full century after his original appearance in this book. So many recent social observers and critics have compared our own era to the gilded age that it seems an appropriate, if essentially unanswerable, question. Is it not true that in our time, too, we see an almost religious reliance on the free workings of the marketplace? Do we not also observe a social conservatism that has, as two of its manifestations, a reduction of sympathy for the sufferings of the poor and a spirited rejection of the notion that our government has a responsibility to help alleviate their pain? Are the centers of our cities more attractive than they were in the 1890s? Are the products that crowd our stores and our homes more tasteful, more carefully and conscientiously made? Are our citizens less hypnotized by the beckoning and seductive lure of more and more possessions, more and more money? Do the wealthiest and most powerful citizens exercise any less influence on our lawmakers, on our democratic processes, than they did a hundred years ago? Are we noticeably more devoted to civic responsibilities, noticeably less devoted to private and selfish pursuits? And do we not feel occasionally torn between the seductive allure of wealth and comfort and the uneasiness that comes from a suspicion of our extravagance or perhaps from a memory of the higher ideals to which we once aspired? To whatever extent the answers to these questions are troubling, to that extent at least it will perhaps pay us to reconsider the words of that gentle radical William Dean Howells and his inquisitive creation, the traveler from Altruria.

PART TWO

The Document

A Traveler from Altruria
by William Dean Howells

CHAPTER I

I confess that with all my curiosity to meet an Altrurian, I was in no hospitable mood towards the traveler when he finally presented himself, pursuant to the letter of advice sent me by the friend who introduced him. It would be easy enough to take care of him in the hotel; I had merely to engage a room for him, and have the clerk tell him his money was not good if he tried to pay for anything. But I had swung fairly into my story; its people were about me all the time; I dwelt amidst its events and places, and I did not see how I could welcome my guest among them, or abandon them for him. Still, when he actually arrived, and I took his hand as he stepped from the train, I found it less difficult to say that I was glad to see him than I expected. In fact, I was glad, for I could not look upon his face without feeling a glow of kindness for him. I had not the least trouble in identifying him, he was so unlike all the Americans who dismounted from the train with him, and who all looked hot, worried, and anxious. He was a man no longer young, but in what we call the heyday of life, when our own people are so absorbed in making provision for the future that they may be said not to live in the present at all. This Altrurian's whole countenance, and especially his quiet, gentle eyes, expressed a vast contemporaneity, with bounds of leisure removed to the end of time; or, at least, this was the effect of something in them which I am obliged to report in rather fantastic terms. He was above the middle height, and he carried himself vigorously. His face was sun-burnt, or sea-burnt, where it was not bearded; and although I knew from my friend's letter that he was a man of learning and distinction in his own country, I should never have supposed him a person of scholarly life, he was so far from sicklied over with anything like the pale cast of thought. When he took the hand I offered him in my half-hearted welcome he gave it a grasp that decided me to confine our daily greetings to something much less muscular.

"Let me have your bag," I said, as we do when we meet people at the train, and he instantly bestowed a rather heavy valise upon me, with a smile in his benignant eyes, as if it had been the greatest favor. "Have you got any checks?" I asked.

"Yes," he said, in very good English, but with an accent new to me: "I bought two." He gave them to me, and I passed them to our hotel porter, who was waiting there with the baggage cart. Then I proposed that we should walk across the meadow to the house, which is a quarter of a mile or so from the station. We started, but he stopped suddenly and looked back over his shoulder. "Oh, you needn't be troubled about your trunks," I said. "The porter will get them to the house all right. They'll be in your room by the time we get there."

"But he's putting them into the wagon himself," said the Altrurian.

"Yes; he always does that. He's a strong young fellow. He'll manage it. You needn't — " I could not finish saying he need not mind the porter; he was rushing back to the station, and I had the mortification of seeing him take an end of each trunk and help the porter toss it into the wagon; some lighter pieces he put in himself, and he did not stop till all the baggage the train had left was disposed of.

I stood holding his valise, unable to put it down in my embarrassment at this eccentric performance, which had been evident not to me alone, but to all the people who arrived by the train, and all their friends who came from the hotel to meet them. A number of these passed me on the tally-ho coach; and a lady, who had got her husband with her for over Sunday, and was in very good spirits, called gayly down to me: "Your friend seems fond of exercise!"

"Yes," I answered dryly; the sparkling repartee which ought to have come to my help failed to show up. But it was impossible to be vexed with the Altrurian when he returned to me, unruffled by his bout with the baggage, and serenely smiling.

"Do you know," he said, "I fancied that good fellow was ashamed of my helping him. I hope it didn't seem a reflection upon him in any way before your people? I ought to have thought of that."

"I guess we can make it right with him. I dare say he felt more surprised than disgraced. But we must make haste a little now; your train was half an hour late, and we shall not stand so good a chance for supper if we are not there pretty promptly."

"No?" said the Altrurian. "Why?"

"Well," I said, with evasive lightness, "first come, first served, you know. That's human nature."

"Is it?" he returned, and he looked at me as one does who suspects another of joking.

"Well, isn't it?" I retorted; but I hurried to add: "Besides, I want to have time after supper to show you a bit of our landscape. I think you'll enjoy it." I knew he had arrived in Boston that morning by steamer, and I now thought it high time to ask him: "Well, what do you think of America, anyway?" I ought really to have asked him this the moment he stepped from the train.

"Oh," he said, "I'm intensely interested," and I perceived that he spoke with a certain reservation. "As the most advanced country of its time, I've always been very curious to see it."

The last sentence raised my dashed spirits again, and I said confidently: "You must find our system of baggage checks delightful." I said this because it is one of the first things we brag of to foreigners, and I had the habit of it. "By-the-way," I ventured to add, "I suppose you meant to say you *brought* two checks when I asked you for them at the train just now? But you really said you *bought* them."

"Yes," the Altrurian replied, "I gave half a dollar apiece for them at the station in Boston. I saw other people doing it," he explained, noting my surprise. "Isn't it the custom?"

"I'm happy to say it isn't yet, on most of our roads. They were tipping the baggage man, to make sure that he checked their baggage in time, and put it on the train. I had to do that myself when I came up; otherwise it might have got along here some time next day. But the system is perfect."

"The poor man looked quite worn out," said the Altrurian, "and I am glad I gave him something. He seemed to have several hundred pieces of baggage to look after, and he wasn't embarrassed like your porter by my helping him put my trunks into the car. May I confess that the meanness of the station, its insufficient facilities, its shabby waiting-rooms, and its whole crowded and confused appearance gave me rather a bad impression?"

"I know," I had to own, "it's shameful; but you wouldn't have found another station in the city so bad."

"Ah, then," said the Altrurian, "I suppose this particular road is too poor to employ more baggage men, or build new stations; they seemed rather shabby all the way up."

"Well, no," I was obliged to confess, "it's one of the richest roads in the country. The stock stands at about 180. But I'm really afraid we shall be late to supper, if we don't get on," I broke off; though I was not altogether sorry to arrive after the porter had disposed of the baggage. I dreaded another display of active sympathy on the part of my strange companion; I have often felt sorry myself for the porters of hotels, but I have never thought of offering to help them handle the heavy trunks that they manage.

The Altrurian was delighted with the hotel; and in fact it did look extremely pretty with its branching piazzas full of well-dressed people, and its green lawns where the children were playing. I led the way to the room which I had taken for him next my own; it was simply furnished, but it was sweet with matting, fresh linen, and pure white-washed walls. I flung open the window-blinds and let him get a glimpse of the mountains purpling under the sunset, the lake beneath, and the deeply foliaged shores.

"Glorious! glorious!" he sighed.

"Yes," I modestly assented. "We think that's rather fine." He stood tranced before the window, and I thought I had better say, "Well, now I can't give you much time to get the dust of travel off; the dining-room doors close at eight, and we must hurry down."

"I'll be with you in a moment," he said, pulling off his coat.

I waited impatiently at the foot of the stairs, avoiding the question I met on the lips and in the eyes of my acquaintance. The fame of my friend's behavior at the station must have spread through the whole place; and everybody wished to know who he was. I answered simply he was a traveler from Altruria; and in some cases I went farther and explained that the Altrurians were peculiar.

In much less time than it seemed my friend found me; and then I had a little compensation for my suffering in his behalf. I could see that, whatever people said of him, they felt the same mysterious liking at sight of him that I had felt. He had made a little change in his dress, and I perceived that the women thought him not only good-looking, but well-dressed. They followed him with their eyes as we went into the dining-room, and I was rather proud of being with him, as if I somehow shared the credit of his clothes and good looks. The Altrurian himself seemed most struck with the head waiter, who showed us to our places, and while we were waiting for our supper I found a chance to explain that he was a divinity student from one of the fresh-water colleges, and was serving here during his summer vacation. This seemed to interest my friend so much that I went on to tell him that many of the waitresses, whom he saw standing there subject to the order of the guests, were country school-mistresses in the winter.

"Ah, that is as it should be," he said; "that is the kind of thing I expected to meet with in America."

"Yes," I responded, in my flattered national vanity, "if America means anything at all it means the honor of work and the recognition of personal worth everywhere. I hope you are going to make a long stay with us. We like to have travelers visit us who can interpret the spirit of our institutions as well as read their letter. As a rule, Europeans never quite get our point of view. Now a great many of these waitresses are ladies, in the true sense of the word: self-respectful, intelligent, refined, and fit to grace — "

I was interrupted by the noise my friend made in suddenly pushing back his chair and getting to his feet. "What's the matter?" I asked. "You're not ill, I hope?"

But he did not hear me. He had run half down the dining-hall toward the slender young girl who was bringing us our supper. I had ordered rather generously, for my friend had owned to a good appetite, and I was hungry myself with waiting for him, so that the tray the girl carried was piled up with heavy dishes. To my dismay I saw, rather than heard at that distance, the Altrurian enter into a polite controversy with her, and then, as if overcoming all her scruples by sheer strength of will, possess himself of the tray and make off with it toward our table. The poor child followed him, blushing to her hair; the head waiter stood looking helplessly on; the guests, who at that late hour were fortunately few, were simply aghast at the scandal; the Altrurian alone seemed to think his conduct the most natural thing in the world. He put the tray on the side table near us, and in spite of our waitress's protests insisted upon arranging the little bird-bath dishes before our plates. Then at last he sat down, and the girl, flushed and tremulous, left the room, as I could not help suspecting, to have a good cry in the kitchen. She did not come back, and the head waiter, who was perhaps afraid to send another in her place, looked after our few wants himself. He kept a sharp eye on my friend, as if he were not quite sure he was safe, but the Altrurian resumed the conversation with all that lightness of spirits which I noticed in him after he helped the porter with the baggage. I did not think it the moment to take him to task for what he had just done; I was not even sure that it was the part of a host to do so at all, and between the one doubt and the other I left the burden of the talk to him.

"What a charming young creature!" he began. "I never saw anything prettier than the way she had of refusing my help, absolutely without coquetry or affectation of any kind. She is, as you said, a perfect lady, and she graces her work, as I am sure she would grace any exigency of life.

She quite realizes my ideal of an American girl, and I see now what the spirit of your country must be from such an expression of it." I wished to tell him that while a country school-teacher who waits at table in a summer hotel is very much to be respected in her sphere, she is not regarded with that high honor which some other women command among us; but I did not find this very easy, after what I had said of our esteem for labor; and while I was thinking how I could hedge, my friend went on. "I liked England greatly, and I liked the English, but I could not like the theory of their civilization, or the aristocratic structure of their society. It seemed to me iniquitous, for we believe that inequality and iniquity are the same in the last analysis."

At this I found myself able to say: "Yes, there is something terrible, something shocking, in the frank brutality with which Englishmen affirm the essential inequality of men. The affirmation of the essential equality of men was the first point of departure with us when we separated from them."

"I know," said the Altrurian. "How grandly it is expressed in your glorious Declaration."

"Ah, you have read our Declaration of Independence then?"

"Every Altrurian has read that," answered my friend.

"Well," I went on smoothly, and I hoped to render what I was going to say the means of enlightening him without offense concerning the little mistake he had just made with the waitress; "of course we don't take that in its closest literality."

"I don't understand you," he said.

"Why, you know it was rather the political than the social traditions of England that we broke with, in the revolution."

"How is that?" he returned. "Didn't you break with monarchy and nobility, and ranks and classes?"

"Yes, we broke with all those things."

"But I found them a part of the social as well as the political structure in England. You have no kings or nobles here. Have you any ranks or classes?"

"Well, not exactly in the English sense. Our ranks and classes, such as we have, are what I may call voluntary."

"Oh, I understand. I suppose that from time to time certain ones among you feel the need of serving, and ask leave of the commonwealth to subordinate themselves to the rest of the state, and perform all the lowlier offices in it. Such persons must be held in peculiar honor. Is it something like that?"

"Well, no, I can't say it's quite like that. In fact, I think I'd better let you trust to your own observation of our life."

"But I'm sure," said the Altrurian, with a simplicity so fine that it was a long time before I could believe it quite real, "that I shall approach it so much more intelligently with a little instruction from you. You say that your social divisions are voluntary. But do I understand that those who serve among you do not wish to do so?"

"Well, I don't suppose they would serve if they could help it," I replied.

"Surely," said the Altrurian, with a look of horror, "you don't mean that they are slaves."

"Oh, no! oh, no!" I said; "the war put an end to that. We are all free, now, black and white."

"But if they do not wish to serve, and are not held in peculiar honor for serving — "

"I see that my word 'voluntary' has misled you," I put in. "It isn't the word exactly. The divisions among us are rather a process of natural selection. You will see, as you get better acquainted with the workings of our institutions, that there are no arbitrary distinctions here, but the fitness of the work for the man and the man for the work determines the social rank that each one holds."

"Ah, that is fine!" cried the Altrurian with a glow of enthusiasm. "Then I suppose that these intelligent young people who teach school in winter and serve at table in the summer are in a sort of provisional state, waiting for the process of natural selection to determine whether they shall finally be teachers or waiters."

"Yes, it might be stated in some such terms," I assented, though I was not altogether easy in my mind. It seemed to me that I was not quite candid with this most candid spirit. I added, "You know we are a sort of fatalists here in America. We are great believers in the doctrine that it will all come out right in the end."

"Ah, I don't wonder at that," said the Altrurian, "if the process of natural selection works so perfectly among you as you say. But I am afraid I don't understand this matter of your domestic service yet. I believe you said that all honest work is honored in America. Then no social slight attaches to service, I suppose?"

"Well, I can't say that, exactly. The fact is, a certain social slight does attach to service, and that is one reason why I don't quite like to have students wait at table. It won't be pleasant for them to remember it in after life, and it won't be pleasant for their children to remember it."

"Then the slight would descend?"

"I think it would. One wouldn't like to think one's father or mother had been at service."

The Altrurian said nothing for a moment. Then he remarked, "So it seems that while all honest work is honored among you, there are some kinds of honest work that are not honored so much as others."

"Yes."

"Why?"

"Because some occupations are more degrading than others."

"But why?" he persisted, as I thought, a little unreasonably.

"Really," I said, "I think I must leave you to imagine."

"I am afraid I can't," he said sadly. "Then, if domestic service is degrading in your eyes, and people are not willingly servants among you, may I ask why any are servants?"

"It is a question of bread and butter. They are obliged to be."

"That is, they are forced to do work that is hateful and disgraceful to them because they cannot live without?"

"Excuse me," I said, not at all liking this sort of pursuit, and feeling it fair to turn even upon a guest who kept it up. "Isn't it so with you in Altruria?"

"It was so once," he admitted, "but not now. In fact, it is like a waking dream to find one's self in the presence of conditions here that we outlived so long ago."

There was an unconscious superiority in this speech that nettled me, and stung me to retort: "We do not expect to outlive them. We regard them as final, and as indestructibly based in human nature itself."

"Ah," said the Altrurian with a delicate and caressing courtesy, "have I said something offensive?"

"Not at all," I hastened to answer. "It is not surprising that you do not get our point of view exactly. You will by and by, and then, I think, you will see that it is the true one. We have found that the logic of our convictions would not be applied to the problem of domestic service. It is everywhere a very curious and perplexing problem. The simple old solution of the problem was to own your servants; but we found that this was not consistent with the spirit of our free institutions. As soon as it was abandoned the anomaly began. We had outlived the primitive period when the housekeeper worked with her domestics and they were her help, and were called so; and we had begun to have servants to do all the household work, and to call them so. This state of things never seemed right to some of our purest and best people. They fancied, as you seem to have done, that to compel people through their necessities to do your hateful drudgery, and to wound and shame them with a name which every American instinctively resents, was neither republican nor Christian. Some of our thinkers tried to mend matters by making their domestics a part of their families; and in the life of Emerson you'll find an amusing account of his attempt to have his servant eat at the same table with himself and his wife. It wouldn't work. He and his wife could stand it, but the servant couldn't."

I paused, for this was where the laugh ought to have come in. The Altrurian did not laugh, he merely asked: "Why?"

"Well, because the servant knew, if they didn't, that they were a whole world apart in their traditions, and were no more fit to associate than New-Englanders and New-Zealanders. In the mere matter of education — "

"But I thought you said that these young girls who wait at table here were teachers."

"Oh, I beg your pardon; I ought to have explained. By this time it had become impossible, as it now is, to get American girls to take service except on some such unusual terms as we have in a summer hotel; and the domestics were already ignorant foreigners, fit for nothing else. In such a place as this it isn't so bad. It is more as if the girls worked in a shop or a factory. They command their own time, in a measure; their hours are tolerably fixed, and they have each other's society. In a private family they would be subject to order at all times, and they would have no social life. They would be in the family, but not of it. American girls understand this, and so they won't go out to service in the usual way. Even in a summer hotel the relation has its odious aspects. The system of giving fees seems to me degrading to those who have to take them. To offer a student or a teacher a dollar for personal service — it isn't right, or I can't make it so. In fact, the whole thing is rather anomalous to us. The best that you can say of it is that it works, and we don't know what else to do."

"But I don't see yet," said the Altrurian, "just why domestic service is degrading in a country where all kinds of work are honored."

"Well, my dear fellow, I have done my best to explain. As I intimated before, we distinguish; and in the different kinds of labor we distinguish against domestic service. I dare say it is partly because of the loss of independence which it involves. People naturally despise a dependant."

"Why?" asked the Altrurian, with that innocence of his which I was beginning to find rather trying.

"Why?" I retorted. "Because it implies weakness."

"And is weakness considered despicable among you?" he pursued.

"In every community it is despised practically, if not theoretically," I tried to explain. "The great thing that America has done is to offer the race an opportunity: the opportunity for any man to rise above the rest, and to take the highest place, if he is able." I had always been proud of this fact, and I thought I had put it very well, but the Altrurian did not seem much impressed by it.

He said: "I do not see how it differs from any country of the past in that. But perhaps you mean that to rise carries with it an obligation to those below. 'If any is first among you, let him be your servant.' Is it something like that?"

"Well, it is not quite like that," I answered, remembering how very little our self-made men as a class had done for others. "Every one is expected to look out for himself here. I fancy that there would be very little rising if men were expected to rise for the sake of others, in America. How is it with you in Altruria?" I demanded, hoping to get out of a certain discomfort I felt, in that way. "Do your risen men generally devote themselves to the good of the community after they get to the top?"

"There is no rising among us," he said, with what seemed a perception of the harsh spirit of my question; and he paused a moment before he asked in his turn, "How do men rise among you?"

"That would be rather a long story," I replied. "But putting it in the rough, I should say that they rose by their talents, their shrewdness, their ability to seize an advantage and turn it to their own account."

"And is that considered noble?"

"It is considered smart. It is considered at the worst far better than a dead level of equality. Are all men equal in Altruria? Are they all alike gifted or beautiful, or short or tall?"

"No, they are only equal in duties and in rights. But, as you said just now, that is a very long story. Are they equal in nothing here?"

"They are equal in opportunities."

"Ah!" breathed the Altrurian, "I am glad to hear that."

I began to feel a little uneasy, and I was not quite sure that this last assertion of mine would hold water. Everybody but ourselves had now left the dining-room, and I saw the head waiter eying us impatiently. I pushed back my chair and said, "I'm sorry to seem to hurry you, but I should like to show you a very pretty sunset effect we have here before it is too dark. When we get back, I want to introduce you to a few of my friends. Of course, I needn't tell you that there is a good deal of curiosity about you, especially among the ladies."

"Yes, I found that the case in England, largely. It was the women who cared most to meet me. I understand that in America society is managed even more by women than it is in England."

"It's entirely in their hands," I said, with the satisfaction we all feel in the fact. "We have no other leisure class. The richest men among us are generally hard workers; devotion to business is the rule; but as soon as a man reaches the point where he can afford to pay for domestic service, his wife and daughters expect to be released from it to the cultivation of their minds and the enjoyment of social pleasures. It's quite right. That is what makes them so delightful to foreigners. You must have heard their praises chanted in England. The English find our men rather stupid, I believe; but they think our women are charming."

"Yes, I was told that the wives of their nobility were sometimes Americans," said the Altrurian. "The English think that you regard such marriages as a great honor, and that they are very gratifying to your national pride."

"Well, I suppose that is so in a measure," I confessed. "I imagine that it will not be long before the English aristocracy derives as largely from American millionaires as from kings' mistresses. Not," I added virtuously, "that we approve of aristocracy."

"No, I understand that," said the Altrurian. "I shall hope to get your point of view in this matter more distinctly by and by. As yet, I'm a little vague about it."

"I think I can gradually make it clear to you," I returned.

CHAPTER II

We left the hotel, and I began to walk my friend across the meadow toward the lake. I wished him to see the reflection of the afterglow in its still waters, with the noble lines of the mountain range that glassed itself there; the effect is one of the greatest charms of that lovely region, the sojourn of the sweetest summer in the world, and I am always impatient to show it to strangers.

We climbed the meadow wall and passed through a stretch of woods, to a path leading down to the shore, and as we loitered along in the tender gloom of the forest, the music of the hermit-thrushes rang all round us, like crystal bells, like silver flutes, like the drip of fountains, like the choiring of still-eyed cherubim. We stopped from time to time and listened, while the shy birds sang unseen in their covert of shadows; but we did not speak till we emerged from the trees and suddenly stood upon the naked knoll overlooking the lake.

Then I explained, "The woods used to come down to the shore here, and we had their mystery and music to the water's edge; but last winter the owner cut the timber off. It looks rather ragged now." I had to recognize the fact, for I saw the Altrurian staring about him over the clearing, in a kind of horror. It was a squalid ruin, a graceless desolation, which not even the pitying twilight could soften. The stumps showed their hideous mutilation everywhere; the brush had been burned, and the fires had scorched and blackened the lean soil of the hill slope, and blasted it with sterility. A few weak saplings, withered by the flames, drooped and straggled about; it would be a century before the forces of nature could repair the waste.

"You say the owner did this," said the Altrurian. "Who is the owner?"

"Well, it does seem too bad," I answered evasively. "There has been a good deal of feeling about it. The neighbors tried to buy him off before he began the destruction, for they knew the value of the woods as an attraction to summer-boarders; the city cottagers, of course, wanted to save them, and together they offered for the land pretty nearly as much as the timber was worth. But he had got it into his head that the land here by the lake would sell for building lots if it was cleared, and he could make money on that as well as on the trees; and so they had to go. Of course, one might say that he was deficient in public spirit, but I don't blame him, altogether."

"No," the Altrurian assented, somewhat to my surprise, I confess.

I resumed, "There was no one else to look after his interests, and it was not only his right but his duty to get the most he could for himself and his own, according to his best light. That is what I tell people when they fall foul of him for his want of public spirit."

"The trouble seems to be, then, in the system that obliges each man to be the guardian of his own interests. Is that what you blame?"

"No, I consider it a very perfect system. It is based upon individuality, and we believe that individuality is the principle that differences civilized men from savages, from the lower animals, and makes us a nation instead of a tribe or a herd. There isn't one of us, no matter how much he censured this man's want of public spirit, but would resent the slightest interference with his property rights. The woods were his; he had the right to do what he pleased with his own."

"Do I understand you that, in America, a man may do what is wrong with his own?"

"He may do anything with his own."

"To the injury of others?"

"Well, not in person or property. But he may hurt them in taste and sentiment as much as he likes. Can't a man do what he pleases with his own in Altruria?"

"No, he can only do right with his own."

"And if he tries to do wrong, or what the community thinks is wrong?"

"Then the community takes his own from him." Before I could think of anything to say to this he went on: "But I wish you would explain to me why it was left to this man's neighbors to try and get him to sell his portion of the landscape?"

"Why, bless my soul!" I exclaimed, "who else was there? You wouldn't have expected to take up a collection among the summer-boarders?"

"That wouldn't have been so unreasonable; but I didn't mean that. Was there no provision for such an exigency in your laws? Wasn't the state empowered to buy him off at the full value of his timber and his land?"

"Certainly not," I replied. "That would be rank paternalism."

It began to get dark, and I suggested that we had better be going back to the hotel. The talk seemed already to have taken us away from all pleasure in the prospect; I said, as we found our way through the rich, balsam-scented twilight of the woods, where one joy-haunted thrush was still singing, "You know that in America the law is careful not to meddle with a man's private affairs, and we don't attempt to legislate personal virtue."

"But marriage," he said, "surely you have the institution of marriage?"

I was really annoyed at this. I returned sarcastically, "Yes, I am glad to say that there we can meet your expectation; we have marriage, not only consecrated by the church, but established and defended by the state. What has that to do with the question?"

"And you consider marriage," he pursued, "the citadel of morality, the fountain of all that is pure and good in your private life, the source of home and the image of heaven?"

"There are some marriages," I said with a touch of our national humor, "that do not quite fill the bill, but that is certainly our ideal of marriage."

"Then why do you say that you have not legislated personal virtue in America?" he asked. "You have laws, I believe, against theft and murder, and slander and incest, and perjury and drunkenness?"

"Why, certainly."

"Then it appears to me that you have legislated honesty, regard for human life, regard for character, abhorrence of unnatural vice, good faith and sobriety. I was told on the train coming up, by a gentleman who was shocked at the sight of a man beating his horse, that you even had laws against cruelty to animals."

"Yes, and I am happy to say that they are enforced to such a degree that a man cannot kill a cat cruelly without being punished for it." The Altrurian did not follow up his advantage, and I resolved not to be outdone in magnanimity. "Come, I will own that you have the best of me on those points. I must say you've trapped me very neatly, too; I can enjoy a thing of that kind when it's well done, and I frankly knock under. But I had in mind something altogether different when I spoke. I was thinking of those idealists who want to bind us hand and foot, and render us the slaves of a state where the most intimate relations of life shall be penetrated by legislation, and the very hearthstone shall be a tablet of laws."

"Isn't marriage a rather intimate relation of life?" asked the Altrurian. "And I understood that gentleman on the train to say that you had laws against cruelty to children, and societies established to see them enforced. You don't consider such laws an invasion of the home, do you, or a violation of its immunities? I imagine," he went on, "that the difference between your civilization and ours is only one of degree, after all, and that America and Altruria are really one at heart."

I thought his compliment a bit hyperbolical, but I saw that it was honestly meant, and as we Americans are first of all patriots, and vain for our country before we are vain for ourselves, I was not proof against the flattery it conveyed to me civically if not personally.

We were now drawing near the hotel, and I felt a certain glow of pleasure in its gay effect on the pretty knoll where it stood. In its artless and accidental architecture it was not unlike one of our immense coast-wise steamboats. The twilight had thickened to dusk, and the edifice was brilliantly lighted with electrics, story above story, which streamed into the gloom around like the lights of saloon and state-room. The corner of wood making into the meadow hid the station; there was no other building in sight; the hotel seemed riding at anchor on the swell of a placid sea. I was going to call the Altrurian's attention to this fanciful resemblance when I remembered that he had not been in our country long enough to have seen a Fall River boat,[1] and I made toward the house without wasting the comparison upon him. But I treasured it up in my own mind, intending some day to make a literary use of it.

The guests were sitting in friendly groups about the piazzas or in rows against the walls, the ladies with their gossip and the gentlemen with their cigars. The night had fallen cool after a hot day, and they all had the effect of having cast off care with the burden of the week that was past, and to be steeping themselves in the innocent and simple enjoyment of the hour. They were mostly middle-aged married folk, but some were old enough to have sons and daughters among the young people who went and came in a long, wandering promenade of the piazzas, or wove themselves through the waltz past the open windows of the great parlor; the music seemed one with the light that streamed far out on the lawn flanking the

---

[1] Howells refers to one of the elegant steamboats being produced by the Fall River Steamship Line of Massachusetts. See Roger W. McAdams, *The Old Fall River Line* (New York: Stephen Daye Press, 1955), chap. 2.

piazzas. Every one was well dressed and comfortable and at peace, and I felt that our hotel was in some sort a microcosm of the republic.

We involuntarily paused, and I heard the Altrurian murmur, "Charming, charming! This is really delightful!"

"Yes, isn't it?" I returned, with a glow of pride. "Our hotel here is a type of the summer hotel everywhere; it's characteristic in not having anything characteristic about it; and I rather like the notion of the people in it being so much like the people in all the others that you would feel yourself at home wherever you met such a company in such a house. All over the country, north and south, wherever you find a group of hills or a pleasant bit of water or a stretch of coast, you'll find some such refuge as this for our weary toilers. We began to discover some time ago that it would not do to cut open the goose that laid our golden eggs, even if it looked like an eagle, and kept on perching on our banners just as if nothing had happened. We discovered that, if we continued to kill ourselves with hard work, there would be no Americans pretty soon."

The Altrurian laughed. "How delightfully you put it! How quaint! How picturesque! Excuse me, but I can't help expressing my pleasure in it. Our own humor is so very different."

"Ah," I said; "what is your humor like?"

"I could hardly tell you, I'm afraid; I've never been much of a humorist myself."

Again a cold doubt of something ironical in the man went through me, but I had no means of verifying it, and so I simply remained silent, waiting for him to prompt me if he wished to know anything further about our national transformation from bees perpetually busy into butterflies occasionally idle. "And when you had made that discovery?" he suggested.

"Why, we're nothing if not practical, you know, and as soon as we made that discovery we stopped killing ourselves and invented the summer resort. There are very few of our business or professional men now who don't take their four or five weeks' vacation. Their wives go off early in the summer, and if they go to some resort within three or four hours of the city, the men leave town Saturday afternoon and run out, or come up, and spend Sunday with their families. For thirty-eight hours or so a hotel like this is a nest of happy homes."

"That is admirable," said the Altrurian. "You are truly a practical people. The ladies come early in the summer, you say?"

"Yes, sometimes in the beginning of June."

"What do they come for?" asked the Altrurian.

"What for? Why, for rest!" I retorted, with some little temper.

"But I thought you told me a while ago that as soon as a husband could afford it he relieved his wife and daughters from all household work."

"So he does."

"Then what do the ladies wish to rest from?"

"From care. It is not work alone that kills. They are not relieved from household care even when they are relieved from household work. There is nothing so killing as household care. Besides, the sex seems to be born tired. To be sure, there are some observers of our life who contend that with the advance of athletics among our ladies, with boating and bathing, and lawn-tennis and mountain climbing and freedom from care, and these long summers of repose, our women are likely to become as superior to the men physically as they now are intellectually. It is all right. We should like to see it happen. It would be part of the national joke."

"Oh, have you a national joke?" asked the Altrurian. "But, of course! You have so much humor. I wish you could give me some notion of it."

"Well, it is rather damaging to any joke to explain it," I replied, "and your only hope of getting at ours is to live into it. One feature of it is the confusion of foreigners at the sight of our men's willingness to subordinate themselves to our women."

"Oh, I don't find that very bewildering," said the Altrurian. "It seems to me a generous and manly trait of the American character. I'm proud to say that it is one of the points at which your civilization and our own touch. There can be no doubt that the influence of women in your public affairs must be of the greatest advantage to you; it has been so with us."

I turned and stared at him, but he remained insensible to my astonishment, perhaps because it was now too dark for him to see it. "Our women have no influence in public affairs," I said quietly, after a moment.

"They haven't? Is it possible? But didn't I understand you to imply just now that your women are better educated than your men?"

"Well, I suppose that, taking all sorts and conditions among us, the women are as a rule better schooled, if not better educated."

"Then, apart from the schooling, they are not more cultivated?"

"In a sense you might say they were. They certainly go in for a lot of things: art and music, and Browning and the drama, and foreign travel and psychology, and political economy and Heaven knows what all. They have more leisure for it; they have all the leisure there is, in fact; our young men have to go into business. I suppose you may say our women are more cultivated than our men; yes, I think there's no questioning that. They are the great readers among us. We poor devils of authors would be badly off if it were not for our women. In fact, no author could make a reputation among us without them. American literature exists because American women appreciate it and love it."

"But surely your men read books?"

"Some of them; not many, comparatively. You will often hear a complacent ass of a husband and father say to an author: 'My wife and daughters know your books, but I can't find time for anything but the papers nowadays. I skim them over at breakfast, or when I'm going in to business on the train.' He isn't the least ashamed to say that he reads nothing but the newspapers."

"Then you think that it would be better for him to read books?"

"Well, in the presence of four or five thousand journalists with drawn scalping-knives I should not like to say so. Besides, modesty forbids."

"No, but really," the Altrurian persisted, "you think that the literature of a book is more carefully pondered than the literature of a daily newspaper?"

"I suppose even the four or five thousand journalists with drawn scalping-knives would hardly deny that."

"And it stands to reason, doesn't it, that the habitual reader of carefully pondered literature ought to be more thoughtful than the readers of literature which is not carefully pondered, and which they merely skim over on their way to business?"

"I believe we began by assuming the superior culture of our women, didn't we? You'll hardly find an American that isn't proud of it."

"Then," said the Altrurian, "if your women are generally better schooled than your men, and more cultivated and more thoughtful, and are relieved of household work in such great measure, and even of domestic cares, why have they no part in your public affairs?"

I laughed, for I thought I had my friend at last. "For the best of all possible reasons; they don't want it."

"Ah, that's no reason," he returned. "Why don't they want it?"

"Really," I said, out of all patience, "I think I must let you ask the ladies themselves," and I turned and moved again toward the hotel, but the Altrurian gently detained me.

"Excuse me," he began.

"No, no," I said:

" 'The feast is set, the guests are met,
  May'st hear the merry din.'

Come in and see the young people dance!"

"Wait," he entreated, "tell me a little more about the old people first. This digression about the ladies has been very interesting, but I thought you were going to speak of the men here. Who are they, or rather, what are they?"

"Why, as I said before, they are all business men and professional men; people who spend their lives in studies and counting-rooms and offices, and have come up here for a few weeks or a few days of well-earned repose. They are of all kinds of occupations: they are lawyers and doctors, and clergymen and merchants, and brokers and bankers. There's hardly any calling you won't find represented among them. As I was thinking just now, our hotel is a sort of microcosm of the American republic."

"I am most fortunate in finding you here, where I can avail myself of your intelligence in making my observations of your life under such advantageous circumstances. It seems to me that with your help I might penetrate the fact of American life, possess myself of the mystery of your national joke, without stirring beyond the piazza of your hospitable hotel," said my friend. I doubted it, but one does not lightly put aside a compliment like that to one's intelligence, and I said I should be very happy to be of use to him. He thanked me, and said, "Then, to begin with, I understand that these gentlemen are here because they are all overworked."

"Of course. You can have no conception of how hard our business men and our professional men work. I suppose there is nothing like it anywhere else in the world. But, as I said before, we are beginning to find that we cannot burn the candle at both ends and have it last long. So we put one end out for a little while every summer. Still, there are frightful wrecks of men strewn all along the course of our prosperity, wrecks of mind and body. Our insane asylums are full of madmen who have broken under the tremendous strain, and every country in Europe abounds in our dyspeptics." I was rather proud of this terrible fact; there is no doubt but we Americans are proud of overworking ourselves; Heaven knows why.

The Altrurian murmured, "Awful! Shocking!" But I thought somehow he had not really followed me very attentively in my celebration of our national violation of the laws of life and its consequences. "I am glad," he went on, "that your business men and professional men are beginning to realize the folly and wickedness of overwork. Shall I find some of your other weary workers here, too?"

"What other weary workers?" I asked in turn, for I imagined I had gone over pretty much the whole list.

"Why," said the Altrurian, "your mechanics and day laborers, your iron moulders and glass blowers, your miners and farmers, your printers and mill operatives, your trainmen and quarry hands. Or do they prefer to go to resorts of their own?"

CHAPTER III

It was not easy to make sure of such innocence as prompted this inquiry of my Altrurian friend. The doubt whether he could really be in earnest was something that I had already felt; and it was destined to beset me, as it did now, again and again. My first thought was that of course he was trying a bit of cheap irony on me, a mixture of the feeble sarcasm and false sentiment that makes us smile when we find it in the philippics of the industrial agitators. For a moment I did not know but I had fallen victim to a walking-delegate[2] on his vacation, who was employing his summer leisure in going about the country in the guise of a traveler from Altruria, and foisting himself upon people who would have had nothing to do with him in his real character. But in another moment I perceived that this was impossible. I could not suppose that the friend who had introduced him to me would be capable of seconding so poor a joke, and besides I could not imagine why a walking-delegate should wish to address his clumsy satire to me particularly. For the present, at least, there was nothing for it but to deal with this inquiry as if it were made in good faith, and in the pursuit of useful information. It struck me as grotesque; but it would not have been decent to treat it as if it were so. I was obliged to regard it seriously, and so I decided to shirk it.

"Well," I said, "that opens up rather a large field, which lies somewhat outside of the province of my own activities. You know, I am a writer of romantic fiction, and my time is so fully occupied in manipulating the destinies of the good old-fashioned hero and heroine, and trying always to make them end in a happy marriage, that I hardly had a chance to look much into the lives of agriculturists or artisans; and, to tell you the truth, I don't know what they do with their leisure. I'm pretty certain, though, you won't meet any of them in this hotel; they couldn't afford it, and I fancy they would find themselves out of their element among our guests. We respect them thoroughly; every American does; and we know that the prosperity of the country rests with them; we have a theory that they are politically sovereign, but we see very little of them, and we don't associate with them. In fact, our cultivated people have so little interest in them socially that they don't like to meet them, even in fiction; they prefer refined and polished ladies and gentlemen, whom they can have some sympathy with; and I always go to the upper classes for my types. It won't do to suppose, though, that we are indifferent to the working-classes in their place. Their condition is being studied a good deal just

[2] A walking-delegate is appointed by a labor union to travel around the country and represent its cause.

now, and there are several persons here who will be able to satisfy your curiosity on the points you have made, I think. I will introduce you to them."

The Altrurian did not try to detain me this time. He said he should be very glad indeed to meet my friends, and I led the way toward a little group at the corner of the piazza. They were men whom I particularly liked, for one reason or another; they were intelligent and open-minded, and they were thoroughly American. One was a banker; another was a minister; there was a lawyer, and there was a doctor; there was a professor of political economy in one of our colleges; and there was a retired manufacturer — I do not know what he used to manufacture: cotton or iron, or something like that. They all rose politely as I came up with my Altrurian, and I fancied in them a sensation of expectancy created by the rumor of his eccentric behavior which must have spread through the hotel. But they controlled this if they had it, and I could see, as the light fell upon his face from a spray of electrics on the nearest pillar, that sort of liking kindle in theirs which I had felt myself at first sight of him.

I said, "Gentlemen, I wish to introduce my friend, Mr. Homos," and then I presented them severally to him by name. We all sat down, and I explained: "Mr. Homos is from Altruria. He is visiting our country for the first time, and is greatly interested in the working of our institutions. He has been asking me some rather hard questions about certain phases of our civilization; and the fact is that I have launched him upon you because I don't feel quite able to cope with him."

They all laughed civilly at this sally of mine, but the professor asked, with a sarcasm that I thought I hardly merited, "What point in our polity can be obscured to the author of 'Glove and Gauntlet' and 'Airs and Graces'?"

They all laughed again, not so civilly, I felt, and then the banker asked my friend, "Is it long since you left Altruria?"

"It seems a great while ago," the Altrurian answered, "but it is really only a few weeks."

"You came by way of England, I suppose?"

"Yes; there is no direct line to America," said the Altrurian.

"That seems rather odd," I ventured, with some patriotic grudge.

"Oh, the English have direct lines everywhere," the banker instructed me.

"The tariff has killed our shipbuilding," said the professor. No one took up this firebrand, and the professor added, "Your name is Greek, isn't it, Mr. Homos?"

"Yes; we are of one of the early Hellenic families," said the Altrurian.

"And do you think," asked the lawyer, who, like most lawyers, was a lover of romance, and was well read in legendary lore especially, "that there is any reason for supposing that Altruria is identical with the fabled Atlantis?"

"No, I can't say that I do. We have no traditions of a submergence of the continent, and there are only the usual evidences of a glacial epoch which you find everywhere to support such a theory. Besides, our civilization is strictly Christian, and dates back to no earlier period than that of the first Christian commune after Christ. It is a matter of history with us that one of these communists, when they were dispersed, brought the gospel to our continent; he was cast away on our eastern coast on his way to Britain."

"Yes, we know that," the minister intervened, "but it is perfectly astonishing that an island so large as Altruria should have been lost to the knowledge of the rest of the world ever since the beginning of our era. You would hardly think that there was a space of the ocean's surface a mile square which had not been traversed by a thousand keels since Columbus sailed westward."

"No, you wouldn't. And I wish," the doctor suggested in his turn, "that Mr. Homos would tell us something about his country, instead of asking us about ours."

"Yes," I coincided, "I'm sure we should all find it a good deal easier. At least I should; but I brought our friend up in the hope that the professor would like nothing better than to train a battery of hard facts upon a defenseless stranger." Since the professor had given me that little stab, I was rather anxious to see how he would handle the desire for information in the Altrurian which I had found so prickly.

This turned the laugh on the professor, and he pretended to be as curious about Altruria as the rest, and said he would rather hear of it. But the Altrurian said: "I hope you will excuse me. Some time I shall be glad to talk of Altruria as long as you like; or if you will come to us, I shall be still happier to show you many things that I couldn't make you understand at a distance. But I am in America to learn, not to teach, and I hope you will have patience with my ignorance. I begin to be afraid that it is so great as to seem a little incredible. I have fancied in my friend here," he went on, with a smile toward me, "a suspicion that I was not entirely single in some of the inquiries I have made, but that I had some ulterior motive, some wish to censure or satirize."

"Oh, not at all!" I protested, for it was not polite to admit a conjecture so accurate. "We are so well satisfied with our condition that we have nothing but pity for the darkened mind of the foreigner, though we believe in it fully: we are used to the English tourist."

My friends laughed, and the Altrurian continued: "I am very glad to hear it, for I feel myself at a peculiar disadvantage among you. I am not only a foreigner, but I am so alien to you in all the traditions and habitudes that I find it very difficult to get upon common ground with you. Of course I know theoretically what you are, but to realize it practically is another thing. I had read so much about America and understood so little that I could not rest without coming to see for myself. Some of the apparent contradictions were so colossal — "

"We have everything on a large scale here," said the banker, breaking off the ash of his cigar with the end of his little finger, "and we rather pride ourselves on the size of our inconsistencies, even. I know something of the state of things in Altruria, and, to be frank with you, I will say that it seems to me preposterous. I should say it was impossible, if it were not an accomplished fact; but I always feel bound to recognize the thing done. You have hitched your wagon to a star, and you have made the star go; there is never any trouble with wagons, but stars are not easily broken to harness, and you have managed to get yours well in hand. As I said, I don't believe in you, but I respect you." I thought this charming, myself; perhaps because it stated my own mind about Altruria so exactly and in terms so just and generous.

"Pretty good," said the doctor, in a murmur of satisfaction, at my ear, "for a bloated bond-holder."

"Yes," I whispered back, "I wish I had said it. What an American way of putting it! Emerson would have liked it himself. After all, *he* was our prophet."

"He must have thought so from the way we kept stoning him," said the doctor, with a soft laugh.

"Which of our contradictions," asked the banker, in the same tone of gentle bonhomie, "has given you and our friend pause, just now?"

The Altrurian answered after a moment: "I am not sure that it is a contradiction, for as yet I have not ascertained the facts I was seeking. Our friend was telling me of the great change that had taken place in regard to work, and the increased leisure that your professional people are now allowing themselves; and I was asking him where your working-men spent their leisure."

He went over the list of those he had specified, and I hung my head in shame and pity; it really had such an effect of mawkish sentimentality. But my friends received it in the best possible way. They did not laugh; they heard him out, and then they quietly deferred to the banker, who made answer for us all:

"Well, I can be almost as brief as the historian of Iceland in his chapter on snakes: those people have no leisure to spend."

"Except when they go out on a strike," said the manufacturer, with a certain grim humor of his own; I never heard anything more dramatic than the account he once gave of the way he broke up a labor-union. "I have seen a good many of them at leisure then."

"Yes," the doctor chimed in, "and in my younger days, when I necessarily had a good deal of charity-practice, I used to find them at leisure when they were 'laid off.' It always struck me as such a pretty euphemism. It seemed to minify the harm of the thing so. It seemed to take all the hunger and cold and sickness out of the fact. To be simply 'laid off' was so different from losing your work and having to face beggary or starvation!"

"Those people," said the professor, "never put anything by. They are wasteful and improvident, almost to a man; and they learn nothing by experience, though they know as well as we do that it is simply a question of demand and supply, and that the day of overproduction is sure to come, when their work must stop unless the men that give them work are willing to lose money."

"And I've seen them lose it, sometimes, rather than shut down," the manufacturer remarked; "lose it hand over hand, to keep the men at work; and then as soon as the tide turned the men would strike for higher wages. You have no idea of the ingratitude of those people." He said this towards the minister, as if he did not wish to be thought hard; and in fact he was a very kindly man.

"Yes," replied the minister, "that is one of the most sinister features of the situation. They seem really to regard their employers as their enemies. I don't know how it will end."

"I know how it would end if I had my way," said the professor. "There wouldn't be any labor-unions, and there wouldn't be any strikes."

"That is all very well," said the lawyer, from that judicial mind which I always liked in him, "as far as the strikes are concerned, but I don't understand that the abolition of the unions would affect the impersonal process of 'laying-off.' The law of demand and supply I respect as much as any one — it's something like the constitution; but all the same I should object extremely to have my income stopped by it every now and then. I'm probably not so wasteful as a workingman generally is; still I haven't laid by enough to make it a matter of indifference to me whether my income went on or not. Perhaps the professor has." The professor did not say, and we all took leave to laugh. The lawyer concluded, "I don't see how those fellows stand it."

"They don't, all of them," said the doctor. "Or their wives and children don't. Some of them die."

"I wonder," the lawyer pursued, "what has become of the good old American fact that there is always work for those who are willing to work? I notice that wherever five thousand men strike in the forenoon, there are five thousand men to take their places in the afternoon — and not men who are turning their hands to something new, but men who are used to doing the very thing the strikers have done."

"That is one of the things that teach the futility of strikes," the professor made haste to interpose, as if he had not quite liked to appear averse to the interests of the workman; no one likes to do that. "If there were anything at all to be hoped from them it would be another matter."

"Yes, but that isn't the point, quite," said the lawyer.

"By the way, what is the point?" I asked, with my humorous lightness.

"Why, I supposed," said the banker, "it was the question how the working-classes amused their elegant leisure. But it seems to be almost anything else."

We all applauded the neat touch, but the Altrurian eagerly entreated: "No, no! never mind that, now. That is a matter of comparatively little interest. I would so much rather know something about the status of the workingman among you."

"Do you mean his political status? It's that of every other citizen."

"I don't mean that. I suppose that in America you have learned, as we have in Altruria, that equal political rights are only means to an end, and as an end have no value or reality. I meant the economic status of the workingman, and his social status."

I do not know why we were so long girding up our loins to meet this simple question. I myself could not have hopefully undertaken to answer it: but the others were each in their way men of affairs, and practically acquainted with the facts, except perhaps the professor; but he had devoted a great deal of thought to them, and ought to have been qualified to make some sort of response. But even he was silent; and I had a vague feeling that they were all somehow reluctant to formulate their knowledge, as if it were uncomfortable or discreditable. The banker continued to smoke quietly on for a moment; then he suddenly threw his cigar away.

"I like to free my mind of cant," he said, with a short laugh, "when I can afford it, and I propose to cast all sorts of American cant out of it, in answering your question. The economic status of the workingman among us is essentially the same as that of the workingman all over the civilized world. You will find plenty of people here, especially about election time, to tell you differently, but they will not be telling you the truth, though a great many of them think they are. In fact, I suppose most Americans honestly believe because we have a republican form of government, and manhood-suffrage, and so on, that our economic conditions are peculiar, and that our workingman has a status higher and better than that of the workingman anywhere else. But he has nothing of the kind. His circumstances are better, and provisionally his wages are higher, but it is only a question of years or decades when his circumstances will be the same and his wages the same as the European workingman's. There is nothing in our conditions to prevent this."

"Yes, I understood from our friend here," said the Altrurian, nodding toward me, "that you had broken only with the political tradition of Europe, in your revolution; and he has explained to me that you do not hold all kinds of labor in equal esteem; but — "

"What kind of labor did he say we did hold in esteem?" asked the banker.

"Why, I understood him to say that if America meant anything at all it meant the honor of work, but that you distinguished and did not honor some kinds of work so much as others: for instance, domestic service, or personal attendance of any kind."

The banker laughed again. "Oh, he drew the line there, did he? Well, we all have to draw the line somewhere. Our friend is a novelist, and I will tell you in strict confidence that the line he has drawn is imaginary. We don't honor any kind of work any more than any other people. If a fellow gets up,[3] the papers make a great ado over his having been a wood-chopper, or a bobbin-boy, or something of that kind, but I doubt if the fellow himself likes it; he doesn't, if he's got any sense. The rest of us feel that it's *infra dig.*, and hope nobody will find out that we ever worked with our hands for a living. I'll go farther," said the banker, with the effect of whistling prudence down the wind, "and I will challenge any of you to gainsay me from his own experience or observation. How does esteem usually express itself? When we wish to honor a man, what do we do?"

"Ask him to dinner," said the lawyer.

"Exactly. We offer him some sort of social recognition. Well, as soon as a fellow gets up, if he gets up high enough, we offer him some sort of social recognition; in fact, all sorts; but upon condition that he has left off working with his hands for a living. We forgive all you please to his past on account of the present. But there isn't a workingman, I venture to say, in any city, or town, or even large village, in the whole length and breadth of the United States who has any social recognition, if he is still working

[3] Here *to get up* means to rise in the world, to succeed.

at his trade. I don't mean, merely, that he is excluded from rich and fashionable society, but from the society of the average educated and cultivated people. I'm not saying he is fit for it; but I don't care how intelligent and agreeable he might be — and some of them are astonishingly intelligent, and so agreeable in their tone of mind, and their original way of looking at things, that I like nothing better than to talk with them — all of our invisible fences are up against him."

The minister said: "I wonder if that sort of exclusiveness is quite natural? Children seem to feel no sort of social difference among themselves."

"We can hardly go to children for a type of social order," the professor suggested.

"True," the minister meekly admitted. "But somehow there is a protest in us somewhere against these arbitrary distinctions; something that questions whether they are altogether right. We know that they must be, and always have been, and always will be, and yet — well, I will confess it — I never feel at peace when I face them."

"Oh," said the banker, "if you come to the question of right and wrong, that is another matter. I don't say it's right. I'm not discussing that question; though I'm certainly not proposing to level the fences; I should be the last to take my own down. I say simply that you are no more likely to meet a workingman in American society than you are to meet a colored man. Now you can judge," he ended, turning directly to the Altrurian, "how much we honor labor. And I hope I have indirectly satisfied your curiosity as to the social status of the workingman among us."

We were all silent. Perhaps the others were occupied like myself in trying to recall some instance of a workingman whom they had met in society, and perhaps we said nothing because we all failed.

The Altrurian spoke at last.

"You have been so very full and explicit that I feel as if it were almost unseemly to press any further inquiry; but I should very much like to know how your workingmen bear this social exclusion."

"I'm sure I can't say," returned the banker. "A man does not care much to get into society until he has something to eat, and how to get that is always the first question with the workingman."

"But you wouldn't like it yourself?"

"No, certainly, I shouldn't like it myself. I shouldn't complain of not being asked to people's houses, and the workingmen don't; you can't do that; but I should feel it an incalculable loss. We may laugh at the emptiness of society, or pretend to be sick of it, but there is no doubt that society is the flower of civilization, and to be shut out from it is to be denied the best privilege of a civilized man. There are society-women — we have all met them — whose graciousness and refinement of presence are something of incomparable value; it is more than a liberal education to have been admitted to it, but it is as inaccessible to the workingman as — what shall I say? The thing is too grotesquely impossible for any sort of comparison. Merely to conceive of its possibility is something that passes a joke; it is a kind of offence."

Again we were silent.

"I don't know," the banker continued, "how the notion of our social equality originated, but I think it has been fostered mainly by the expectation of foreigners, who argued it from our political equality. As a matter of fact, it never existed, except in our poorest and most primitive communities, in the pioneer days of the West, and among the gold-hunters of California. It was not dreamt of in our colonial society, either in Virginia, or Pennsylvania, or New York, or Massachusetts; and the fathers of the republic, who were mostly slave-holders, were practically as stiffnecked aristocrats as any people of their day. We have not a political aristocracy, that is all; but there is as absolute a division between the orders of men, and as little love, in this country as in any country on the globe. The severance of the man who works for his living with his hands, from the man who does not work for his living with his hands, is so complete, and apparently so final, that nobody even imagines anything else, not even in fiction. Or, how is that?" he asked, turning to me. "Do you fellows still put the intelligent, high-spirited, handsome young artisan, who wins the millionaire's daughter into your books? I used sometimes to find him there."

"You might still find him in the fiction of the weekly story-papers; but," I was obliged to own, "he would not go down with my readers. Even in the story-paper fiction he would leave off working as soon as he married the millionaire's daughter, and go to Europe, or he would stay here and become a social leader, but he would not receive workingmen in his gilded halls."

The others rewarded my humor with a smile, but the banker said: "Then I wonder you were not ashamed of filling our friend up with that stuff about our honoring some kinds of labor. It is true that we don't go about openly and explicitly despising any kind of honest toil — people don't do that anywhere now; but we contemn it in terms quite as unmistakable. The workingman acquiesces as completely as anybody else. He does not remain a workingman a moment longer than he can help; and after he gets up, if he is weak enough to be proud of having been one, it is because he feels that his low origin is a proof of his prowess in rising to the top against unusual odds. I don't suppose there is a man in the whole civilized world — outside of Altruria, of course — who is proud of working at a trade, except the shoemaker Tolstoï,[4] and he is a count, and he does not make very good shoes."

We all laughed again: those shoes of Count Tolstoï's are always such an infallible joke. The Altrurian, however, was cocked and primed with another question; he instantly exploded it. "But are all the workingmen in America eager to rise above their condition? Is there none willing to remain among the mass because the rest could not rise with him, and from the hope of yet bringing labor to honor?"

The banker answered: "I never heard of any. No, the American ideal is not to change the conditions for all, but for each to rise above the rest if he can."

"Do you think it is really so bad as that?" asked the minister, timidly.

The banker answered: "Bad? Do you call that bad? I thought it was very good. But good or bad, I don't think you'll find it deniable, if you look into the facts. There may be workingmen willing to remain so for other workingmen's sake, but I have never met any — perhaps because the workingman never goes into society."

The unfailing question of the Altrurian broke the silence which ensued: "Are there many of your workingmen who are intelligent and agreeable — of the type you mentioned a moment since?"

"Perhaps;" said the banker, "I had better refer you to one of our friends here, who has had a great deal more to do with them than I have. He is a manufacturer and he has had to do with all kinds of work-people."

"Yes, for my sins," the manufacturer assented; and he added, "They are often confoundly intelligent, though I haven't often found them very agreeable, either in their tone of mind, or their original way of looking at things."

The banker amiably acknowledged his thrust, and the Altrurian asked, "Ah, they are opposed to your own?"

"Well, we have the same trouble here that you must have heard of in England. As you know now that the conditions are the same here, you won't be surprised at the fact."

"But the conditions," the Altrurian pursued; "do you expect them always to continue the same?"

"Well, I don't know," said the manufacturer. "We can't expect them to

---

[4] In his later years, Leo Tolstoy (1828–1910), who was born into a noble family, preached Christian socialism and the simple life exemplified by Christ. As part of his philosophy, he labored in the fields and learned the art of the shoe cobbler — although one commentator remarked that the boots he made "couldn't be worse."

change of themselves, and I shouldn't know how to change them. It was expected that the rise of the trusts and the syndicates would break the unions, but somehow they haven't. The situation remains the same. The unions are not cutting one another's throats now any more than we are. The war is on a larger scale — that's all."

"Then let me see," said the Altrurian, "whether I clearly understand the situation, as regards the workingman in America. He is dependent upon the employer for his chance to earn a living, and he is never sure of this. He may be thrown out of work by his employer's disfavor or disaster, and his willingness to work goes for nothing; there is no public provision of work for him; there is nothing to keep him from want, nor the prospect of anything."

"We are all in the same boat," said the professor.

"But some of us have provisioned ourselves rather better and can generally weather it through till we are picked up," the lawyer put in.

"I am always saying the workingman is improvident," returned the professor.

"There are the charities," the minister suggested.

"But his economical status," the Altrurian pursued, "is in a state of perpetual uncertainty, and to save himself in some measure he has organized, and so has constituted himself a danger to the public peace?"

"A very great danger," said the professor.

"I guess we can manage him," the manufacturer remarked.

"And socially he is non-existent?"

The Altrurian turned with this question to the banker, who said, "He is certainly not in society."

"Then," said my guest, "if the workingman's wages are provisionally so much better here than in Europe, why should they be discontented? What is the real cause of their discontent?"

I have always been suspicious, in the company of practical men, of an atmosphere of condescension to men of my calling, if nothing worse. I fancy they commonly regard artists of all kinds as a sort of harmless eccentrics, and that literary people they look upon as something droll, as weak and soft, as not quite right. I believed that this particular group, indeed, was rather abler to conceive of me as a rational person than most others, but I knew that if even they had expected me to be as reasonable as themselves they would not have been greatly disappointed if I were not; and it seemed to me that I had put myself wrong with them in imparting to the Altrurian that romantic impression that we hold labor in honor here. I had really thought so, but I could not say so now, and I wished to retrieve myself somehow. I wished to show that I was a practical man, too, and so I made answer: "What is the cause of the workingman's discontent? It is very simple: the walking-delegate."

CHAPTER IV

I suppose I could not have fairly claimed any great originality for my notion that the walking-delegate was the cause of the labor troubles: he is regularly assigned as the reason of a strike in the newspapers, and is reprobated for his evil agency by the editors, who do not fail to read the workingmen many solemn lessons, and fervently warn them against him, as soon as the strike begins to go wrong — as it nearly always does. I understand from them that the walking-delegate is an irresponsible tyrant, who emerges from the mystery that habitually hides him and from time to time orders a strike in mere rancor of spirit and plenitude of power, and then leaves the workingmen and their families to suffer the consequences, while he goes off somewhere and rolls in the lap of luxury, careless of the misery he has created. Between his debauches of vicious idleness and his accesses of baleful activity he is employed in poisoning the mind of the workingmen against his real interests and real friends. This is perfectly easy, because the American workingman, though singularly shrewd and sensible in other respects, is the victim of an unaccountable obliquity of vision which keeps him from seeing his real interests and real friends — or at least from knowing them when he sees them.

There could be no doubt, I thought, in the mind of any reasonable person that the walking-delegate was the source of the discontent among our proletariat, and I alleged him with a confidence which met the approval of the professor, apparently, for he nodded, as if to say that I had hit the nail on the head this time; and the minister seemed to be freshly impressed with a notion that could not be new to him. The lawyer and the doctor were silent, as if waiting for the banker to speak again; but he was silent, too. The manufacturer, to my chagrin, broke into a laugh. "I'm afraid," he said, with a sardonic levity which surprised me, "you'll have to go a good deal deeper than the walking-delegate. He's a symptom; he isn't the disease. The thing keeps on and on, and it seems to be always about wages; but it isn't about wages at the bottom. Some of those fellows know it and some of them don't, but the real discontent is with the whole system, with the nature of things. I had a curious revelation on that point the last time I tried to deal with my men as a union. They were always bothering me about this and about that, and there was no end to the bickering. I yielded point after point, but it didn't make any difference. It seemed as if the more I gave the more they asked. At last I made up my mind to try to get at the real inwardness of the matter, and I didn't wait for their committee to come to me — I sent for their leading man, and said I wanted to have it out with him. He wasn't a bad fellow, and when I got at him, man to man that way, I found he had sense, and he had ideas — it's no use pretending those fellows are fools; he had thought about his side of the question, any way. I said: 'Now what does it all mean? Do you want the earth, or don't you? When is it going to end?' I offered him something to take, but he said he didn't drink, and we compromised on cigars. 'Now when is it going to end?' said I, and I pressed it home, and wouldn't let him fight off from the point. 'Do you mean when it is all going to end?' said he. 'Yes,' said I, 'all. I'm sick of it. If there's any way out I'd like to know it.' 'Well,' said he, 'I'll tell you, if you want to know. It's all going to end when you get the same amount of money for the same amount of work as we do.'"

We all laughed uproariously. The thing was deliciously comical; and nothing, I thought, attested the Altrurian's want of humor like his failure to appreciate this joke. He did not even smile in asking, "And what did you say?"

"Well," returned the manufacturer, with cosy enjoyment, "I asked him if the men would take the concern and run it themselves." We laughed again; this seemed even better than the other joke. "But he said 'No;' they would not like to do that. And then I asked him just what they would like, if they could have their own way, and he said they would like to have me run the business, and all share alike. I asked him what was the sense of that, and why, if I could do something that all of them put together couldn't do, I shouldn't be paid more than all of them put together; and he said that if a man did his best he ought to be paid as much as the best man. I asked him if that was the principle their union was founded on, and he said 'Yes,' that the very meaning of their union was the protection of the weak by the strong, and the equalization of earnings among all who do their best."

We waited for the manufacturer to go on, but he made a dramatic pause at this point, as if to let it sink into our minds; and he did not speak until the Altrurian prompted him with the question, "And what did you finally do?"

"I saw there was only one way out for me, and I told the fellow I did not think I could do business on that principle. We parted friends, but the next Saturday I locked them out and smashed their union. They came back, most of them — they had to — but I've treated with them ever since 'as individuals.' "

"And they're much better off in your hands than they were in the union," said the professor.

"I don't know about that," said the manufacturer, "but I'm sure I am."

We laughed with him, all but the minister, whose mind seemed to have caught upon some other point, and who sat absently by.

"And is it your opinion, from what you know of the workingmen generally, that they all have this twist in their heads?" the professor asked.

"They have, until they begin to rise. Then they get rid of it mighty soon. Let a man save something — enough to get a house of his own, and take a boarder or two, and perhaps have a little money at interest — and he sees the matter in another light."

"Do you think he sees it more clearly?" asked the minister.

"He sees it differently."

"What do you think?" the minister pursued, turning to the lawyer. "You are used to dealing with questions of justice — "

"Rather more with questions of law, I'm afraid," the other returned pleasantly, putting his feet together before him and looking down at them, in a way he had. "But still, I have a great interest in questions of justice, and I confess that I find a certain wild equity in this principle, which I see nobody could do business on. It strikes me as idyllic — it's a touch of real poetry in the rough-and-tumble prose of our economic life."

He referred this to me as something I might appreciate in my quality of literary man, and I responded in my quality of practical man, "There's certainly more rhyme than reason in it."

He turned again to the minister:

"I suppose the ideal of the Christian state is the family?"

"I hope so," said the minister, with the gratitude that I have seen people of his cloth show when men of the world conceded premises which the world usually contests; it has seemed to me pathetic.

"And if that is the case, why the logic of the postulate is that the prosperity of the weakest is the sacred charge and highest happiness of all the stronger. But the law has not recognized any such principle, in economics at least, and if the labor unions are based upon it they are outlaw, so far as any hope of enforcing it is concerned; and it is bad for men to feel themselves outlaw. How is it," the lawyer continued, turning to the Altrurian, "in your country? We can see no issue here, if the first principle of organized labor antagonizes the first principle of business."

"But I don't understand precisely yet what the first principle of business is," returned my guest.

"Ah, that raises another interesting question," said the lawyer. "Of course every business man solves the problem practically according to his temperament and education, and I suppose that on first thoughts every business man would answer you accordingly. But perhaps the personal equation is something you wish to eliminate from the definition."

"Yes, of course."

"Still, I would rather not venture upon it first," said the lawyer. "Professor, what should you say was the first principle of business?"

"Buying in the cheapest market and selling in the dearest," the professor promptly answered.

"We will pass the parson and the doctor and the novelist as witnesses of no value. They can't possibly have any cognizance of the first principle of business; their affair is to look after the souls and bodies and fancies of other people. But what should you say it was?" he asked the banker.

"I should say it was an enlightened conception of one's own interests."

"And you?"

The manufacturer had no hesitation in answering: "The good of Number One first, last, and all the time. There may be a difference of opinion about the best way to get at it; the long way may be the better, or the short way; the direct way or the oblique way, or the purely selfish way, or the partly selfish way; but if you ever lose sight of that end you might as well shut up shop. That seems to be the first law of nature, as well as the first law of business."

"Ah, we mustn't go to nature for our morality," the minister protested.

"We were not talking of morality," said the manufacturer, "we were talking of business."

This brought the laugh on the minister, but the lawyer cut it short: "Well, then, I don't really see why the trades-unions are not as business-like as the syndicates in their dealings with all those outside of themselves. Within themselves they practice an altruism of the highest order, but it is a tribal altruism; it is like that which prompts a Sioux to share his last mouthful with a starving Sioux, and to take the scalp of a starving Apache. How is it with your trades-unions in Altruria?" he asked my friend.

"We have no trades-unions in Altruria," he began.

"Happy Altruria!" cried the professor.

"We had them formerly," the Altrurian went on, "as you have them now. They claimed, as I suppose yours do, that they were forced into existence by the necessities of the case; that without union the working-man was unable to meet the capitalist on anything like equal terms, or to withstand his encroachments and oppressions. But to maintain themselves they had to extinguish industrial liberty among the workingmen themselves, and they had to practice great cruelties against those who refused to join them or who rebelled against them."

"They simply destroy them here," said the professor.

"Well," said the lawyer, from his judicial mind, "the great syndicates have no scruples in destroying a capitalist who won't come into them, or who tries to go out. They don't club him or stone him, but they undersell him and freeze him out; they don't break his head, but they bankrupt him. The principle is the same."

"Don't interrupt Mr. Homos," the banker entreated. "I am very curious to know just how they got rid of labor unions in Altruria."

"We had syndicates, too, and finally we had the reductio ad absurdum — we had a federation of labor unions and a federation of syndicates, that divided the nation into two camps. The situation was not only impossible, but it was insupportably ridiculous."

I ventured to say, "It hasn't become quite so much of a joke with us yet."

"Isn't it in a fair way to become so?" asked the doctor; and he turned to the lawyer: "What should you say was the logic of events among us for the last ten or twenty years?"

"There's nothing so capricious as the logic of events. It's like a woman's reasoning — you can't tell what it's aimed at, or where it's going to fetch up; all that you can do is to keep out of the way if possible. We may come to some such condition of things as they have in Altruria, where the faith of the whole nation is pledged to secure every citizen in the pursuit of happiness; or we may revert to some former condition, and the master may again own the man; or we may hitch and joggle along indefinitely, as we are doing now."

"But come, now," said the banker, while he laid a caressing touch on the Altrurian's shoulder, "you don't mean to say honestly that everybody works with his hands in Altruria?"

"Yes, certainly. We are mindful, as a whole people, of the divine law, 'In the sweat of thy brow shalt thou eat bread.' "

"But the capitalists? I'm anxious about Number One, you see."

"We have none."

"I forgot, of course. But the lawyers, the doctors, the parsons, the novelists?"

"They all do their share of hand work."

The lawyer said: "That seems to dispose of the question of the workingman in society. But how about your minds? When do you cultivate your minds? When do the ladies of Altruria cultivate their minds, if they have to do their own work, as I suppose they do? Or is it only the men who work, if they happen to be the husbands and fathers of the upper classes?"

The Altrurian seemed to be sensible of the kindly skepticism which persisted in our reception of his statements, after all we had read of Altruria. He smiled indulgently, and said: "You mustn't imagine that work in Altruria is the same as it is here. As we all work, the amount that each one need do is very little, a few hours each day at the most, so that every man and woman has abundant leisure and perfect spirits for the higher pleasures which the education of their whole youth has fitted them to enjoy. If you can understand a state of things where the sciences and arts and letters are cultivated for their own sake, and not as a means of livelihood — "

"No," said the lawyer, smiling, "I'm afraid we can't conceive of that. We consider the pinch of poverty the highest incentive that a man can have. If our gifted friend here," he said, indicating me, "were not kept like a toad under the harrow, with his nose on the grindstone, and the poorhouse staring him in the face — "

"For Heaven's sake," I cried out, "don't mix your metaphors so, anyway!"

"If it were not for that and all the other hardships that literary men undergo — 'Toil, envy, want, the patron and the jail' — his novels probably wouldn't be worth reading."

"Ah!" said the Altrurian, as if he did not quite follow this joking; and to tell the truth, I never find the personal thing in very good taste. "You will understand, then, how extremely difficult it is for me to imagine a condition of things like yours — although I have it under my very eyes — where the money consideration is the first consideration."

"Oh, excuse me!" urged the minister, "I don't think that's quite the case."

"I beg your pardon," said the Altrurian, sweetly; "you can see how easily I go astray."

"Why, I don't know," the banker interposed, "that you are so far out in what you say. If you had said that money was always the first motive, I should have been inclined to dispute you, too; but when you say that money is the first consideration, I think you are quite right. Unless a man secures his financial basis for his work, he can't do his work. It's nonsense to pretend otherwise. So the money consideration is the first consideration. People here have to live by their work, and to live they must have money. Of course, we all recognize a difference in the qualities, as well as in the kinds, of work. The work of the laborer may be roughly defined as the necessity of his life; the work of the business man as the means, and the work of the artist and scientist as the end. We might refine upon these definitions and make them closer, but they will serve for illustration as they are. I don't think there can be any question as to which is the highest kind of work; some truths are self-evident. He is a fortunate man whose work is an end, and every business man sees this, and owns it to himself, at least when he meets some man of an æsthetic or scientific occupation. He knows that this luckier fellow has a joy in his work, which he can never feel in business; that his success in it can never be embittered by the thought that it is the failure of another; that if he does it well, it is pure good; that there cannot be any competition in it — there can be only a noble emulation, as far as the work itself is concerned. He can always look up to his work, for it is something above him; and a business man often has to look down upon his business, for it is often beneath him, unless he is a pretty low fellow."

I listened to all this in surprise; I knew that the banker was a cultivated man, a man of university training, and that he was a reader and a thinker; but he had always kept a certain reserve in his talk, which he now seemed to have thrown aside for the sake of the Altrurian, or because the subject had a charm that lured him out of himself. "Well, now," he continued, "the question is of the money consideration, which is the first consideration with us all: does it, or doesn't it degrade the work, which is the life, of those among us whose work is the highest? I understand that this is the misgiving which troubles you in view of our conditions?"

The Altrurian assented, and I thought it a proof of the banker's innate delicacy that he did not refer the matter, so far as it concerned the æsthetic life and work, to me; I was afraid he was going to do so. But he courteously proposed to keep the question impersonal, and he went on to consider it himself. "Well, I don't suppose any one can satisfy you fully. But I should say that it put such men under a double strain, and perhaps that is the reason why so many of them break down in a calling that is certainly far less exhausting than business. On one side, the artist is kept to the level of the workingman, of the animal, of the creature whose sole affair is to get something to eat and somewhere to sleep. This is through his necessity. On the other side, he is exalted to the height of beings who have no concern but with the excellence of their work, which they were born and divinely authorized to do. This is through his purpose. Between the two, I should say that he got mixed, and that his work shows it."

None of the others said anything, and since I had not been personally appealed to, I felt the freer to speak. "If you will suppose me to be speaking from observation rather than experience," I began.

"By all means," said the banker, "go on," and the rest made haste in various forms to yield me the word.

"I should say that such a man certainly got mixed, but that his work kept itself pure from the money consideration, as it were, in spite of him. A painter, or actor, or even a novelist, is glad to get all he can for his work, and, such is our fallen nature, he does get all he knows how to get; but when he has once fairly passed into his work, he loses himself in it. He does not think whether it will pay or not, whether it will be popular or not, but whether he can make it good or not."

"Well, that is conceivable," said the banker. "But wouldn't he rather do something he would get less for, if he could afford it, than the thing he knows he will get more for? Doesn't the money consideration influence his choice of subject?"

"Oddly enough, I don't believe it does," I answered, after a moment's reflection. "A man makes his choice once for all when he embraces the æsthetic life, or rather it is made for him; no other life seems possible. I know there is a general belief that an artist does the kind of thing he has made go because it pays; but this only shows the prevalence of business ideals. If he did not love to do the thing he does he could not do it well, no matter how richly it paid."

"I am glad to hear it," said the banker, and he added to the Altrurian: "So you see we are not so bad as one would think. We are illogically better, in fact."

"Yes," the other assented. "I knew something of your literature as well as your conditions before I left home, and I perceived that by some anomaly the one was not tainted by the other. It is a miraculous proof of the divine mission of the poet."

"And the popular novelist," the lawyer whispered in my ear, but loud enough for the rest to hear, and they all testified their amusement at my cost.

The Altrurian, with his weak sense of humor, passed the joke. "It shows no signs of corruption from greed, but I can't help thinking that, fine as it is, it might have been much finer if the authors who produced it had been absolutely freed to their work, and had never felt the spur of need."

"Are they absolutely freed to it in Altruria?" asked the professor. "I understood you that everybody had to work for his living in Altruria."

"That is a mistake. Nobody works for his living in Altruria; he works for others' living."

"Ah, that is precisely what our workingmen object to doing here!" said the manufacturer. "In that last interview of mine with the walking-delegate he had the impudence to ask me why my men should work for my living as well as their own."

"He couldn't imagine that you were giving them the work to do — the very means of life," said the professor.

"Oh, no, that's the last thing those fellows want to think of."

"Perhaps," the Altrurian suggested, "they might not have found it such a hardship to work for your living if their own had been assured, as it is with us. If you will excuse my saying it, we should think it monstrous in Altruria for any man to have another's means of life in his power; and in our condition it is hardly imaginable. Do you really have it in your power to take away a man's opportunity to earn a living?"

The manufacturer laughed uneasily. "It is in my power to take away his life; but I don't habitually shoot my fellow-men, and I never dismissed a man yet without good reason."

"Oh, I beg your pardon," said the Altrurian. "I didn't dream of accusing you of such inhumanity. But, you see, our whole system is so very different that, as I said, it is hard for me to conceive of yours, and I am very curious to understand its workings. If you shot your fellow-man, as you say, the law would punish you; but if, for some reason that you decided to be good, you took away his means of living, and he actually starved to death — "

"Then the law would have nothing to do with it," the professor replied for the manufacturer, who did not seem ready to answer. "But that is not the way things fall out. The man would be supported in idleness, probably, till he got another job, by his union, which would take the matter up."

"But I thought that our friend did not employ union labor," returned the Altrurian.

I found all this very uncomfortable, and tried to turn the talk back to a point that I felt curious about. "But in Altruria, if the literary class is not exempt from the rule of manual labor where do they find time and strength to write?"

"Why, you must realize that our manual labor is never engrossing or exhausting. It is no more than is necessary to keep the body in health. I do not see how you remain well here, you people of sedentary occupations."

"Oh, we all take some sort of exercise. We walk several hours a day, or we row, or we ride a bicycle, or a horse, or we fence."

"But to us," returned the Altrurian, with a growing frankness which nothing but the sweetness of his manner would have excused, "exercise for exercise would appear stupid. The barren expenditure of force that began and ended in itself, and produced nothing, we should — if you will excuse my saying so — look upon as childish, if not insane or immoral."

CHAPTER V

At this moment, the lady who had hailed me so gayly from the top of the coach while I stood waiting for the Altrurian to help the porter with the baggage, just after the arrival of the train, came up with her husband to our little group and said to me: "I want to introduce my husband to you. He adores your books." She went on much longer to this effect, while the other men grinned round and her husband tried to look as if it were all true, and her eyes wandered to the Altrurian, who listened gravely. I knew perfectly well that she was using her husband's zeal for my fiction to make me present my friend; but I did not mind that, and I introduced him to both of them. She took possession of him at once and began walking him off down the piazza, while her husband remained with me, and the members of our late conference drifted apart. I was not sorry to have it broken up for the present; it seemed to me that it had lasted quite long enough, and I lighted a cigar with the husband, and we strolled together in the direction his wife had taken.

He began, apparently in compliment to literature in my person, "Yes, I like to have a book where I can get at it when we're not going out to the theatre, and I want to quiet my mind down after business. I don't care much what the book is; my wife reads to me till I drop off, and then she finishes the book herself and tells me the rest of the story. You see, business takes it out of you so! Well, I let my wife do most of the reading, anyway. She knows pretty much everything that's going in that line. We haven't got any children, and it occupies her mind. She's up to all sorts of things — she's artistic, and she's musical, and she's dramatic, and she's literary. Well, I like to have her. Women are funny, anyway."

He was a good-looking, good-natured, average American of the money-making type; I believe he was some sort of a broker, but I do not quite know what his business was. As we walked up and down the piazza, keeping a discreet little distance from the corner where his wife had run off to with her capture, he said he wished he could get more time with her in the summer — but he supposed I knew what business was. He was glad she could have the rest, anyway; she needed it.

"By-the-way," he asked, "who is this friend of yours? The women are all crazy about him, and it's been an even thing between my wife and Miss Groundsel which would fetch him first. But I'll bet on my wife every time, when it comes to a thing like that. He's a good-looking fellow — some kind of foreigner, I believe; pretty eccentric, too, I guess. Where is Altruria, anyway?"

I told him, and he said: "Oh, yes. Well, if we are going to restrict immigration, I suppose we sha'n't see many more Altrurians, and we'd better make the most of this one. Heigh?"

I do not know why this innocent pleasantry piqued me to say: "If I understand the Altrurians, my dear fellow, nothing could induce them to emigrate to America. As far as I can make out, they would regard it very much as we should regard settling among the Esquimaux."

"Is that so?" asked my new acquaintance, with perfect good temper. "Why?"

"Really, I can't say, and I don't know that I've explicit authority for my statement."

"They are worse than the English used to be," he went on. "I didn't know that there were any foreigners who looked at us in that light now. I thought the war settled all that."

I sighed. "There are a good many things that the war didn't settle so definitely as we've been used to thinking, I'm afraid. But for that matter, I fancy an Altrurian would regard the English as a little lower in the scale of savagery than ourselves even."

"Is that so? Well, that's pretty good on the English, anyway," said my companion, and he laughed with an easy satisfaction that I envied him.

"My dear!" his wife called to him from where she was sitting with the Altrurian, "I wish you would go for my shawl. I begin to feel the air a little."

"I'll go if you'll tell me where," he said, and he confided to me, "Never knows where her shawl is one-quarter of the time."

"Well, I think I left it in the office somewhere. You might ask at the desk; or, perhaps it's in the rack by the dining room door — or maybe up in our room."

"I thought so," said her husband, with another glance at me, as if it were the greatest fun in the world, and he started amiably off.

I went and took a chair by the lady and the Altrurian, and she began at once: "Oh, I'm so glad you've come! I have been trying to enlighten Mr. Homos about some of the little social peculiarities among us that he finds so hard to understand. He was just now," the lady continued, "wanting to know why all the natives out here were not invited to go in and join our young people in the dance, and I've been trying to tell him that we consider it a great favor to let them come and take up so much of the piazza and look in at the windows."

She gave a little laugh of superiority, and twitched her pretty head in the direction of the young country girls and country fellows who were thronging the place that night in rather unusual numbers. They were well enough looking, and as it was Saturday night they were in their best. I suppose their dress could have been criticised; the young fellows were clothed by the ready-made clothing store, and the young girls after their own devices from the fashion-papers; but their general effect was good, and their behavior was irreproachable; they were very quiet — if anything, too quiet. They took up a part of the piazza that was yielded them by common usage, and sat watching the hop inside, not so much enviously, I thought, as wistfully; and for the first time it struck me as odd that they should have no part in the gayety. I had often seen them there before, but I had never thought it strange they should be shut out. It had always seemed quite normal, but now, suddenly, for one baleful moment, it seemed abnormal. I suppose it was the talk we had been having about the workingmen in society which caused me to see the thing as the Altrurian must have seen it; but I was, nevertheless, vexed with him for having asked such a question, after he had been so fully instructed upon the point. It was malicious of him, or it was stupid. I hardened my heart, and answered: "You might have told him, for one thing, that they were not dancing because they had not paid the piper."

"Then the money consideration enters even into your social pleasures?" asked the Altrurian.

"Very much. Doesn't it with you?"

He evaded this question, as he evaded all straightforward questions concerning his country: "We have no money considerations, you know. But do I understand that all your social entertainments are paid for by the guests?"

"Oh, no, not so bad as that, quite. There are a great many that the host pays for. Even here, in a hotel, the host furnishes the music and the room free to the guests of the house."

"And none are admitted from the outside?"

"Oh, yes, people are welcome from all the other hotels and boarding-houses and the private cottages. The young men are especially welcome; there are not enough young men in the hotel to go round, you see." In fact, we could see that some of the pretty girls within were dancing with other girls; half-grown boys were dangling from the waists of tall young ladies and waltzing on tiptoe.

"Isn't that rather droll?" asked the Altrurian.

"It's grotesque!" I said, and I felt ashamed of it. "But what are you to do? The young men are hard at work in the cities, as many as can get work there, and the rest are out West, growing up with the country. There are twenty young girls for every young man at all the summer-resorts in the East."

"But what would happen if these young farmers — I suppose they are farmers — were invited in to take part in the dance?" asked my friend.

"But that is impossible."

"Why?"

"Really, Mrs. Makely, I think I shall have to give him back to you!" I said.

The lady laughed. "I am not sure that I want him back."

"Oh, yes," the Altrurian entreated, with unwonted perception of the humor. "I know that I must be very trying with my questions; but do not abandon me to the solitude of my own conjectures. They are dreadful!"

"Well, I won't," said the lady, with another laugh. "And I will try to tell you what would happen if those farmers, or farm hands, or whatever they are, were asked in. The mammas would be very indignant, and the young ladies would be scared, and nobody would know what to do, and the dance would stop."

"Then the young ladies prefer to dance with one another and with little boys — "

"No, they prefer to dance with young men of their own station; they would rather not dance at all than dance with people beneath them. I don't say anything against the natives here; they are very civil and decent. But they have not the same social traditions as the young ladies; they would be out of place with them, and they would feel it."

"Yes, I can see that they are not fit to associate with them," said the Altrurian, with a gleam of common-sense that surprised me, "and that as long as your present conditions endure, they never can be. You must excuse the confusion which the difference between your political ideals and your economic ideals constantly creates in me. I always think of you politically first, and realize you as a perfect democracy; then come these other facts, in which I cannot perceive that you differ from the aristocratic countries of Europe in theory or practice. It is very puzzling. Am I right in supposing that the effect of your economy is to establish insuperable inequalities among you, and to forbid the hope of the brotherhood which your polity proclaims?"

Mrs. Makely looked at me as if she were helpless to grapple with his meaning, and for fear of worse, I thought best to evade it. I said, "I don't believe that anybody is troubled by those distinctions. We are used to them, and everybody acquiesces in them, which is a proof that they are a very good thing."

Mrs. Makely now came to my support. "The Americans are very high-spirited, in every class, and I don't believe one of those nice farm boys would like being asked in any better than the young ladies. You can't imagine how proud some of them are."

"So that they suffer from being excluded as inferiors?"

"Oh, I assure you they don't feel themselves inferior! They consider themselves as good as anybody. There are some very interesting characters among them. Now, there is a young girl sitting at the first window, with her profile outlined by the light, whom I feel it an honor to speak to. That's her brother, standing there with her — that tall, gaunt young man with a Roman face; it's such a common type here in the mountains. Their father was a soldier, and he distinguished himself so in one of the last battles that he was promoted. He was badly wounded, but he never took a pension; he just came back to his farm and worked on till he died. Now the son has the farm, and he and his sister live there with their mother. The daughter takes in sewing, and in that way they manage to make both ends meet. The girl is really a first-rate seamstress and *so* cheap! I give her a good deal of my work in the summer, and we are quite friends. She's very fond of reading; the mother is an invalid, but she reads aloud while the daughter sews, and you've no idea how many books they get through. When she comes for sewing, I like to talk with her about them; I always have her sit down; it's hard to realize that she isn't a lady. I'm a good deal criticised, I know, and I suppose I do spoil her a little; it puts notions into such people's heads, if you meet them in that way; they're pretty free and independent as it is. But when I'm with Lizzie I forget that there is any difference between us; I can't help loving the child. You must take Mr. Homos to see them, Mr. Twelvemough. They've got the father's sword hung up over the head of the mother's bed; it's very touching. But the poor little place *is* so bare!"

Mrs. Makely sighed, and there fell a little pause, which she broke with a question she had the effect of having kept back.

"There is one thing I should like to ask you, too, Mr. Homos. Is it true that everybody in Altruria does some kind of manual labor?"

"Why, certainly," he answered, quite as if he had been an American.

"Ladies, too? Or perhaps you have none!"

I thought this rather offensive, but I could not see that the Altrurian had taken it ill. "Perhaps we had better try to understand each other clearly before I answer that question. You have no titles of nobility as they have in England — "

"No, indeed! I hope we have outgrown those superstitions," said Mrs. Makely, with a republican fervor that did my heart good. "It is a word that we apply first of all to the moral qualities of a person."

"But you said just now that you sometimes forgot that your seamstress was not a lady. Just what did you mean by that?"

Mrs. Makely hesitated. "I meant — I suppose I meant — that she had not the surroundings of a lady; the social traditions."

"Then it has something to do with social as well as moral qualities — with ranks and classes?"

"Classes, yes; but, as you know, we have no ranks in America." The Altrurian took off his hat and rubbed an imaginable perspiration from his forehead. He sighed deeply. "It is all very difficult."

"Yes," Mrs. Makely assented, "I suppose it is. All foreigners find it so. In fact it is something that you have to live into the notion of; it can't be explained."

"Well, then, my dear madam, will you tell me without further question what you understand by a lady, and let me live into the notion of it at my leisure?"

"I will do my best," said Mrs. Makely. "But it would be so much easier to tell you *who* was or who was not a lady! However, your acquaintance is so limited yet that I must try to do something in the abstract and impersonal for you. In the first place, a lady must be above the sordid anxieties in every way. She need not be very rich, but she must have enough, so that she need not be harassed about making both ends meet, when she ought to be devoting herself to her social duties. The time is past with us when a lady could look after the dinner, and perhaps cook part of it herself, and then rush in to receive her guests, and do the amenities. She must have a certain kind of house, so that her entourage won't seem cramped and mean, and she must have nice frocks, of course, and plenty of them. She needn't be of the smart set; that isn't at all necessary; but she can't afford to be out of the fashion. Of course she must have a certain training. She must have cultivated tastes; she must know about art, and literature, and music, and all those kind of things, and though it isn't necessary to go in for anything in particular, it won't hurt her to have a fad or two. The nicest kind of fad is charity; and people go in for that a great deal. I think sometimes they use it to work up with, and there are some who use religion in the same way; I think it's horrid; but it's perfectly safe; you can't accuse them of doing it. I'm happy to say, though, that mere church association doesn't count socially so much as it used to. Charity is a great deal more insidious. But you see how hard it is to define a lady. So much has to be left to the nerves, in all these things! And then it's changing all the time; Europe's coming in, and the old American ideals are passing away. Things that people did ten years ago would be impossible now, or at least ridiculous. You wouldn't be considered vulgar, quite, but you would certainly be considered a back number, and that's almost as bad. Really," said Mrs. Makely, "I don't believe I can tell you what a lady is."

We all laughed together at her frank confession. The Altrurian asked, "But do I understand that one of her conditions is that she shall have nothing whatever to do?"

"Nothing to *do!*" cried Mrs. Makely. "A lady is busy from morning till night! She always goes to bed perfectly worn out."

"But with what?" asked the Altrurian.

"With making herself agreeable and her house attractive, with going to lunches and teas and dinners and concerts and theatres and art exhibitions, and charity meetings and receptions, and with writing a thousand and one notes about them, and accepting and declining, and giving lunches and dinners, and making calls and receiving them, and I don't know what all. It's the most hideous slavery!" Her voice rose into something like a shriek; one could see that her nerves were going at the mere thought of it all. "You don't have a moment to yourself; your life isn't your own!"

"But the lady isn't allowed to do any useful kind of work?"

"*Work!* Don't you call all that work, and *useful?* I'm sure I envy the cook in my kitchen at times; I envy the woman that scrubs my floors. Stop! Don't ask why I don't go into my kitchen, or get down on my knees with the mop! It isn't possible! You simply can't! Perhaps you could if you were very *grande dame*, but if you're anywhere near the line of necessity, or ever have been, you can't. Besides, if we did do our own household work, as I understand your Altrurian ladies do, what would become of the servant class? We should be taking away their living, and that would be wicked."

"It would certainly be wrong to take away the living of a fellow-creature," the Altrurian gravely admitted, "and I see the obstacle in your way."

"It's a mountain," said the lady, with exhaustion in her voice, but a returning amiability; his forbearance must have placated her.

"May I ask what the use of your society life is?" he ventured, after a moment.

"Use? Why should it have any? It kills time."

"Then you are shut up to a hideous slavery without use, except to kill time, and you cannot escape from it without taking away the living of those dependent on you?"

"Yes," I put in, "and that is a difficulty that meets us at every turn. It is something that Matthew Arnold urged with great effect in his paper on that crank of a Tolstoï. He asked what would become of the people who need the work, if we served and waited on ourselves, as Tolstoï preached. The question is unanswerable."

"That is true; in your conditions, it is unanswerable," said the Altrurian.

"I think," said Mrs. Makely, "that under the circumstances we do pretty well."

"Oh, I don't presume to censure you. And if you believe that your conditions are the best — "

"We believe them the best in the best of all possible worlds," I said devoutly; and it struck me that if ever we came to have a national church, some such affirmation as that concerning our economical conditions ought to be in the confession of faith.

The Altrurian's mind had not followed mine so far. "And your young girls?" he asked of Mrs. Makely, "how is their time occupied?"

"You mean after they come out in society?"

"I suppose so."

She seemed to reflect. "I don't know that it is very differently occupied. Of course, they have their own amusements; they have their dances, and little clubs, and their sewing societies. I suppose that even an Altrurian would applaud their sewing for the poor?" Mrs. Makely asked, rather satirically.

"Yes," he answered; and then he asked, "Isn't it taking work away from some needy seamstress, though? But I suppose you excuse it to the thoughtlessness of youth."

Mrs. Makely did not say, and he went on: "What I find it so hard to understand is how you ladies can endure a life of mere nervous exertion, such as you have been describing to me. I don't see how you keep well."

"We *don't* keep well," said Mrs. Makely, with the greatest amusement. "I don't suppose that when you get above the working classes, till you reach the very rich, you would find a perfectly well woman in America."

"Isn't that rather extreme?" I ventured to ask.

"No," said Mrs. Makely, "it's shamefully moderate," and she seemed to delight in having made out such a bad case for her sex. You can't stop a woman of that kind when she gets started; I had better left it alone.

"But," said the Altrurian, "if you are forbidden by motives of humanity from doing any sort of manual labor, which you must leave to those who live by it, I suppose you take some sort of exercise?"

"Well," said Mrs. Makely, shaking her head gayly, "we prefer to take medicine."

"You must approve of that," I said to the Altrurian, "as you consider exercise for its own sake insane or immoral. But, Mrs. Makely," I entreated, "you're giving me away at a tremendous rate. I have just been telling Mr. Homos that you ladies go in for athletics so much now in your summer outings that there is danger of your becoming physically as well as intellectually superior to us poor fellows. Don't take that consolation from me!"

"I won't, altogether," she said. "I couldn't have the heart to, after the pretty way you've put it. I don't call it very athletic, sitting around on hotel piazzas all summer long, as nineteen-twentieths of us do. But I don't deny that there is a Remnant, as Matthew Arnold calls them, who do go in for tennis, and boating, and bathing, and tramping, and climbing." She paused, and then she concluded gleefully, "And you ought to see what wrecks they get home in the fall!"

The joke was on me; I could not help laughing, though I felt rather sheepish before the Altrurian. Fortunately, he did not pursue the inquiry; his curiosity had been given a slant aside from it.

"But your ladies," he asked, "they have the summer for rest, however they use it. Do they generally leave town? I understood Mr. Twelvemough to say so," he added, with a deferential glance at me.

"Yes, you may say it is the universal custom in the class that can afford it," said Mrs. Makely. She proceeded as if she felt a tacit censure in his question. "It wouldn't be the least use for us to stay and fry through our summers in the city simply because our fathers and brothers had to. Besides, we are worn out at the end of the season, and they want us to come away as much as we want to come."

"Ah, I have always heard that the Americans are beautiful in their attitude towards women."

"They are perfect dears," said Mrs. Makely, "and here comes one of the best of them."

At that moment her husband came up and laid her shawl across her shoulders. "Whose character is it you're blasting?" he asked, jocosely.

"Where in the world did you find it?" she asked, meaning the shawl.

"It was where you left it; on the sofa, in the side parlor. I had to take my life in my hand when I crossed among all those waltzers in there. There must have been as many as three couples on the floor. Poor girls! I pity them, off at these places. The fellows in town have a good deal better time. They've got their clubs, and they've got the theatre, and when the weather gets too much for them, they can run off down to the shore for the night. The places anywhere within an hour's ride are full of fellows. The girls don't have to dance with one another there, or with little boys. Of course, that's all right if they like it better." He laughed at his wife, and winked at me, and smoked swiftly, in emphasis of his irony.

"Then the young gentlemen whom the young ladies here usually meet in society are all at work in the cities?" the Altrurian asked him, rather needlessly, as I had already said so.

"Yes, those who are not out West, growing up with the country, except, of course, the fellows who have inherited a fortune. They're mostly off on yachts."

"But why do your young men go West to grow up with the country?" pursued my friend.

"Because the East is *grown* up. They have got to hustle, and the West is the place to hustle. To make money," added Makely, in response to a puzzled glance of the Altrurian.

"Sometimes," said his wife, "I almost hate the name of money."

"Well, so long as you don't hate the thing, Peggy."

"Oh, we must have it, I suppose," she sighed. "They used to say about the girls who grew into old maids just after the Rebellion that they had lost their chance in the war for the union. I think quite as many lose their chance now in the war for the dollar."

"Mars hath slain his thousands, but Mammon hath slain his tens of thousands," I suggested lightly; we all like to recognize the facts, so long as we are not expected to do anything about them; then, we deny them.

"Yes, quite as bad as that," said Mrs. Makely.

"Well, my dear, you are expensive, you know," said her husband, "and if we want to have you, why we've got to hustle first."

"Oh, I don't blame you, you poor things! There's nothing to be done about it; it's just got to go on and on; I don't see how it's ever to end."

The Altrurian had been following us with that air of polite mystification which I had begun to dread in him. "Then, in your good society you postpone, and even forego, the happiness of life in the struggle to be rich?"

"Well, you see," said Makely, "a fellow don't like to ask a girl to share a home that isn't as nice as the home she has left."

"Sometimes," his wife put in, rather sadly, "I think that it's all a mistake, and that we'd be willing to share the privations of the man we loved."

"Well," said Makely, with a laugh, "we wouldn't like to risk it."

I laughed with him, but his wife did not, and in the silence that ensued there was nothing to prevent the Altrurian from coming in with another of his questions. "How far does this state of things extend downward? Does it include the working-classes, too?"

"Oh, no!" we all answered together, and Mrs. Makely said: "With your Altrurian ideas I suppose you would naturally sympathize a great deal more with the lower classes, and think they had to endure all the hardships in our system; but if you could realize how the struggle goes on in the best society, and how we all have to fight for what we get, or don't get, you would be disposed to pity our upper classes, too."

"I am sure I should," said the Altrurian.

Makely remarked, "I used to hear my father say that slavery was harder on the whites than it was on the blacks, and that he wanted it done away with for the sake of the masters."

Makely rather faltered in conclusion, as if he were not quite satisfied with his remark, and I distinctly felt a want of proportion in it; but I did not wish to say anything. His wife had no reluctance.

"Well, there's no comparison between the two things, but the struggle certainly doesn't affect the working classes as it does us. They go on marrying and giving in marriage in the old way. They have nothing to lose, and so they can afford it."

"Blessed am dem what don't expect nuffin! Oh, I tell you it's a workingman's country," said Makely, through his cigar smoke. "You ought to see them in town, these summer nights, in the parks and squares and cheap theatres. Their girls are not off for their health, anywhere, and their fellows are not off growing up with the country. Their day's work is over and they're going in for a good time. And, then, walk through the streets where they live, and see them out on the stoops with their wives and children! I tell you, it's enough to make a fellow wish he was poor himself."

"Yes," said Mrs. Makely, "it's astonishing how strong and well those women keep, with their great families and their hard work. Sometimes I really envy them."

"Do you suppose," said the Altrurian, "that they are aware of the sacrifices which the ladies of the upper classes make in leaving all the work to them, and suffering from the nervous debility which seems to be the outcome of your society life?"

"They have not the remotest idea of it! They have no conception of what a society woman goes through with. They think we do nothing. They envy us, too, and sometimes they're so ungrateful and indifferent, if you try to help them, or get on terms with them, that I believe they hate us."

"But that comes from ignorance?"

"Yes, though I don't know that they are really any more ignorant of us than we are of them. It's the other half on both sides."

"Isn't that a pity, rather?"

"Of course it's a pity, but what can you do? You can't know what people are like unless you live like them, and then the question is whether the game is worth the candle. I should like to know how you manage in Altruria."

"Why, we have solved the problem in the only way, as you say, that it can be solved. We all live alike."

"Isn't that a little, just a very trifling little bit monotonous?" Mrs. Makely asked, with a smile. "But there is everything, of course, in being used to it. To an unregenerate spirit — like mine, for example — it seems intolerable."

"But why? When you were younger, before you were married, you all lived at home together. — Or, perhaps, you were an only child?"

"Oh, no, indeed! There were ten of us."

"Then you all lived alike, and shared equally?"

"Yes, but we were a family."

"We do not conceive of the human race except as a family."

"Now, excuse me, Mr. Homos, that is all nonsense. You cannot have the family feeling without love, and it is impossible to love other people. That talk about the neighbor, and all that, is all well enough — " She stopped herself, as if she dimly remembered who began that talk, and then went on: "Of course I accept it as a matter of faith, and the spirit of it, nobody denies that; but what I mean is, that you must have frightful quarrels all the time." She tried to look as if this were where she really meant to bring up, and he took her on the ground she had chosen.

"Yes, we have quarrels. Hadn't you at home?"

"We fought like little cats and dogs, at times."

Makely and I burst into a laugh at her magnanimous frankness. The Altrurian remained serious. "But because you lived alike, you knew each other; and so you easily made up your quarrels. It is quite as simple with us, in our life as a human family."

This notion of a human family seemed to amuse Mrs. Makely more and more; she laughed and laughed again. "You must excuse me!" she panted, at last. "But I cannot imagine it! No, it is too ludicrous. Just fancy the jars of an ordinary family multiplied by the population of a whole continent! Why, you must be in a perpetual squabble! You can't have any peace of your lives! It's worse, far worse, than our way!"

"But, madam," he began, "you are supposing our family to be made up of people with all the antagonistic interests of your civilization. As a matter of fact — "

"No, no! *I know human nature*, Mr. Homos!" She suddenly jumped up and gave him her hand. "Good-night!" she said, sweetly, and as she drifted off on her husband's arm, she looked back at us and nodded in gay triumph.

The Altrurian turned upon me with unabated interest. "And have you no provision in your system for finally making the lower classes understand the sufferings and sacrifices of the upper classes in their behalf? Do you expect to do nothing to bring them together in mutual kindness?"

"Well, not this evening," I said, throwing the end of my cigar away. "I'm going to bed, aren't you?"

"Not yet."

"Well, good-night. Are you sure you can find your room?"

"Oh, yes. Good-night."

CHAPTER VI

I left my guest abruptly, with a feeling of vexation not very easily definable. His repetition of questions about questions which society has so often answered, and always in the same way, was not so bad in him as it would have been in a person of our civilization; he represented a wholly different state of things, the inversion of our own, and much could be forgiven him for that reason, just as in Russia much could be forgiven to an American if he formulated his curiosity concerning imperialism from a purely republican experience. I knew that in Altruria, for instance, the possession of great gifts, of any kind of superiority, involved the sense of obligation to others, and the wish to identify one's self with the great mass of men, rather than the ambition to distinguish one's self from them; and that the Altrurians honored their gifted men in the measure they did this. A man reared in such a civilization must naturally find it difficult to get our point of view; with social inclusion as the ideal, he could with difficulty conceive of our ideal of social exclusion; but I think we had all been very patient with him; we should have made short work with an American who had approached us with the same inquiries. Even from a foreigner, the citizen of a republic founded on the notion, elsewhere exploded ever since Cain, that one is his brother's keeper, the things he asked seemed inoffensive only because they were puerile; but they certainly were puerile. I felt that it ought to have been self-evident to him that when a commonwealth of sixty million Americans based itself upon the great principle of self-seeking, self-seeking was the best thing, and whatever hardship it seemed to work, it must carry with it unseen blessings in tenfold measure. If a few hundred thousand favored Americans enjoyed the privilege of socially contemning all the rest, it was as clearly right and just that they should do so as that four thousand American millionaires should be richer than all the other Americans put together. Such a status, growing out of our political equality and our material prosperity, must evince a divine purpose to any one intimate with the designs of Providence, and it seemed a kind of impiety to doubt its perfection. I excused the misgivings, which I could not help seeing in the Altrurian to his alien traditions, and I was aware that my friends had done so too. But if I could judge from myself he must have left them all sensible of their effort; and this was not pleasant. I could not blink the fact that although I had openly disagreed with him on every point of ethics and economics, I was still responsible for him as a guest. It was as if an English gentleman had introduced a blatant American Democrat into Tory society; or, rather, as if a Southerner of the olden time had harbored a Northern Abolitionist, and permitted him to inquire into the workings of slavery among his neighbors. People would tolerate him as my guest for a time, but there must be an end of their patience with the tacit enmity of his sentiments and the explicit vulgarity of his ideals, and when the end came I must be attained with him.

I did not like the notion of this, and I meant to escape it if I could. I confess that I would have willingly disowned him, as I had already disavowed his opinions, but there was no way of doing it short of telling him to go away, and I was not ready to do that. Something in the man, I do not know what, mysteriously appealed to me. He was not contemptibly puerile without being lovably childlike, and I could only make up my mind to be more and more frank with him, and to try and shield him, as well as myself, from the effects I dreaded.

I fell asleep planning an excursion farther into the mountains, which should take up the rest of the week that I expected him to stay with me, and would keep him from following up his studies of American life where they would be so injurious to both of us as they must in our hotel. A knock at my door roused me, and I sent a drowsy "Come in!" towards it from the bedclothes without looking that way.

"Good-morning!" came back in the rich, gentle voice of the Altrurian. I lifted my head with a jerk from the pillow, and saw him standing against the closed door, with my shoes in his hand. "Oh, I am sorry I waked you! I thought — "

"Not at all, not at all!" I said. "It's quite time, I dare say. But you oughtn't to have taken the trouble to bring my shoes in!"

"I wasn't altogether disinterested in it," he returned. "I wished you to compliment me on them. Don't you think they are pretty well done, for an amateur?" He came towards my bed, and turned them about in his hands, so that they would catch the light, and smiled down upon me.

"I don't understand," I began.

"Why," he said, "I blacked them, you know."

"You blacked them!"

"Yes," he returned, easily. "I thought I would go into the baggage-room, after we parted last night, to look for a piece of mine that had not been taken to my room, and I found the porter there, with his wrist bound up. He said he had strained it in handling a lady's Saratoga — he said a Saratoga was a large trunk — and I begged him to let me relieve him at the boots he was blacking. He refused at first, but I insisted upon trying my hand at a pair, and then he let me go on with the men's boots; he said he could varnish the ladies' without hurting his wrist. It needed less skill than I supposed, and after I had done a few pairs he said I could black boots as well as he."

"Did anybody see you?" I gasped, and I felt a cold perspiration break out on me.

"No, we had the whole midnight hour to ourselves. The porter's work with the baggage was all over, and there was nothing to interrupt the delightful chat we fell into. He is a very intelligent man, and he told me all about that custom of feeing which you deprecate. He says that the servants hate it as much as the guests; they have to take the tips now because the landlords figure on them in the wages, and they cannot live without them. He is a fine, manly fellow, and — "

"Mr. Homos," I broke in, with the strength I found in his assurance that no one had seen him helping the porter black boots, "I want to speak very seriously with you, and I hope you will not be hurt if I speak very plainly about a matter in which I have your good solely at heart." This was not quite true, and I winced inwardly a little when he thanked me with that confounded sincerity of his, which was so much like irony; but I went on: "It is my duty to you, as my guest, to tell you that this thing of doing for others is not such a simple matter here, as your peculiar training leads you to think. You have been deceived by a superficial likeness; but really, I do not understand how you could have read all you have done about us, and not realize before coming here that America and Altruria are absolutely distinct and diverse in their actuating principles. They are both republics, I know; but America is a republic where every man is for himself, and you cannot help others as you do at home; it is dangerous — it is ridiculous. You must keep this fact in mind, or you will fall into errors that will be very embarrassing to you in your stay among us, and," I was forced to add, "to all your friends. Now, I certainly hoped, after what I had said to you, and what my friends had explained of our civilization, that you would not have done a thing of this kind. I will see the porter, as soon as I am up, and ask him not to mention the matter to any one, but I confess I don't like to take an apologetic tone with him; your conditions are so alien to ours that they will seem incredible to him, and he will think I am stuffing him."

"I don't believe he will think that," said the Altrurian, "and I hope you won't find the case so bad as it seems to you. I am extremely sorry to have done wrong — "

"Oh, the thing wasn't wrong in itself. It was only wrong under the circumstances. Abstractly, it is quite right to help a fellow-being who needs help; no one denies that, even in a country where every one is for himself."

"I am so glad to hear it," said the Altrurian. "Then at least, I have not gone radically astray; and I do not think you need to take the trouble to explain the Altrurian ideas to the porter. I have done that already, and they seemed quite conceivable to him; he said that poor folks had to act upon them, even here, more or less, and that if they did not act upon them, there would be no chance for them at all. He says they have to help each other, very much as we do at home, and that it is only the rich folks among you who are independent. I really don't think you need speak to him at all, unless you wish; and I was very careful to guard my offer of help at the point where I understood from you and your friends that it might do harm. I asked him if there was not some one who would help him out with his boot-blacking for money, because in that case I should be glad to pay him; but he said there was no one about who would take the job; that he had to agree to black the boots, or else he would not have got the place of porter, but that all the rest of the help would consider it a disgrace, and would not help him for love or money. So it seemed quite safe to offer him my services."

I felt that the matter was almost hopeless, but I asked, "And what he said, didn't that suggest anything else to you?"

"How anything else?" asked the Altrurian, in his turn.

"Didn't it occur to you that if none of his fellow-servants were willing to help him black boots, and if he did it only because he was obliged to, it was hardly the sort of work for you?"

"Why, no," said the Altrurian, with absolute simplicity. He must have perceived the despair I fell into at this answer, for he asked, "Why should I have minded doing for others what I should have been willing to do for myself?"

"There are a great many things we are willing to do for ourselves that we are not willing to do for others. But even on that principle, which I think false and illogical, you could not be justified. A gentleman is not willing to black *his own* boots. It is offensive to his feelings, to his self-respect; it is something he will not do if he can get anybody else to do it for him."

"Then in America," said the Altrurian, "it is not offensive to the feelings of a gentleman to let another do for him what he would not do for himself?"

"Certainly not."

"Ah," he returned, "then we understand something altogether different by the word gentleman in Altruria. I see, now, how I have committed a mistake. I shall be more careful hereafter."

I thought I had better leave the subject, and, "By-the-way," I said, "how would you like to take a little tramp with me to-day farther up into the mountains?"

"I should be delighted," said the Altrurian so gratefully that I was ashamed to think why I was proposing the pleasure to him.

"Well, then, I shall be ready to start as soon as we have had breakfast. I will join you down-stairs in half an hour."

He left me at this hint, though really I was half afraid he might stay and offer to lend me a hand at my toilet, in the expression of his national character. I found him with Mrs. Makely, when I went down, and she began, with a parenthetical tribute to the beauty of the mountains in the morning light, "Don't be surprised to see me up at this unnatural hour. I don't know whether it was the excitement of our talk last night, or what it was, but my sulfonal[5] wouldn't act, though I took fifteen grains, and I was up with the lark, or should have been, if there had been any lark outside of literature to be up with. However, this air is so glorious that I don't mind losing a night's sleep now and then. I believe that with a little practice one could get along without any sleep at all here; at least *I* could. I'm sorry to say poor Mr. Makely *can't*, apparently. He's making up for his share of my vigils, and I'm going to breakfast without him. Do you know, I've done a very bold thing: I've got the head waiter to give you places at our table; I know you'll hate it, Mr. Twelvemough, because you naturally want to keep Mr. Homos to yourself, and I don't blame you at all; but I'm simply not going to *let* you, and that's all there is about it."

The pleasure I felt at this announcement was not unmixed, but I tried to keep Mrs. Makely from thinking so, and I was immensely relieved when she found a chance to say to me in a low voice, "I know just how you're feeling, Mr. Twelvemough, and I'm going to help you keep him from doing anything ridiculous if I can. I *like* him, and I think it's a perfect

---

[5] Sulfonal is an organic compound that was used as a sedative.

shame to have people laughing at him. I know we can manage him
between us."

We so far failed, however, that the Altrurian shook hands with the head
waiter when he pressed open the wire-netting door to let us into the
dining-room, and made a bow to our waitress of the sort one makes to a
lady. But we thought it best to ignore these little errors of his, and reserve
our moral strength for anything more spectacular. Fortunately we got
through our breakfast with nothing worse than his jumping up and
stooping to hand the waitress a spoon she let fall; but this could easily
pass for some attention to Mrs. Makely at a little distance. There were
not many people down to breakfast yet; but I could see that there was a
good deal of subdued sensation among the waitresses, standing with
folded arms behind their tables, and that the head waiter's handsome face
was red with anxiety.

Mrs. Makely asked if we were going to church. She said she was
driving that way, and would be glad to drop us. "I'm not going myself,"
she explained, "because I couldn't make anything of the sermon, with my
head in the state it is, and I'm going to compromise on a good action. I
want to carry some books and papers over to Mrs. Camp. Don't you think
that will be quite as acceptable, Mr. Homos?"

"I should venture to hope it," he said, with a tolerant seriousness not
altogether out of keeping with her lightness.

"Who is Mrs. Camp?" I asked, not caring to commit myself on the
question.

"Lizzie's mother. You know I told you about them last night. I think
she must have got through the books I lent her, and I know Lizzie didn't
like to ask me for more, because she saw me talking with you, and didn't
want to interrupt us. Such a nice girl! I think the Sunday papers must have
come, and I'll take them over, too; Mrs. Camp is always so glad to get
them, and she is so delightful when she gets going about public events.
But perhaps you don't approve of Sunday papers, Mr. Homos."

"I'm sure I don't know, madam. I haven't seen them yet. You know this
is the first Sunday I've been in America."

"Well, I'm sorry to say you won't see the old Puritan Sabbath," said
Mrs. Makely, with an abrupt deflection from the question of the Sunday
papers. "Though you ought to, up in these hills. The only thing left of it
is rye-and-Indian bread, and these baked beans and fish-balls."

"But they are very good?"

"Yes, I dare say they are not the worst of it."

She was a woman who tended to levity, and I was a little afraid she
might be going to say something irreverent, but if she were, she was

forestalled by the Altrurian asking, "Would it be very indiscreet, madam, if I were to ask you some time to introduce me to that family?"

"The Camps?" she returned. "Not at all. I should be perfectly delighted." The thought seemed to strike her, and she asked, "Why not go with me this morning, unless you are inflexibly bent on going to church, you and Mr. Twelvemough?"

The Altrurian glanced at me, and I said I should be only too glad, if I could carry some books, so that I could compromise on a good action, too. "Take one of your own," she instantly suggested.

"Do you think they wouldn't be too severe upon it?" I asked.

"Well, Mrs. Camp might," Mrs. Makely consented, with a smile. "She goes in for rather serious fiction; but I think Lizzie would enjoy a good, old-fashioned love-story, where everybody got married, as they do in your charming books."

I winced a little, for every one likes to be regarded seriously, and I did not enjoy being remanded to the young-girl public; but I put a bold face on it, and said, "My good action shall be done in behalf of Miss Lizzie."

Half an hour later, Mrs. Makely having left word with the clerk where we were gone, so that her husband need not be alarmed when he got up, we were striking into the hills on a two-seated buckboard, with one of the best teams of our hotel, and one of the most taciturn drivers. Mrs. Makely had the Altrurian get into the back seat with her, and, after some attempts to make talk with the driver, I leaned over and joined in their talk. The Altrurian was greatly interested, not so much in the landscape — though he owned its beauty, when we cried out over it from point to point — but in the human incidents and features. He noticed the cattle in the fields, and the horses we met on the road, and the taste and comfort of the buildings, the variety of the crops, and the promise of the harvest. I was glad of the respite his questions gave me from the study of the intimate character of our civilization, for they were directed now at these more material facts, and I willingly joined Mrs. Makely in answering them. We explained that the finest teams we met were from the different hotels or boarding-houses, or at least from the farms where the people took city people to board; and that certain shabby equipages belonged to the natives who lived solely by cultivating the soil. There was not very much of the soil cultivated, for the chief crop was hay, with here and there a patch of potatoes or beans, and a few acres in sweet-corn. The houses of the natives, when they were for their use only, were no better than their turnouts; it was where the city boarder had found shelter that they were modern and pleasant. Now and then we came to a deserted homestead, and I tried to make the Altrurian understand how farming in New England had yielded to the competition of the immense agricultural operations of the West. "You know," I said, "that agriculture is really an operation out there, as much as coal-mining is in Pennsylvania, or finance in Wall Street; you have no idea of the vastness of the scale." Perhaps I swelled a little with pride in my celebration of the national prosperity, as it flowed from our Western farms of five and ten and twenty thousand acres; I could not very well help putting on the pedal in these passages. Mrs. Makely listened almost as eagerly as the Altrurian, for, as a cultivated American woman, she was necessarily quite ignorant of her own country, geographically, politically, and historically. "The only people left in the hill country of New England," I concluded, "are those who are too old or too lazy to get away. Any young man of energy would be ashamed to stay, unless he wanted to keep a boarding-house or live on the city vacationists in summer. If he doesn't, he goes West and takes up some of the new land, and comes back in middle-life, and buys a deserted farm to spend his summers on."

"Dear me!" said the Altrurian, "Is it so simple as that? Then we can hardly wonder at their owners leaving these worn-out farms; though I suppose it must be with the pang of exile, sometimes."

"Oh, I fancy there isn't much sentiment involved," I answered, lightly.

"Whoa!" said Mrs. Makely, speaking to the horses before she spoke to the driver, as some women will. He pulled them up, and looked round at her.

"Isn't that Reuben Camp, *now*, over there by that house?" she asked, as if we had been talking of him; that is another way some women have.

"Yes, ma'am," said the driver.

"Oh, well, then!" and "Reuben!" she called to the young man who was prowling about the door-yard of a sad-colored old farm-house, and peering into a window here and there. "Come here a moment — won't you, please?"

He lifted his head and looked round, and when he had located the appeal made to him, he came down the walk to the gate and leaned over it, waiting for further instructions. I saw that it was the young man whom we had noticed with the girl Mrs. Makely called Lizzie on the hotel piazza the night before.

"Do you know whether I should find Lizzie at home this morning?"

"Yes, she's there with mother," said the young fellow, with neither liking nor disliking in his tone.

"Oh, I'm so glad!" said the lady. "I didn't know but she might be at church. What in the world has happened here? Is there anything unusual going on inside?"

"No, I was just looking to see if it was all right. The folks wanted I should come round."

"Why, where are they?"

"Oh, they're gone."

"Gone?"

"Yes; gone West. They've left the old place, because they couldn't make a living here any longer."

"Why, this is quite a case in point," I said. "Now, Mr. Homos, here is a chance to inform yourself at first hand about a very interesting fact of our civilization;" and I added in a low voice, to Mrs. Makely, "Won't you introduce us?"

"Oh, yes! Mr. Camp, this is Mr. Twelvemough, the author — you know his books, of course; and Mr. Homos, a gentleman from Altruria."

The young fellow opened the gate he leaned on, and came out to us. He took no notice of me, but he seized the Altrurian's hand and wrung it. "I've heard of *you*," he said. "Mrs. Makely, were you going to our place?"

"Why, yes."

"So do, then! Mother would give almost anything to see Mr. Homos. We've heard of Altruria, over our way," he added, to our friend. "Mother's been reading up all she can about it. She'll want to talk with you, and she won't give the rest of us much of a chance, I guess."

"Oh, I shall be glad to see her," said the Altrurian, "and to tell her everything I can. But won't you explain to me first something about your deserted farms here? It's quite a new thing to me."

"It isn't a new thing to us," said the young fellow, with a short laugh. "And there isn't much to explain about it. You'll see them all through New England. When a man finds he can't get his funeral expenses out of the land, he don't feel like staying to be buried in it, and he pulls up and goes."

"But people used to get their living expenses here," I suggested. "Why can't they now?"

"Well, they didn't use to have Western prices to fight with; and then the land wasn't worn out so, and the taxes were not so heavy. How would you like to pay twenty to thirty dollars on the thousand, and assessed up to the last notch, in the city?"

"Why, what in the world makes your taxes so heavy?"

"Schools and roads. We've got to have schools, and you city folks want good roads when you come here in the summer, don't you? Then the season is short, and sometimes we can't make a crop. The frost catches the corn in the field, and you have your trouble for your pains. Potatoes are the only thing we can count on, except grass, and when everybody raises potatoes, you know where the price goes."

"Oh, but now, Mr. Camp," said Mrs. Makely, leaning over towards him, and speaking in a cosey and coaxing tone, as if he must not really keep the truth from an old friend like her, "isn't it a good deal because the farmers' daughters want pianos, and the farmers' sons want buggies? I heard Professor Lumen saying, the other day, that if the farmers were willing to work, as they used to work, they could still get a good living off their farms, and that they gave up their places because they were too lazy, in many cases, to farm them properly."

"He'd better not let *me* hear him saying that," said the young fellow, while a hot flush passed over his face. He added, bitterly, "If he wants to see how easy it is to make a living up here, he can take this place and try, for a year or two; he can get it cheap. But I guess he wouldn't want it the year round; he'd only want it a few months in the summer, when he could enjoy the sightliness of it, and see me working over there on my farm, while he smoked on his front porch." He turned round and looked at the old house in silence a moment. Then, as he went on, his voice lost its angry ring. "The folks here bought this place from the Indians, and they'd been here more than two hundred years. Do you think they left it because they were too lazy to run it, or couldn't get pianos and buggies out of it, or were such fools as not to know whether they were well off ? It was their *home*; they were born, and lived and died here. There is the family burying-ground, over there."

Neither Mrs. Makely nor myself was ready with a reply, and we left the word with the Altrurian, who suggested, "Still I suppose they will be more prosperous in the West on the new land they take up?"

The young fellow leaned his arms on the wheel by which he stood. "What do you mean by taking up new land?"

"Why, out of the public domain — "

"There *ain't* any public domain that's worth having. All the good land is in the hands of railroads and farm syndicates and speculators; and if you want a farm in the West you've got to buy it; the East is the only place where folks give them away, because they ain't worth keeping. If you haven't got the ready money, you can buy one on credit, and pay ten, twenty, and thirty per cent interest, and live in a dug-out on the plains — till your mortgage matures." The young man took his arms from the wheel and moved a few steps backward, as he added, "I'll see you over at the house later."

The driver touched his horses, and we started briskly off again. But I confess I had quite enough of his pessimism, and as we drove away I leaned back toward the Altrurian, and said, "Now, it is all perfect nonsense to pretend that things are at that pass with us. There are more millionaires in America, probably, than there are in all the other civilized countries of the globe, and it is not possible that the farming population should be in such a hopeless condition. All wealth comes out of the earth, and you may be sure they get their full share of it."

"I am glad to hear you say so," said the Altrurian. "What is the meaning of this new party in the West that seems to have held a convention lately? I read something of it in the train yesterday."

"Oh, that is a lot of crazy Hayseeds, who don't want to pay back the money they have borrowed, or who find themselves unable to meet their interest. It will soon blow over. We are always having these political flurries. A good crop will make it all right with them."[6]

"But is it true that they have to pay such rates of interest as our young friend mentioned?"

"Well," I said, seeing the thing in the humorous light, which softens for us Americans so many of the hardships of others, "I suppose that man likes to squeeze his brother man when he gets him in his grip. That's human nature, you know."

"Is it?" asked the Altrurian.

It seemed to me that he had asked something like that before when I alleged human nature in defense of some piece of every-day selfishness. But I thought best not to notice it, and I went on: "The land is so rich out there that a farm will often pay for itself with a single crop."

"Is it possible?" cried the Altrurian. "Then I suppose it seldom really happens that a mortgage is foreclosed, in the way our young friend insinuated?"

"Well, I can't say that exactly," and having admitted so much, I did not feel bound to impart a fact that popped perversely into my mind. I was once talking with a Western money-lender, a very good sort of fellow, frank and open as the day; I asked him whether the farmers generally paid off their mortgages, and he answered me that if the mortgage was to the value of a fourth of the land, the farmer might pay it off, but if it were to a half or a third even, he never paid it, but slaved on and died in his debts. "You may be sure, however," I concluded, "that our young friend takes a jaundiced view of the situation."

"Now, really," said Mrs. Makely, "I must insist upon dropping this everlasting talk about money. I think it is perfectly disgusting, and I

---

[6] Mr. Twelvemough refers disparagingly here to the new People's (or Populist) party that sprang up in agricultural regions of the South and Midwest. The party demanded significant political and economic reform but was dismissed by many middle-class Americans as the work of ignorant and unsophisticated farmers who wanted to escape their legitimate debts. *Hayseed* is the equivalent, in slang, of *rube* or *hick*.

believe it was Mr. Makely's account of his speculations that kept me awake last night. My brain got running on figures till the dark seemed to be all sown with dollar-marks, like the stars in the milky way. I — ugh! What in the world is it? Oh, you dreadful little things!"

Mrs. Makely passed swiftly from terror to hysterical laughter as the driver pulled up short, and a group of barefooted children broke in front of his horses, and scuttled out of the dust into the road-side bushes like a covey of quails. There seemed to be a dozen of them, nearly all the same in size, but there turned out to be only five or six; or at least no more showed their gleaming eyes and teeth through the underbrush in quiet enjoyment of the lady's alarm.

"Don't you know that you might have got killed?" she demanded, with that severity good women feel for people who have just escaped with their lives. "How lovely the dirty little dears are!" she added, in the next wave of emotion. One bold fellow of six showed a half length above the bushes, and she asked, "Don't you know that you oughtn't to play in the road when there are so many teams passing? Are all those your brothers and sisters?"

He ignored the first question. "One's my cousin." I pulled out a half-dozen coppers and held my hand toward him. "See if there is one for each." They had no difficulty in solving the simple mathematical problem except the smallest girl, who cried for fear and baffled longing. I tossed the coin to her, and a little fat dog darted out at her feet and caught it up in his mouth. "Oh, good gracious!" I called out in my light, humorous way. "Do you suppose he's going to spend it for candy?" The little people thought that a famous joke, and they laughed with the gratitude that even small favors inspire. "Bring your sister here," I said to the boldest boy, and when he came up with the little woman, I put another copper into her hand. "Look out that the greedy dog doesn't get it," I said, and my gayety met with fresh applause. "Where do you live?" I asked, with some vague purpose of showing the Altrurian the kindliness that exists between our upper and lower classes.

"Over there," said the boy. I followed the twist of his head, and glimpsed a wooden cottage on the border of the forest, so very new that the sheathing had not yet been covered with clapboards. I stood up in the buckboard and saw that it was a story and a half high, and could have had four or five rooms in it. The bare, curtainless windows were set in the unpainted frames, but the front door seemed not to be hung yet. The people meant to winter there, however, for the sod was banked up against the wooden underpinning; a stove-pipe struck out of the roof of a little wing behind. While I gazed a young-looking woman came to the door, as if she had been drawn by our talk with the children, and then she jumped down from the threshold, which still wanted a doorstep, and came slowly out to us. The children ran to her with their coppers, and then followed her back to us.

Mrs. Makely called to her before she reached us, "I hope you weren't frightened. We didn't drive over any of them."

"Oh, I wasn't frightened," said the young woman. "It's a very safe place to bring up children, in the country, and I never feel uneasy about them."

"Yes, if they are not under the horses' feet," said Mrs. Makely, mingling instruction and amusement very judiciously in her reply. "Are they all yours?"

"Only five," said the mother, and she pointed to the alien in her flock. "He's my sister's. She lives just below here." Her children had grouped themselves about her, and she kept passing her hands caressingly over their little heads as she talked. "My sister has nine children, but she has the rest at church with her to-day."

"You don't speak like an American," Mrs. Makely suggested.

"No, we're English. Our husbands work in the quarry. That's *my* little palace." The woman nodded her head toward the cottage.

"It's going to be very nice," said Mrs. Makely, with an evident perception of her pride in it.

"Yes, if we ever get money to finish it. Thank you for the children!"

"Oh, it was this gentleman." Mrs. Makely indicated me, and I bore the merit of my good action as modestly as I could.

"Then thank *you*, sir," said the young woman, and she asked Mrs. Makely, "You're not living about here, ma'am?"

"Oh, no, we're staying at the hotel."

"At the hotel! It must be very dear, there."

"Yes, it is expensive," said Mrs. Makely, with a note of that satisfaction in her voice which we all feel in spending a great deal of money.

"But I suppose you can afford it," said the woman, whose eye was running hungrily over Mrs. Makely's pretty costume. "Some are poor, and some are rich. That's the way the world has to be made up, isn't it?"

"Yes," said Mrs. Makely, very dryly, and the talk languished from this point, so that the driver felt warranted in starting up his horses. When we had driven beyond ear-shot she said, "I knew she was not an American, as soon as she spoke, by her accent, and then those foreigners have no self-respect. That was a pretty bold bid for a contribution to finish up her 'little palace!' I'm glad you didn't give her anything, Mr. Twelvemough. I was afraid your sympathies had been wrought upon."

"Oh, not at all!" I answered. "I saw the mischief I had done with the children."

The Altrurian, who had not asked anything for a long time, but had listened with eager interest to all that passed, now came up smiling with his question: "Will you kindly tell me what harm would have been done by offering the woman a little money to help finish up her cottage?"

I did not allow Mrs. Makely to answer, I was so eager to air my political economy. "The very greatest harm. It would have pauperized her. You have no idea how quickly they give way to the poison of that sort of thing. As soon as they get any sort of help they expect more; they count upon it, and they begin to live upon it. The sight of those coppers which I gave her children — more out of joke than charity — demoralized the woman. She took us for rich people, and wanted us to build her a house. You have to guard against every approach to a thing of that sort."

"I don't believe," said Mrs. Makely, "that an American would have hinted, as she did."

"No, an American would not have done that, I'm thankful to say. They take fees, but they don't ask charity, yet." We went on to exult in the noble independence of the American character in all classes, at some length. We talked at the Altrurian, but he did not seem to hear us. At last he asked, with a faint sigh, "Then, in your condition, a kindly impulse to aid one who needs your help is something to be guarded against as possibly pernicious?"

"Exactly," I said. "And now you see what difficulties beset us in dealing with the problem of poverty. We cannot let people suffer, for that would be cruel; and we cannot relieve their need without pauperizing them."

"I see," he answered. "It is a terrible quandary."

"I wish," said Mrs. Makely, "that you would tell us just how you manage with the poor in Altruria."

"We have none," he replied.

"But the comparatively poor — you have some people who are richer than others?"

"No. We should regard that as the worst incivism."

"What is incivism?"

I interpreted, "Bad citizenship."

"Well then, if you will excuse me, Mr. Homos," she said, "I think that is simply impossible. There *must* be rich and there *must* be poor. There always have been, and there always will be. That woman said it as well as anybody. Didn't Christ himself say, 'The poor ye have always with you'?"

CHAPTER VII

The Altrurian looked at Mrs. Makely with an amazement visibly heightened by the air of complacency she put on after delivering this poser: "Do you really think Christ meant that you *ought* always to have the poor with you?" he asked.

"Why, of course!" she answered triumphantly. "How else are the sympathies of the rich to be cultivated? The poverty of some and the wealth of others, isn't that what forms the great tie of human brotherhood? If we were all comfortable, or all shared alike, there could not be anything like charity, and Paul said 'the greatest of these is charity.' I believe it's 'love' in the new version, but it comes to the same thing."

The Altrurian gave a kind of gasp, and then lapsed into a silence that lasted until we came in sight of the Camp farm-house. It stood on the crest of a roadside upland, and looked down the beautiful valley, bathed in Sabbath sunlight, and away to the ranges of hills, so far that it was hard to say whether it was sun or shadow that dimmed their distance. Decidedly, the place was what the country people call sightly. The old house, once painted a Brandon red, crouched low to the ground, with its lean-to in the rear, and its flat-arched wood-sheds and wagon-houses stretching away at the side to the barn, and covering the approach to it with an unbroken roof. There were flowers in the beds along the underpinning of the house, which stood close to the street, and on one side of the door was a clump of Spanish willow; an old-fashioned June rose climbed over it from the other. An aged dog got stiffly to its feet from the threshold stone and whimpered as our buckboard drew up; the poultry picking about the path and among the chips lazily made way for us, and as our wheels ceased to crunch upon the gravel we heard hasty steps, and Reuben Camp came round the corner of the house in time to give Mrs. Makely his hand and help her spring to the ground, which she did very lightly; her remarkable mind had kept her body in a sort of sympathetic activity, and at thirty-five she had the gracile case and self-command of a girl.

"Ah, Reuben," she sighed, permitting herself to call him by his first name, with the emotion which expressed itself more definitely in the words that followed, "how I envy you all this dear old home-like place! I never come here without thinking of my grandfather's farm in Massachusetts, where I used to go every summer when I was a little girl. If I had a place like this, I should never leave it."

"Well, Mrs. Makely," said young Camp, "you can have this place cheap, if you really want it. Or almost any other place in the neighborhood."

"Don't say such a thing!" she returned. "It makes one feel as if the foundations of the great deep were giving way. I don't know what that means, exactly, but I suppose it's equivalent to mislaying George's hatchet,[7] and going back on the Declaration generally; and I don't like to hear you talk so."

Camp seemed to have lost his bitter mood, and he answered pleasantly, "The Declaration is all right, as far as it goes, but it don't help us to compete with the Western farm operations."

"Why, you believe every one was born free and equal, don't you?" Mrs. Makely asked.

"Oh, yes, I believe that; but — "

"Then why do you object to free and equal competition?"

The young fellow laughed, and said, as he opened the door for us: "Walk right into the parlor, please. Mother will be ready for you in a minute." He added, "I guess she's putting on her best cap for you, Mr. Homos. It's a great event for her, your coming here. It is for all of us. We're glad to have you."

"And I'm glad to be here," said the Altrurian, as simply as the other. He looked about the best room of a farm-house that had never adapted itself to the tastes or needs of the city boarder, and was as stiffly repellent in its upholstery and as severe in its decoration as haircloth chairs and dark brown wall-paper of a trellis-pattern, with drab roses, could make it. The windows were shut tight, and our host did not offer to open them. A fly or two crossed the doorway into the hall, but made no attempt to penetrate the interior, where we sat in an obscurity that left the high-hung family photographs on the walls vague and uncertain. I made a mental note of it as a place where it would be very characteristic to have a rustic funeral take place; and I was pleased to have Mrs. Makely drop into a sort of mortuary murmur, as she said: "I hope your mother is as well as usual this morning?" I perceived that this murmur was produced by the sepulchral influence of the room.

"Oh, yes," said Camp, and at that moment a door opened from the room across the hall, and his sister seemed to bring in some of the light from it to us where we sat. She shook hands with Mrs. Makely, who introduced me to her, and then presented the Altrurian. She bowed very civilly to me, but with a touch of severity, such as country people find necessary for the assertion of their self-respect with strangers. I thought it very pretty, and

---

[7] Mrs. Makely refers to the mythical story of young George Washington chopping down a cherry tree and then admitting it to his father because he could not tell a lie.

instantly saw that I could work it into some picture of character; and I was not at all sorry that she made a difference in favor of the Altrurian.

"Mother will be so glad to see you," she said to him, and, "Won't you come right in?" she added to us all.

We followed her and found ourselves in a large, low, sunny room on the southeast corner of the house, which had no doubt once been the living-room, but which was now open up to the bed-ridden invalid; a door opened into the kitchen behind, where the table was already laid for the midday meal, with the plates turned down in the country fashion, and some netting drawn over the dishes to keep the flies away.

Mrs. Makely bustled up to the bedside with her energetic, patronizing cheerfulness. "Ah, Mrs. Camp, I am glad to see you looking so well this morning. I've been meaning to run over for several days past, but I couldn't find a moment till this morning, and I knew you didn't object to Sunday visits." She took the invalid's hand in hers, and with the air of showing how little she felt any inequality between them, she leaned over and kissed her, where Mrs. Camp sat propped against her pillows. She had a large, nobly-moulded face of rather masculine contour, and at the same time the most motherly look in the world. Mrs. Makely bubbled and babbled on, and every one waited patiently till she had done, and turned and said, toward the Altrurian, "I have ventured to bring my friend, Mr. Homos, with me. He is from Altruria." Then she turned to me, and said, "Mr. Twelvemough, you know already through his delightful books;" but although she paid me this perfunctory compliment, it was perfectly apparent to me that in the esteem of this disingenuous woman the distinguished stranger was a far more important person than the distinguished author. Whether Mrs. Camp read my perception of this fact in my face or not I cannot say, but she was evidently determined that I should not feel a difference in her. She held out her hand to me first, and said that I never could know how many heavy hours I had helped to lighten for her, and then she turned to the Altrurian, and took his hand. "Oh!" she said, with a long, deep-drawn sigh, as if that were the supreme moment of her life. "And are you really from Altruria? It seems too good to be true!" Her devout look and her earnest tone gave the commonplace words a quality that did not inhere in them, but Mrs. Makely took them on their surface.

"Yes, doesn't it?" she made haste to interpose, before the Altrurian could say anything. "That is just the way we all feel about it, Mrs. Camp. I assure you, if it were not for the accounts in the papers, and the talk about it everywhere, I couldn't believe there *was* any such place as

Altruria; and if it were not for Mr. Twelvemough here — who has to keep all his inventions for his novels, as a mere matter of business routine, — I might really suspect him and Mr. Homos of — well, *working* us, as my husband calls it."

The Altrurian smiled politely, but vaguely, as if he had not quite caught her meaning, and I made answer for both: "I am sure, Mrs. Makely, if you could understand my peculiar state of mind about Mr. Homos, you would never believe that I was in collusion with him. I find him quite as incredible as you do. There are moments when he seems so entirely subjective with me that I feel as if he were no more definite or tangible than a bad conscience."

"Exactly!" said Mrs. Makely, and she laughed out her delight in my illustration.

The Altrurian must have perceived that we were joking, though the Camps all remained soberly silent. "I hope it isn't so bad as that," he said, "though I have noticed that I seem to affect you all with a kind of misgiving. I don't know just what it is; but if I could remove it, I should be very glad to do so."

Mrs. Makely very promptly seized her chance: "Well, then, in the first place, my husband and I were talking it over last night after we left you, and that was one of the things that kept us awake; it turned into money afterward. It isn't so much that a whole continent, as big as Australia, remained undiscovered till within such a very few years, as it is the condition of things among you: this sort of all living for one another, and not each one for himself. My husband says that is simply moonshine; such a thing never was and never can be; it is opposed to human nature, and would take away incentive, and all motive for exertion and advancement and enterprise. I don't know *what* he didn't say against it; but one thing: he says it's perfectly un-American." The Altrurian remained silent, gravely smiling, and Mrs. Makely added with her most engaging little manner: "I hope you won't feel hurt, personally or patriotically, by what I've repeated to you. I know my husband is awfully Philistine, though he *is* such a good fellow, and I don't, by any means, agree with him on all those points; but I *would* like to know what you think of them. The trouble is, Mrs. Camp," she said, turning to the invalid, "that Mr. Homos is so dreadfully reticent about his own country, and I am so curious to hear of it at first hands that I consider it justifiable to use any means to make him open up about it."

"There is no offense," the Altrurian answered for himself, "in what Mr. Makely says, though, from the Altrurian point of view, there is a good deal of error. Does it seem so strange to you," he asked, addressing himself to Mrs. Camp, "that people should found a civilization on the idea of living for one another instead of each for himself?"

"No, indeed!" she answered. "Poor people have always had to live that way, or they could not have lived at all."

"That was what I understood your porter to say last night," said the Altrurian to me. He added, to the company generally: "I suppose that even in America there are more poor people than there are rich people?"

"Well, I don't know about that," I said. "I suppose there are more people independently rich than there are people independently poor."

"We will let that formulation of it stand. If it is true, I do not see why the Altrurian system should be considered so very un-American. Then, as to whether there is or ever was really a practical altruism, a civic expression of it, I think it cannot be denied that among the first Christians, those who immediately followed Christ, and might be supposed to be directly influenced by his life, there was an altruism practised as radical as that which we have organized into a national polity and a working economy in Altruria."

"Ah, but you know," said Mrs. Makely, with the air of advancing a point not to be put aside, "they had to drop *that*. It was a dead failure. They found that they couldn't make it go at all, among cultivated people, and that, if Christianity was to advance, they would have to give up all that crankish kind of idolatry of the mere letter. At any rate," she went on, with the satisfaction we all feel in getting an opponent into close quarters, "you must confess that there is a much greater play of individuality here."

Before the Altrurian could reply, young Camp said: "If you want to see American individuality, the real, simon-pure article, you ought to go down to one of our big factory towns, and look at the mill-hands coming home in droves after a day's work, young girls and old women, boys and men, all fluffed over with cotton, and so dead-tired that they can hardly walk. They come shambling along with all the individuality of a flock of sheep."

"Some," said Mrs. Makely, heroically, as if she were one of these, "must be sacrificed. Of course, some are not so individual as others. A great deal depends upon temperament."

"A great deal more depends upon capital," said Camp, with an offensive laugh. "If you have capital in America, you can have individuality; if you haven't, you can't."

His sister, who had not taken part in the talk before, said demurely: "It seems to me you've got a good deal of individuality, Reub, and you haven't got a great deal of capital, either," and the two young people laughed together.

Mrs. Makely was one of those fatuous women whose eagerness to make a point excludes the consideration even of their own advantage. "I'm sure," she said, as if speaking for the upper classes, "*we* haven't got any individuality at all. We are as like as so many peas or pins. In fact, you have to be so in society. If you keep asserting your own individuality too much, people avoid you. It's very vulgar, and the greatest bore."

"Then you don't find individuality so desirable, after all," said the Altrurian.

"I perfectly detest it!" cried the lady, and evidently she had not the least notion where she was in the argument. "For my part, I'm never happy except when I've forgotten myself and the whole individual bother."

Her declaration seemed somehow to close the incident, and we were all silent a moment, which I employed in looking about the room, and taking in with my literary sense the simplicity and even bareness of its furnishing. There was the bed where the invalid lay, and near the head a table with a pile of books and a kerosene lamp on it, and I decided that she was a good deal wakeful, and that she read by that lamp when she could not sleep at night. Then there were the hard chairs we sat on, and some home-made hooked rugs, in rounds and ovals, scattered about the clean floor; there was a small melodeon pushed against the wall; the windows had paper shades, and I recalled that I had not seen any blinds on the outside of the house. Over the head of the bed hung a cavalryman's sword, with its belt; the sword that Mrs. Makely had spoken of. It struck me as a room where a great many things might have happened, and I said: "You can't think, Mrs. Camp, how glad I am to see the inside of your house. It seems to me so typical."

A pleased intelligence showed itself in her face, and she answered: "Yes, it is a real old-fashioned farm-house. We have never taken boarders, and so we have kept it as it was built pretty much, and only made such changes in it as we needed or wanted for ourselves."

"It's a pity," I went on, following up what I thought a fortunate lead, "that we city people see so little of the farming life when we come into the country. I have been here now for several seasons, and this is the first time I have been inside a farmer's house."

"Is it possible!" cried the Altrurian, with an air of utter astonishment; and when I found the fact appeared so singular to him, I began to be rather proud of its singularity.

"Yes, I suppose that most city people come and go, year after year, in the country, and never make any sort of acquaintance with the people who live there the year round. We keep to ourselves in the hotels, or if we go out at all it is to make a call upon some city cottager, and so we do not get out of the vicious circle of our own over-intimacy with ourselves and our ignorance of others."

"And you regard that as a great misfortune?" asked the Altrurian.

"Why, it's inevitable. There is nothing to bring us together, unless it's some happy accident, like the present. But we don't have a traveler from Altruria to exploit every day, and so we have no business to come into people's houses."

"You would have been welcome in ours long ago, Mr. Twelvemough," said Mrs. Camp.

"But, excuse me!" said the Altrurian. "What you say really seems dreadful to me. Why, it is as if you were not the same race or kind of men!"

"Yes," I answered. "It has sometimes seemed to me as if our big hotel there were a ship, anchored off some strange coast. The inhabitants come out with supplies, and carry on their barter with the ship's steward, and we sometimes see them over the side, but we never speak to them, or have anything to do with them. We sail away at the close of the season, and that is the end of it till next summer."

The Altrurian turned to Mrs. Camp. "And how do you look at it? How does it seem to you?"

"I don't believe we have thought about it very much; but now that Mr. Twelvemough has spoken of it, I can see that it does look that way. And it seems very strange, doesn't it, for we are all the same people, and have the same language and religion and country — the country that my husband fought for, and I suppose I may say, died for; he was never the same man after the war. It does appear as if we had some interests in common, and might find it out if we ever came together."

"It's a great advantage, the city people going into the country so much as they do now," said Mrs. Makely. "They bring five million dollars into the state of New Hampshire, alone, every summer."

She looked round for the general approval which this fact merited, and young Camp said: "And it shows how worthless the natives are, that they can't make both ends meet, with all that money, but have to give up their farms and go West, after all. I suppose you think it comes from wanting buggies and pianos."

"Well, it certainly comes from something," said Mrs. Makely, with the courage of her convictions.

She was evidently not going to be put down by that sour young fellow, and I was glad of it, though I must say I thought the thing she left to rankle in his mind from our former meeting had not been said in very good taste. I thought, too, that she would not fare best in any encounter of wits with him, and I rather trembled for the result. I said, to relieve the strained situation, "I wish there was some way of our knowing each other better. I'm sure there's a great deal of good will on both sides."

"No, there isn't," said Camp, "or at least I can answer for our side that there isn't. You come into the country to get as much for your money as you can, and we mean to let you have as little as we can. That's the whole story, and if Mr. Homos believes anything different, he's very much mistaken."

"I hadn't formed any conclusion in regard to the matter, which is quite new to me," said the Altrurian, mildly. "But why is there no basis of mutual kindness between you?"

"Because it's like everything else with us, it's a question of supply and demand, and there is no room for any mutual kindness in a question of that kind. Even if there were, there is another thing that would kill it. The summer folks, as we call them, look down on the natives, as they call us, and we know it."

"Now, Mr. Camp, I am sure that you cannot say *I* look down on the natives," said Mrs. Makely, with an air of argument.

The young fellow laughed. "Oh, yes, you do," he said, not unamiably, and he added, "and you've got the right to. We're not fit to associate with you, and you know it, and we know it. You've got more money, and you've got nicer clothes, and you've got prettier manners. You talk about things that most natives never heard of, and you care for things they never saw. I know it's the custom to pretend differently, but I'm not going to pretend differently." I recalled what my friend the banker said about throwing away cant, and I asked myself if I were in the presence of some such free spirit again. I did not see how young Camp could afford it; but then I reflected that he had really nothing to lose by it, for he did not expect to make anything out of us; Mrs. Makely would probably not give up his sister as seamstress, if the girl continued to work so well and so cheaply as she said. "Suppose," he went on, "that some old native took you at your word, and came to call upon you at the hotel, with his wife, just as one of the city cottagers would do if he wanted to make your acquaintance?"

"I should be perfectly delighted!" said Mrs. Makely, "and I should receive them with the greatest possible cordiality."

"The same kind of cordiality that you would show to the cottagers?"

"I suppose that I should feel that I had more in common with the cottagers. We should be interested in the same things, and we should probably know the same people and have more to talk about — "

"You would both belong to the same class, and that tells the whole story. If you were out West, and the owner of one of those big twenty-thousand-acre farms called on you with his wife, would you act towards them as you would towards our natives? You wouldn't! You would all be rich people together, and you would understand each other because you had money."

"Now, that is not so," Mrs. Makely interrupted. "There are plenty of rich people one wouldn't wish to know at all, and who really can't get into society; who are ignorant and vulgar. And then when you come to money, I don't see but what country people are as glad to get it as anybody."

"Oh, gladder," said the young man.

"Well?" demanded Mrs. Makely, as if this were a final stroke of logic. The young man did not reply, and Mrs. Makely continued: "Now I will appeal to your sister to say whether she has ever seen any difference in my manner toward her from what I show to all the young ladies in the hotel." The young girl flushed, and seemed reluctant to answer. "Why, Lizzie!" cried Mrs. Makely, and her tone showed that she was really hurt.

The scene appeared to me rather cruel, and I glanced at Mrs. Camp with an expectation that she would say something to relieve it. But she did not. Her large, benevolent face expressed only a quiet interest in the discussion.

"You know every well, Mrs. Makely," said the girl, "you don't regard me as you do the young ladies in the hotel."

There was no resentment in her voice or look, but only a sort of regret, as if, but for this grievance, she could have loved the woman from whom she had probably had much kindness. The tears came into Mrs. Makely's eyes, and she turned toward Mrs. Camp. "And is this the way you *all* feel towards us?" she asked.

"Why shouldn't we?" asked the invalid, in her turn. "But, no, it isn't the way all the country people feel. Many of them feel as you would like to have them feel; but that is because they do not think. When they think, they feel as we do. But I don't blame you. You can't help yourselves any more than we can. We're all bound up together in that, at least."

At this apparent relenting Mrs. Makely tricked her beams a little, and said, plaintively, as if offering herself for further condolence: "Yes, that is what that woman at the little shanty back there said: some have to be rich, and some have to be poor; it takes all kinds to make a world."

"How would you like to be one of those that have to be poor?" asked young Camp, with an evil grin.

"I don't know," said Mrs. Makely, with unexpected spirit; "but I am sure that I should respect the feelings of all, rich or poor."

"I am sorry if we have hurt yours, Mrs. Makely," said Mrs. Camp, with dignity. "You asked us certain questions, and we thought you wished us to reply truthfully. We could not answer you with smooth things."

"But sometimes you do," said Mrs. Makely, and the tears stood in her eyes again. "And you know how fond I am of you all!"

Mrs. Camp wore a bewildered look. "Perhaps we have said more than we ought. But I couldn't help it, and I don't see how the children could, when you asked them here, before Mr. Homos."

I glanced at the Altrurian, sitting attentive and silent, and a sudden misgiving crossed my mind concerning him. Was he really a man, a human entity, a personality like ourselves, or was he merely a sort of spiritual solvent, sent for the moment to precipitate whatever sincerity there was in us, and show us what the truth was concerning our relations to each other? It was a fantastic conception, but I thought it was one that I might employ in some sort of purely romantic design, and I was professionally grateful for it. I said, with a humorous gayety: "Yes, we all seem to have been compelled to be much more honest than we like; and if Mr. Homos is going to write an account of his travels when he gets home, he can't accuse us of hypocrisy, at any rate. And I always used to think it was one of our virtues! What with Mr. Camp, here, and my friend the banker at the hotel, I don't think he'll have much reason to complain even of our reticence."

"Well, whatever he says of us," sighed Mrs. Makely, with a pious glance at the sword over the bed, "he will have to say that, in spite of our division and classes, we are all Americans, and if we haven't the same opinions and ideas on minor matters, we all have the same country."

"I don't know about that," came from Reuben Camp, with shocking promptness. "I don't believe we all have the same country. America is one thing for you, and it's quite another thing for us. America means ease, and comfort, and amusement for you, year in and year out, and if it means work, it's work that you *wish* to do. For us, America means work that we *have* to do, and hard work all the time if we're going to make both ends meet. It means liberty for you; but what liberty has a man got who doesn't know where his next meal is coming from? Once I was in a strike, when I was working on the railroad, and I've seen men come and give up their liberty for a chance to earn their family's living. They knew they were right, and that they ought to have stood up for their rights; but they had to lie down and lick the hand that fed them! Yes, we are all Americans, but I guess we haven't all got the same country, Mrs. Makely. What sort of a country has a black-listed man got?"

"A black-listed man?" she repeated. "I don't know what you mean."

"Well, a kind of man I've seen in the mill towns, that the bosses have all got on their books as a man that isn't to be given work on any account;

that's to be punished with hunger and cold, and turned into the street, for having offended them; and that's to be made to suffer through his helpless family for having offended them."

"Excuse me, Mr. Camp," I interposed, "but isn't a black-listed man usually a man who has made himself prominent in some labor trouble?"

"Yes," the young fellow answered, without seeming sensible of the point I had made.

"Ah!" I returned. "Then you can hardly blame the employers for taking it out of him in any way they can. That's human nature."

"Good heavens!" the Altrurian cried out. "Is it possible that in America it is human nature to take away the bread of a man's family, because he has gone counter to your interest or pleasure on some economical question?"

"Well, Mr. Twelvemough seems to think so," sneered the young man. "But whether it's human nature or not, it's a fact that they do it, and you can guess how much a black-listed man must love the country where such a thing can happen to him. What should you call such a thing as black-listing in Altruria?"

"Oh, yes," Mrs. Makely pleaded, "do let us get him to talking about Altruria on any terms. I think all this about the labor question is so tiresome; don't you, Mrs. Camp?"

Mrs. Camp did not answer; but the Altrurian said, in reply to her son: "We should have no name for such a thing, for with us such a thing would be impossible. There is no crime so heinous with us that the punishment would take away the criminal's chance of earning his living."

"Oh, if he was a criminal," said young Camp, "he would be all right *here*. The state would give him a chance to earn his living then."

"But if he had no other chance of earning his living, and had committed no offense against the laws — "

"Then the state would let him take to the road. Like that fellow!"

He pulled aside the shade of the window where he sat, and we saw pausing before the house, and glancing doubtfully at the door-step, where the dog lay, a vile and loathesome-looking tramp, a blot upon the sweet and wholesome landscape, a scandal to the sacred day. His rags burlesqued the form which they did not wholly hide; his broken shoes were covered with dust; his coarse hair came in a plume through his tattered hat; his red, sodden face, at once fierce and timid, was rusty with a fortnight's beard. He offended the eye like a visible stench, and the wretched carrion seemed to shrink away from our gaze as if he were aware of his loathesomeness.

"Really," said Mrs. Makely, "I thought those fellows were arrested now. It is too bad to leave them at large. They are dangerous." Young Camp left the room and we saw him going out toward the tramp.

"Ah, that's quite right!" said the lady. "I hope Reuben is going to send him about his business. Why, surely he's not going to feed the horrid creature!" she added, as Camp, after a moment's parley with the tramp, turned with him, and disappeared round a corner of the house. "Now, Mrs. Camp, I think that is really a very bad example. It's encouraging them. Very likely he'll go to sleep in your barn, and set it on fire with his pipe. What do you do with tramps in Altruria, Mr. Homos?"

The Altrurian seemed not to have heard her. He said to Mrs. Camp: " Then I understand from something your son let fall that he has not always been at home with you here. Does he reconcile himself easily to the country after the excitement of town life? I have read that the cities in America are draining the country of the young people."

"I don't think he was sorry to come home," said the mother, with a touch of fond pride. "But there was no choice for him after his father died; he was always a good boy, and he has not made us feel that we were keeping him away from anything better. When his father was alive we let him go, because then we were not so dependent, and I wished him to try his fortune in the world, as all boys long to do. But he is rather peculiar, and he seems to have got quite enough of the world. To be sure, I don't suppose he's seen the brightest side of it. He first went to work in the mills down at Ponkwasset, but he was 'laid off' there, when the hard times came, and there was so much overproduction, and he took a job of railroading, and was braking on a freight train when his father left us."

Mrs. Makely said, smiling, "No, I don't think that was the brightest outlook in the world. No wonder he has brought back such gloomy impressions. I am sure that if he could have seen life under brighter auspices he would not have the ideas he has."

"Very likely," said the mother dryly. "Our experiences have a great deal to do with forming our opinions. But I am not dissatisfied with my son's ideas. I suppose Reuben got a good many of his ideas from his father: he's his father all over again. My husband thought slavery was wrong, and he went into the war to fight against it. He used to say when the war was over that the negroes were emancipated, but slavery was not abolished yet."

"What in the world did he mean by that?" demanded Mrs. Makely.

"Something you wouldn't understand as we do. I tried to carry on the farm after he first went, and before Reuben was large enough to help me much, and ought to be in school, and I suppose I overdid. At any rate that was when I had my first shock of paralysis. I never was very strong, and

I presume my health was weakened by my teaching school so much, and studying, before I was married. But that doesn't matter now, and hasn't for many a year. The place was clear of debt then, but I had to get a mortgage put on it. The savings bank down in the village took it, and we've been paying the interest ever since. My husband died paying it, and my son will pay it all my life, and then I suppose the bank will foreclose. The treasurer was an old playmate of my husband's, and he said that as long as either of us lived the mortgage could lie."

"How splendid of him!" said Mrs. Makely. "I should think you had been very fortunate."

"I said that you would not see it as we do," said the invalid patiently.

The Altrurian asked: "Are there mortgages on many of the farms in the neighborhood?"

"Nearly all," said Mrs. Camp. "We seem to own them, but in fact they own us."

Mrs. Makely hastened to say: "My husband thinks it's the best way to have your property. If you mortgage it close up, you have all your capital free, and you can keep turning it over. That's what you ought to do, Mrs. Camp. But what was the slavery that Captain Camp said was not abolished yet?"

The invalid looked at her a moment without replying, and just then the door of the kitchen opened, and young Camp came in, and began to gather some food from the table on a plate.

"Why don't you bring him to the table, Reub?" his sister called to him.

"Oh, he says he'd rather not come in, as long as we have company. He says he isn't dressed for dinner; left his spike-tail in the city."

The young man laughed and his sister with him.

CHAPTER VIII

Young Camp carried out the plate of victuals to the tramp, and Mrs. Makely said to his mother, "I suppose you would make the tramp do some sort of work to earn his breakfast on week-days?"

"Not always," Mrs. Camp replied. "Do the boarders at the hotel always work to earn their breakfast?"

"No, certainly not," said Mrs. Makely, with the sharpness of offence. "But they always pay for it."

"I don't think that paying for a thing is earning it. Perhaps some one else earned the money that pays for it. But I believe there is too much work in the world. If I were to live my life over again, I should not work half so hard. My husband and I took this place when we were young married people, and began working to pay for it. We wanted to feel that it was ours, that we owned it, and that our children should own it afterwards. We both worked all day long like slaves, and many a moonlight night we were up till morning, almost, gathering the stones from our fields, and burying them in deep graves that we had dug for them. But we buried our youth, and strength, and health in those graves, too, and what for? I don't own the farm that we worked so hard to pay for, and my children won't. That is what it has all come to. We were rightly punished for our greed, I suppose. Perhaps no one has a right to own any portion of the earth. Sometimes I think so, but my husband and I earned this farm, and now the savings bank owns it. That seems strange, doesn't it? I suppose you'll say that the bank paid for it. Well, perhaps so; but the bank didn't earn it. When I think of that I don't always think that a person who pays for his breakfast has the best right to a breakfast."

I could see the sophistry of all this, but I had not the heart to point it out; I felt the pathos of it, too. Mrs. Makely seemed not to see the one nor to feel the other very distinctly. "Yes, but surely," she said, "if you give a tramp his breakfast without making him work for it, you must see that it is encouraging idleness. And idleness is very corrupting — the sight of it."

"You mean to the country people? Well, they have to stand a good deal of that. The summer folks that spend four or five months of the year here don't seem to do anything from morning till night."

"Ah, but you must recollect that they are *resting!* You have no idea how hard they all work in town during the winter," Mrs. Makely urged, with an air of argument.

"Perhaps the tramps are resting, too. At any rate, I don't think the sight of idleness in rags, and begging at back doors, is very corrupting to the country people; I never heard of a single tramp who had started from the country; they all come from the cities. It's the other kind of idleness that tempts our young people. The only tramps that my son says he ever envies are the well-dressed, strong young fellows from town that go tramping through the mountains for exercise every summer."

The ladies both paused. They seemed to have got to the end of their tether; at least Mrs. Makely had apparently nothing else to advance, and I said lightly, "But that is just the kind of tramps that Mr. Homos would most disapprove of. He says that in Altruria they would consider exercise for exercise sake a wicked waste of force, and little short of lunacy."

I thought my exaggeration might provoke him to denial, but he seemed not to have found it unjust. "Why, you know," he said to Mrs.

Camp, "in Altruria every one works with his hands, so that the hard work shall not all fall to any one class; and this manual labor of each is sufficient to keep the body in health, as well as to earn a living. After the three hours' work, which constitutes a day's work with us, is done, the young people have all sorts of games and sports, and they carry them as late into life as the temperament of each demands. But what I was saying to Mr. Twelve-mough — perhaps I did not make myself clear — was that we should regard the sterile putting forth of strength in exercise, if others were each day worn out with hard manual labor, as insane or immoral. But I can account for it differently with you, because I understand that in your conditions a person of leisure could not do any manual labor without taking away the work of some one who needed it to live by; and could not even relieve an overworked laborer, and give him the money for the work without teaching him habits of idleness. In Altruria we can all keep ourselves well by doing each his share of hard work, and we can help those who are exhausted, when such a thing happens, without injuring them materially or morally."

Young Camp entered at this moment, and the Altrurian hesitated. "Oh, do go on!" Mrs. Makely entreated. She added to Camp, "We've got him to talking about Altruria at last, and we wouldn't have him stopped for worlds."

The Altrurian looked around at all our faces, and no doubt read our eager curiosity in them. He smiled, and said, "I shall be very glad I'm sure. But I do not think you will find anything so remarkable in our civilization, if you will conceive of it as the outgrowth of the neighborly instinct. In fact, neighborliness is the essence of Altrurianism. If you will imagine having the same feeling toward all," he explained to Mrs. Makely, "as you have toward your next door neighbor — "

"My next door neighbor!" she cried. "But I don't *know* the people next door! We live in a large apartment house, some forty families, and I assure you I do not know a soul among them."

He looked at her with a puzzled air, and she continued, "Sometimes it *does* seem rather hard. One day the people on the same landing with us lost one of their children, and I should never have been a whit the wiser if my cook hadn't happened to mention it. The servants all know each other; they meet in the back elevator, and get acquainted. I don't encourage it. You can't tell what kind of families they belong to."

"But surely," the Altrurian persisted, "you have friends in the city whom you think of as your neighbors?"

"No, I can't say that I have," said Mrs. Makely. "I have my visiting-list, but I shouldn't think of anybody on *that* as a neighbor."

The Altrurian looked so blank and baffled that I could hardly help laughing. "Then I should not know how to explain Altruria to you, I'm afraid."

"Well," she returned lightly, "if it's anything like neighborliness, as I've seen it in small places, deliver me from it! I like being independent. That's why I like the city. You're let alone."

"I was down in New York once, and I went through some of the streets and houses where the poor people live," said young Camp, "and they seemed to know each other, and to be quite neighborly."

"And would you liked to be all messed in with each other, that way?" demanded the lady.

"Well, I thought it was better than living as we do in the country, so far apart that we never see each other, hardly. And it seems to me better than not having any neighbors at all."

"Well, every one to his taste," said Mrs. Makely. "I wish you would tell us how people manage with you, socially, Mr. Homos."

"Why, you know," he began, "we have neither city nor country in your sense, and so we are neither so isolated nor so crowded together. You feel that you lose a great deal in not seeing each other oftener?" he asked Camp.

"Yes. Folks rust out, living alone. It's human nature to want to get together."

"And I understand Mrs. Makely that it is human nature to want to keep apart?"

"Oh, no, but to come together independently," she answered.

"Well that is what we have contrived in our life at home. I should have to say, in the first place, that — "

"Excuse me just one moment, Mr. Homos!" said Mrs. Makely. This perverse woman was as anxious to hear about Altruria as any of us, but she was a woman who would rather hear the sound of her own voice than any other, even if she were dying, as she would call it, to hear the other. The Altrurian stopped politely, and Mrs. Makely went on: "I have been thinking of what Mr. Camp was saying about the black-listed men, and their all turning into tramps — "

"But I didn't say that, Mrs. Makely," the young fellow protested, in astonishment.

"Well, it stands to reason that if the tramps have all been black-listed men — "

"But I didn't say that, either!"

"No matter! What I am trying to get at is this: if a workman has made himself a nuisance to the employers, haven't they a right to punish him in any way they can?"

"I believe there's no law yet against black-listing," said Camp.

"Very well, then, I don't see what they've got to complain of. The employers surely know their own business."

"They claim to know the men's too. That's what they're always saying; they will manage their own affairs in their own way. But no man, or company, that does business on a large scale, has any affairs that are not partly other folks' affairs too. All the saying in the world won't make it different."

"Very well, then," said Mrs. Makely, with a force of argument which she seemed to think was irresistible, "I think the workmen had better leave things to the employers, and then they won't get black-listed. It's as broad as it's long." I confess that, although I agreed with Mrs. Makely in regard to what the workmen had better do, her position had been arrived at by such extraordinary reasoning that I blushed for her; at the same time, I wanted to laugh. She continued triumphantly, "You see, the employers have ever so much more at stake."

"The men have everything at stake; the work of their hands," said the young fellow.

"Oh, but surely," said Mrs. Makely, "you wouldn't set that against capital? You wouldn't compare the two?"

"Yes, I should," said Camp, and I could see his eye kindle and his jaw stiffen.

"Then I suppose you would say that a man ought to get as much for his work as an employer gets for his capital. If you think one has as much at stake as the other, you must think they ought to be paid alike."

"That is *just* what I think," said Camp, and Mrs. Makely burst into a peal of amiable laughter.

"Now, that is too preposterous!"

"Why is it preposterous?" he demanded, with a quivering nostril.

"Why, simply because it *is*," said the lady, but she did not say why, and although I thought so, too, I was glad she did not attempt to do it, for her conclusions seemed to me much better than her reasons.

The old wooden clock in the kitchen began to strike, and she rose briskly to her feet, and went and laid the books she had been holding in her lap on the table beside Mrs. Camp's bed. "We must really be going," she said, as she leaned over and kissed the invalid. "It is your dinner time, and we shall barely get back for lunch, if we go by the Loop road; and I want very much to have Mr. Homos see the Witch's Falls, on the way. I have got two or three of the books here that Mr. Makely brought me last night — I sha'n't have time to read them at once — and I'm smuggling in one of Mr. Twelvemough's, that he's too modest to present for himself."

She turned a gay glance upon me, and Mrs. Camp thanked me, and a number of civilities followed from all sides. In the process of their exchange, Mrs. Makely's spirits perceptibly rose, and she came away in high good-humor with the whole Camp family. "Well, now, I am sure," she said to the Altrurian, as we began the long ascent of the Loop road, "you must allow that you have seen some very original characters. But how *warped* people get living alone so much! That is the great drawback of the country. Mrs. Camp thinks the savings-bank did her a real injury in taking a mortgage on her place, and Reuben seems to have seen just enough of the outside world to get it all wrong! But they are the best-hearted creatures in the world, and I know you won't misunderstand them. That unsparing country bluntness, don't you think it's perfectly delightful? I do like to stir poor Reuben up, and get him talking. He is a good boy, if he *is* so wrong-headed, and he's the most devoted son and brother in the world. Very few young fellows would waste their lives on an old farm like that; I suppose when his mother dies he will marry and strike out for himself in some growing place."

"He did not seem to think the world held out any very bright inducements for him to leave home," the Altrurian suggested.

"Oh, let him get one of these lively, pushing Yankee girls for a wife, and he will think very differently," said Mrs. Makely.

The Altrurian disappeared that afternoon, and I saw little or nothing of him till the next day at supper. Then he said he had been spending the time with young Camp, who had shown him something of the farm work, and introduced him to several of the neighbors; he was very much interested in it all, because at home he was, at present, engaged in farm work himself, and he was curious to contrast the American and Altrurian methods. We began to talk of the farming interest again, later in the day, when the members of our little group came together, and I told them what the Altrurian had been doing. The doctor had been suddenly called back to town; but the minister was there, and the lawyer, and the professor, and the banker, and the manufacturer. It was the banker who began to comment on what I said, and he seemed to be in the frank humor of the Saturday night before. "Yes," he said, "it's a hard life, and they have to look sharp if they expect to make both ends meet. I would not like to undertake it myself with their resources."

The professor smiled, in asking the Altrurian: "Did your agricultural friends tell you anything of the little rural traffic in votes that they carry on about election time? That is one of the side means they have of making both ends meet."

"I don't understand," said the Altrurian.

"Why, you know, you can buy votes among our virtuous yeomen from two dollars up at the ordinary elections. When party feeling runs high, and there are vital questions at stake, the votes cost more."

The Altrurian looked around at us all aghast: "Do you mean that Americans buy votes?"

The professor smiled again. "Oh, no; I only mean that they sell them. Well, I don't wonder that they rather prefer to blink the fact; but it is a fact, nevertheless, and pretty notorious."

"Good heavens!" cried the Altrurian. "And what defense have they for such treason? I don't mean those who sell; from what I have seen of the bareness and hardship of their lives, I could well imagine that there might sometimes come a pinch when they would be glad of the few dollars that they could get in that way; but what have those who buy to say?"

"Well," said the professor, "it isn't a transaction that's apt to be talked about much on either side."

"I think," the banker interposed, "that there is some exaggeration about that business; but it certainly exists, and I suppose it is a growing evil in the country. I fancy it arises, somewhat, from a want of clear thinking on the subject. Then there is no doubt but it comes, sometimes, from poverty. A man sells his vote, as a woman sells her person, for money, when neither can turn virtue into cash. They feel that they must live, and neither of them would be satisfied if Dr. Johnson told them he didn't see the necessity. In fact I shouldn't myself, if I were in their places. You can't have the good of a civilization like ours without having the bad; but I am not going to deny that the bad is bad. Some people like to do that; but I don't find my account in it. In either case, I confess that I think the buyer is worse than the seller — incomparably worse. I suppose you are not troubled with either case in Altruria?"

"Oh, no!" said the Altrurian, with an utter horror, which no repetition of his words can give the sense of. "It would be unimaginable."

"Still," the banker suggested, "you have cakes and ale, and at times the ginger is hot in the mouth?"

"I don't pretend that we have immunity from error; but upon such terms as you have described we have none. It would be impossible."

The Altrurian's voice expressed no contempt, but only a sad patience, a melancholy surprise, such as a celestial angel might feel in being suddenly confronted with some secret shame and horror of the Pit.

"Well," said the banker, "with us the only way is to take the business view and try to strike an average somewhere."

"Talking of business," said the professor, turning to the manufacturer, who had been quietly smoking, "why don't some of you capitalists take hold of farming here in the East, and make a business of it as they do in the West?"

"Thank you," said the other; "if you mean me, I would rather not invest." He was silent a moment, and then he went on, as if the notion were beginning to win upon him: "It may come to something like that though. If it does, the natural course, I should think, would be through the railroads. It would be a very easy matter for them to buy up all the good farms along their lines and put tenants on them, and run them in their own interest. Really, it isn't a bad scheme. The waste in the present method is enormous, and there is no reason why the roads should not own the farms, as they are beginning to own the mines. They could manage them better than the small farmers do in every way. I wonder the thing hasn't occurred to some smart railroad man."

We all laughed a little, perceiving the semi-ironical spirit of his talk; but the Altrurian must have taken it in dead earnest: "But, in that case, the number of people thrown out of work would be very great, wouldn't it? And what would become of them?"

"Well, they would have whatever their farms brought to make a new start with somewhere else; and, besides, that question of what would become of people thrown out of work by a given improvement is something that capital cannot consider. We used to introduce a bit of machinery in the mill, every now and then, that threw out a dozen or a hundred people; but we couldn't stop for that."

"And you never knew what became of them?"

"Sometimes. Generally not. We took it for granted that they would light on their feet somehow."

"And the state — the whole people — the government — did nothing for them?"

"If it became a question of the poor-house, yes."

"Or the jail," the lawyer suggested.

"Speaking of the poor-house," said the professor, "did our exemplary rural friends tell you how they sell out their paupers to the lowest bidder, and get them boarded sometimes as low as a dollar and a quarter a week?"

"Yes, young Mr. Camp told me of that. He seemed to think it was terrible."

"Did he? Well, I'm glad to hear that of young Mr. Camp. From all that I've been told before, he seems to reserve his conscience for the use of capitalists. What does he propose to do about it?"

"He seems to think the state ought to find work for them."

"Oh, paternalism! Well, I guess the state won't."

"That was his opinion, too."

"But they pointed out," said the lawyer, "that the great American fortunes had been made by men who had never had their educational advantages, and they seemed to think that what we call the education of a gentleman was a little too good for money-making purposes."

"Well," said the other, "they can console themselves with the reflection that going into business isn't necessarily making money; it isn't necessarily making a living, even."

"Some of them seem to have caught on to that fact; and they pitied Jack or Jim partly because the chances were so much against him. But they pitied him mostly because in the life before him he would have no use for his academic training, and he had better not gone to college at all. They said he would be none the better for it, and would always be miserable when he looked back to it."

The manufacturer did not reply, and the professor, after a preliminary hemming, held his peace. It was the banker who took the word. "Well, so far as business is concerned, they were right. It is no use to pretend that there is any relation between business and the higher education. There is no business man who will pretend that there is not often an actual incompatibility if he is honest. I know that when we get together at a commercial or financial dinner we talk as if great merchants and great financiers were beneficent geniuses, who evoked the prosperity of mankind by their schemes from the conditions that would otherwise have remained barren. Well, very likely they are, but we must all confess that they do not know it at the time. What they are consciously looking out for then is the main chance. If general prosperity follows, all well and good; they are willing to be given the credit for it. But, as I said, with business as business, the 'education of a gentleman' has nothing to do. That education is always putting the old Ciceronian question: whether the fellow arriving at a starving city with a cargo of grain is bound to tell the people before he squeezes them that there are half a dozen other fellows with grain just below the horizon. As a gentleman he would have to tell them, because he could not take advantage of their necessities; but, as a business man, he would think it bad business to tell them, or no business at all. The principle goes all through; I say, business is business; and I am not going to pretend that business will ever be anything else. In our business battles we don't take off our hats to the other side and say, 'Gentlemen of the French Guard, have the goodness to fire.' That may be war, but it is not business. We seize all the advantages we can; very few of us would actually deceive; but if a fellow believes a thing, and we know he is wrong, we do not usually take the trouble to set him right, if we are

"It seems a hard fate," said the minister, "that the only provision law makes for people who are worn out by sickness or a life of work sho\ be something that assorts them with idiots and lunatics, and brings suc shame upon them that it is almost as terrible as death."

"It is the only way to encourage independence and individuality," said the professor. "Of course it has its dark side. But anything else would be sentimental and unbusinesslike, and, in fact, un-American."

"I am not so sure that it would be un-Christian," the minister timidly ventured, in the face of such an authority on political economy.

"Oh, as to that, I must leave the question to the reverend clergy," said the professor.

A very unpleasant little silence followed. It was broken by the lawyer, who put his feet together, and after a glance down at them, began to say, "I was very much interested this afternoon by a conversation I had with some of the young fellows in the hotel. You know most of them are graduates, and they are taking a sort of supernumerary vacation this summer before they plunge into the battle of life in the autumn. They were talking of some other fellows, classmates of theirs, who were not so lucky, but had been obliged to begin the fight at once. It seems that our fellows here are all going in for some sort of profession: medicine, or law, or engineering, or teaching, or the Church, and they were commiserating those other fellows not only because they were not having the supernu- merary vacation, but because they were going into business. That struck me as rather odd, and I tried to find out what it meant, and, as nearly as I could find out, it meant that most college graduates would not go into business if they could help it. They seemed to feel a sort of incongruity between their education and the business life. They pitied the fellows that had to go into it, and apparently the fellows that had to go in for it pitied themselves, for the talk seemed to have begun about a letter that one of the chaps here had got from poor Jack or Jim somebody, who had been obliged to go into his father's business, and was groaning over it. The fellows who were going to study professions were hugging themselves at the contrast between their fate and his, and were making remarks about business that were, to say the least, unbusinesslike. A few years ago we should have made a summary disposition of the matter, and I believe some of the newspapers still are in doubt about the value of a college education to men who have got to make their way. What do you think?"

The lawyer addressed his question to the manufacturer, who an- swered, with a comfortable satisfaction, that he did not think those young men if they went into business would find that they knew too much.

going to lose anything by undeceiving him. That would not be business. I suppose you think that is dreadful?" He turned smilingly to the minister.

"I wish — I wish," said the minister, gently, "it could be otherwise."

"Well, I wish so, too," returned the banker. "But it isn't. Am I right or am I wrong?" he demanded of the manufacturer, who laughed.

"I am not conducting this discussion. I will not deprive you of the floor."

"What you say," I ventured to put in, "reminds me of the experience of a friend of mine, a brother novelist. He wrote a story where the failure of a business man turned on a point just like that you have instanced. The man could have retrieved himself if he had let some people believe that what was so was not so, but his conscience stepped in and obliged him to own the truth. There was a good deal of talk about the case, I suppose, because it was not in real life, and my friend heard divers criticisms. He heard of a group of ministers who blamed him for exalting a case of common honesty, as if it were something extraordinary; and he heard of some business men who talked it over, and said he had worked the case up splendidly, but he was all wrong in the outcome; the fellow would never have told the other fellows. They said it would not have been business."

We all laughed except the minister and the Altrurian; the manufacturer said, "Twenty-five years hence, the fellow who is going into business may pity the fellows who are pitying him for his hard fate now."

"Very possibly, but not necessarily," said the banker. "Of course, the business man is on top, as far as money goes; he is the fellow who makes the big fortunes; the millionaire lawyers and doctors and ministers are exceptional. But his risks are tremendous. Ninety-five times out of a hundred he fails. To be sure, he picks up and goes on, but he seldom gets there, after all."

"Then in your system," said the Altrurian, "the great majority of those who go into what you call the battle of life are defeated?"

"The killed, wounded, and missing sum up a frightful total," the banker admitted. "But whatever the end is, there is a great deal of prosperity on the way. The statistics are correct, but they do not tell the whole truth. It is not so bad as it seems. Still, simply looking at the material chances, I don't blame those young fellows for not wanting to go into business. And when you come to other considerations! We used to cut the knot of the difficulty pretty sharply; we said a college education was wrong, or the hot and hot American spreadeaglers did. Business is the national ideal, and the successful business man is the American type. It is a business man's country."

"Then, if I understand you," said the Altrurian, "and I am very anxious to have a clear understanding of the matter, the effect of the university with you is to unfit a youth for business life."

"Oh no. It may give him great advantages in it, and that is the theory and expectation of most fathers who send their sons to the university. But, undoubtedly, the effect is to render business-life distasteful. The university nurtures all sorts of lofty ideals, which business has no use for."

"Then the effect is undemocratic?"

"No, it is simply unbusinesslike. The boy is a better democrat when he leaves college than he will be later, if he goes into business. The university has taught him and equipped him to use his own gifts and powers for his advancement; but the first lesson of business, and the last, is to use other men's gifts and powers. If he looks about him at all, he sees that no man gets rich simply by his own labor, no matter how mighty a genius he is, and that if you want to get rich, you must make other men work for you, and pay you for the privilege of doing so. Isn't that true?"

The banker turned to the manufacturer with this question, and the other said, "The theory is, that we give people work," and they both laughed.

The minister said, "I believe that in Altruria no man works for the profit of another?"

"No; each works for the profit of all," replied the Altrurian.

"Well," said the banker, "you seem to have made it go. Nobody can deny that. But we couldn't make it go here."

"Why? I am very curious to know why our system seems so impossible to you!"

"Well, it is contrary to the American spirit. It is alien to our love of individuality."

"But we prize individuality too, and we think we secure it under our system. Under yours, it seems to me that while the individuality of the man who makes other men work for him is safe, except from itself, the individuality of the workers — "

"Well, that is their lookout. We have found that upon the whole, it is best to let every man look out for himself. I know that, in a certain light, the result has an ugly aspect; but, nevertheless, in spite of all, the country is enormously prosperous. The pursuit of happiness, which is one of the inalienable rights secured to us by the Declaration is, and always has been, a dream; but the pursuit of the dollar yields tangible proceeds, and we get a good deal of excitement out of it as it goes on. You can't deny that we are the richest nation in the world. Do you call Altruria a rich country?"

I could not quite make out whether the banker was serious or not in all this talk; sometimes I suspected him of a fine mockery, but the Altrurian took him upon the surface of his words.

"I hardly know whether it is or not. The question of wealth does not enter into our scheme. I can say that we all have enough, and that no one is even in the fear of want."

"Yes, that is very well. But we should think it was paying too much for it if we had to give up the hope of ever having more than we wanted," and at this point the banker uttered his jolly laugh, and I perceived that he had been trying to draw the Altrurian out, and practice upon his patriotism. It was a great relief to find that he had been joking in so much that seemed a dead give-away of our economical position. "In Altruria," he asked, "who is your ideal great man? I don't mean personally, but abstractly."

The Altrurian thought a moment. "With us there is so little ambition for distinction, as you understand it, that your question is hard to answer. But I should say, speaking largely, that it was some man who had been able for the time being, to give the greatest happiness to the greatest number — some artist, or poet, or inventory, or physician."

I was somewhat surprised to have the banker take this preposterous statement seriously, respectfully. "Well, that is quite conceivable with your system. What should you say," he demanded of the rest of us generally, "was our ideal of greatness?"

No one replied at once, or at all, till the manufacturer said, "We will let you continue to run it."

"Well, it is a very curious inquiry, and I have thought it over a good deal. I should say that within a generation our ideal had changed twice. Before the war, and during all the time from the Revolution onward, it was undoubtedly the great politician, the publicist, the statesman. As we grew older and began to have an intellectual life of our own, I think the literary fellows had a pretty good share of the honors that were going; that is, such a man as Longfellow was popularly considered a type of greatness. When the war came, it brought the soldier to the front, and there was a period of ten or fifteen years when he dominated the national imagination. That period passed, and the great era of material prosperity set in. The big fortunes began to tower up, and heroes of another sort began to appeal to our admiration. I don't think there is any doubt but the millionaire is now the American ideal. It isn't very pleasant to think so, even for people who have got on, but it can't very hopefully be denied. It is the man with the most money who now takes the prize in our national cake-walk."[8]

---

[8] A cake-walk was a promenade or march in which the couple who performed the fanciest steps received a cake as a prize.

The Altrurian turned curiously toward me, and I did my best to tell him what a cake-walk was. When I had finished, the banker resumed, only to say, as he rose from his chair to bid us good-night, "In any average assembly of Americans the greatest millionaire would take the eyes of all from the greatest statesman, the greatest poet, or the greatest soldier, we ever had. That," he added to the Altrurian, "will account to you for many things as you travel through our country."

CHAPTER IX

The next time the members of our little group came together, the manufacturer began at once upon the banker:

"I should think that our friend, the professor, here would hardly like that notion of yours, that business, as business, has nothing to do with the education of a gentleman. If this is a business man's country, and if the professor has nothing in stock but the sort of education that business has no use for, I should suppose that he would want to go into some other line."

The banker mutely referred the matter to the professor, who said, with that cold grin of his which I hated:

"Perhaps we shall wait for business to purge and live cleanly. Then it will have some use for the education of a gentleman."

"I see," said the banker, "that I have touched the quick in both of you, when I hadn't the least notion of doing so. But I shouldn't really like to prophesy which will adapt itself to the other: education or business. Let us hope there will be mutual concessions. There are some pessimists who say that business methods, especially on the large scale of the trusts and combinations, have grown worse instead of better; but this may be merely what is called a 'transition state.' Hamlet must be cruel to be kind; the darkest hour comes before dawn — and so on. Perhaps when business gets the whole affair of life into its hands, and runs the republic, as its enemies now accuse it of doing, the process of purging and living cleanly will begin. I have known lots of fellows who started in life rather scampishly; but when they felt secure of themselves, and believed that they could afford to be honest, they became so. There's no reason why the same thing shouldn't happen on a large scale. We must never forget that we are still a very novel experiment, though we have matured so rapidly in some respects that we have come to regard ourselves as an accomplished fact. We are really less so than we were forty years ago, with all the tremendous changes since the war. Before that we could take certain matters for granted. If a man got out of work, he turned his hand to something else; if a man failed in business, he started in again from some other direction; as a last resort, in both cases, he went West, preempted a quarter section of public land, and grew up with the country. Now the country is grown up; the public land is gone; business is full on all sides, and the hand that turned itself to something else has lost its cunning. The struggle for life has changed from a free fight to an encounter of disciplined forces, and the free fighters that are left get ground to pieces between organized labor and organized capital. Decidedly, we are in a transition state, and if the higher education tried to adapt itself to business needs, there are chances that it might sacrifice itself without helping business. After all, how much education does business need? Were our great fortunes made by educated men, or men of university training? I don't know but these young fellows are right about that."

"Yes, that may all be," I put in. "But it seems to me that you give Mr. Homos, somehow, a wrong impression of our economic life by your generalizations. You are a Harvard man yourself."

"Yes, and I am not a rich man. A million or two, more or less; but what is that? I have suffered, at the start and all along, from the question as to what a man with the education of a gentleman ought to do in such and such a juncture. The fellows who have not that sort of education have not that sort of question, and they go in and win."

"So you admit, then," said the professor, "that the higher education elevates a business man's standard of morals?"

"Undoubtedly. That is one of its chief drawbacks," said the banker, with a laugh.

"Well," I said, with the deference due even to a man who had only a million or two, more or less, "we must allow *you* to say such things. But if the case is so bad with the business men who have made the great fortunes — the business men who have never had the disadvantage of a university education — I wish you would explain to Mr. Homos why, in every public exigency, we instinctively appeal to the business sense of the community, as if it were the fountain of wisdom, probity, and equity. Suppose there were some question of vital interest — I won't say financial, but political, or moral, or social — on which it was necessary to rouse public opinion, what would be the first thing to do? To call a meeting over the signatures of the leading business men; because no other names appeal with such force to the public. You might get up a call signed by all the novelists, artists, ministers, lawyers, and doctors in the state, and it would not have a tithe of the effect, with the people at large, that a call signed by a few leading merchants, bank presidents, railroad men, and trust officers would have. What is the reason? It seems strange that I should be asking you to defend yourself against yourself."

"Not at all, my dear fellow, not at all!" the banker replied, with his caressing bonhomie. "Though I will confess, to begin with, that I do not expect to answer your question to your entire satisfaction. I can only do my best — on the installment plan."

He turned to the Altrurian, and then went on:

"As I said the other night, this is a business man's country. We are a purely commercial people; money is absolutely to the fore; and business, which is the means of getting the most money, is the American ideal. If you like, you may call it the American fetish; I don't mind calling it so myself. The fact that business is our ideal, or our fetish, will account for the popular faith in business men, who form its priesthood, its hierarchy. I don't know, myself, any other reason for regarding business men as solider than novelists, or artists, or ministers, not to mention lawyers and doctors. They are supposed to have long heads; but it appears that ninety-five times out of a hundred they haven't. They are supposed to be very reliable; but it is almost invariably a business man of some sort who gets out to Canada while the state examiner is balancing his books, and it is usually the longest-headed business men who get plundered by him. No, it is simply because business is our national ideal that the business man is honored above all other men among us. In the aristocratic countries they forward a public object under the patronage of the nobility and gentry; in a plutocratic country they get the business men to endorse it. I suppose that the average American citizen feels that they wouldn't endorse a thing unless it was safe; and the average American citizen likes to be safe — he is cautious. As a matter of fact, business men are always taking risks, and business is a game of chance, in a certain degree. Have I made myself intelligible?"

"Entirely so," said the Altrurian; and he seemed so thoroughly well satisfied that he forbore asking any further question.

No one else spoke. The banker lighted a cigar, and resumed at the point where he left off when I ventured to enter upon the defense of his class with him. I must say that he had not convinced me at all. At that moment I would rather have trusted him, in any serious matter of practical concern, than all the novelists I ever heard of. But I thought I would leave the word to him, without further attempt to reinstate him in his self-esteem. In fact, he seemed to be getting along very well without it; or else he was feeling that mysterious control from the Altrurian which I had already suspected him of using. Voluntarily or involuntarily, the banker proceeded with his contribution to the Altrurian's stock of knowledge concerning our civilization:

"I don't believe, however, that the higher education is any more of a failure, as a provision for business career, than the lower education is for the life of labor. I suppose that the hypercritical observer might say that in a wholly commercial civilization, like ours, the business man really needed nothing beyond the three R's, and the workingman needed no R at all. As a practical affair, there is a good deal to be said in favor of that view. The higher education is part of the social ideal which we have derived from the past, from Europe. It is part of the provision for the life of leisure, the life of the aristocrat, which nobody of our generation leads, except women. Our women really have some use for the education of a gentleman, but our men have none. How will that do for a generalization?" the banker asked of me.

"Oh," I admitted, with a laugh, "it is a good deal like one of my own. I have always been struck with that phase of our civilization."

"Well, then," the banker resumed, "take the lower education. This is part of the civic ideal which, I suppose, I may say we evolved from the depths of our inner consciousness of what an American citizen ought to be. It includes instruction in all the R's, and in several other letters of the alphabet. It is given free by the state, and no one can deny that it is thoroughly socialistic in conception and application."

"Distinctly so," said the professor. "Now that the text-books are furnished by the state, we have only to go a step farther, and provide a good, hot lunch for the children every day, as they do in Paris."

"Well," the banker returned, "I don't know that I should have much to say against that. It seems as reasonable as anything in the system of education which we force upon the working-classes. *They* know perfectly well, whether we do or not, that the three R's will not make their children better mechanics or laborers, and that, if the fight for a mere living is to go on from generation to generation, they will have no leisure to apply the little learning they get in the public schools for their personal culture. In the meantime we deprive the parents of their children's labor, in order that they may be better citizens for their schooling, as we imagine; I don't know whether they are or not. We offer them no sort of compensation for their time, and I think we ought to feel obliged to them for not wanting wages for their children while we are teaching them to be better citizens."

"You know," said the professor, "that has been suggested by some of their leaders."

"No, really? Well, that is *too* good!" The banker threw back his head and roared, and we all laughed with him. When we had sobered down again, he said: "I suppose that when a workingman makes all the use he can of his lower education he becomes a business man, and then he doesn't need the higher. Professor, you seem to be left out in the cold by our system, whichever way you take it."

"Oh," said the professor, "the law of supply and demand works both ways; it creates the demand, if the supply comes first; and if we keep on giving the sons of business men the education of a gentleman, we may yet make them feel the need of it. We shall evolve a new sort of business man."

"The sort that can't make money, or wouldn't exactly like to, on some terms?" asked the banker. "Well, perhaps we shall work out our democratic salvation in that way. When you have educated your new business man to the point where he can't consent to get rich at the obvious cost of others, you've got him on the way back to work with his hands. He will sink into the ranks of labor, and give the fellow with the lower education a chance. I've no doubt he'll take it. I don't know but you're right, professor."

The lawyer had not spoken as yet. Now he said: "Then it is education, after all, that is to bridge the chasm between the classes and the masses, though it seems destined to go a long way around about it. There was a time, I believe, when we expected religion to do that."

"Well, it may still be doing it, for all I know," said the banker. "What do you say?" he asked, turning to the minister. "You ought to be able to give us some statistics on the subject with that large congregation of yours. You preach to more people than any other pulpit in your city."

The banker named one of the principal cities in the East, and the minister answered, with modest pride: "I am not sure of that; but our society is certainly a very large one."

"Well, and how many of the lower classes are there in it — people who work for their living with their hands?"

The minister stirred uneasily in his chair, and at last he said, with evident unhappiness: "They — I suppose — they have their own churches. I have never thought that such a separation of the classes was right; and I have had some of the very best people — socially and financially — with me in the wish that there might be more brotherliness between the rich and poor among us. But as yet — "

He stopped; the banker pursued: "Do you mean there are *no* working-people in your congregation?"

"I cannot think of any," returned the minister so miserably that the banker forbore to press the point.

The lawyer broke the awkward pause which followed: "I have heard it asserted that there is no country in the world where the separation of the classes is so absolute as in ours. In fact, I once heard a Russian revolutionist, who had lived in exile all over Europe, say that he had never seen anywhere such a want of kindness or sympathy between rich and poor as he had observed in America. I doubted whether he was right. But he believed that, if it ever came to the industrial revolution with us, the fight would be more uncompromising than any such fight that the world had ever seen. There was no respect from low to high, he said, and no consideration from high to low, as there were in countries with traditions and old associations."

"Well," said the banker, "there may be something in that. Certainly, so far as the two forces have come into conflict here, there has been no disposition, on either side, to 'make war with the water of roses.' It's astonishing, in fact, to see how ruthless the fellows who have just got up are towards the fellows who are still down. And the best of us have been up only a generation or two — and the fellows who are still down know it."

"And what do you think would be the outcome of such a conflict?" I asked, with my soul divided between fear of it and the perception of its excellence as material. My fancy vividly sketched the outline of a story which should forecast the struggle and its event, somewhat on the plan of the Battle of Dorking.

"We should beat," said the banker, breaking his cigar-ash off with his little finger; and I instantly cast him, with his ironic calm, for the part of a great patrician leader in my Fall of the Republic. Of course, I disguised him somewhat, and travestied his worldly bonhomie with the bluff sang-froid of the soldier; these things are easily done.

"What makes you think we should beat?" asked the manufacturer, with a certain curiosity.

"Well, all the good jingo reasons: we have got the materials for beating. Those fellows throw away their strength whenever they begin to fight, and they've been so badly generaled, up to the present time, that they have wanted to fight at the outset of every quarrel. They have been beaten in every quarrel, but still they always want to begin by fighting. That is all right. When they have learned enough to begin by *voting,* then we shall have to look out. But if they keep on fighting, and always putting themselves in the wrong and getting the worst of it, perhaps we can fix the voting so we needn't be any more afraid of that than we are of the fighting. It's astonishing how shortsighted they are. They have no conception of any cure for their grievances, except more wages and fewer hours."

"But," I asked, "do you really think they have any just grievances?"

"Of course not, as a business man," said the banker. "If I were a workingman, I should probably think differently. But we will suppose, for the sake of argument, that their day is too long and their pay is too short. How do they go about to better themselves? They strike. Well, a strike is a fight, and in a fight, nowadays, it is always skill and money that win. The workingmen can't stop till they have put themselves outside of the public sympathy which the newspapers say is so potent in their behalf; I never saw that it did them the least good. They begin by boycotting, and breaking the heads of the men who want to work. They destroy property, and they interfere with business — the two absolutely sacred things in the American religion. Then we call out the militia and shoot a few of them, and their leaders declare the strike off. It is perfectly simple."

"But will it be quite as simple," I asked, reluctant in behalf of my projected romance, to have the matter so soon disposed of — "will it be quite so simple if their leaders ever persuade the workingmen to leave the militia, as they threaten to do, from time to time?"

"No, not quite so simple," the banker admitted. "Still, the fight would be comparatively simple. In the first place, I doubt — though I won't be certain about it — whether there are a great many workingmen in the militia now. I rather fancy it is made up, for the most part, of clerks and small tradesmen, and book-keepers, and such employés of business as have time and money for it. I may be mistaken."

No one seemed able to say whether he was mistaken or not; and, after waiting a moment, he proceeded: "I feel pretty sure that it is so in the city companies and regiments, at any rate, and that if every workingman left them it would not seriously impair their effectiveness. But when the workingmen have left the militia, what have they done? They have eliminated the only thing that disqualifies it for prompt and unsparing use against strikes. As long as they are in it we might have our misgivings, but if they were once out of it we should have none. And what would they gain? They would not be allowed to arm and organize as an inimical force. *That* was settled once for all in Chicago, in the case of the International Groups. A few squads of policemen would break them up. Why," the banker exclaimed, with his good-humored laugh, "how preposterous they are when you come to look at it! They are in the majority, the immense majority, if you count the farmers, and they prefer to behave as if they were the hopeless minority. They say they want an eight-hour law, and every now and then they strike and try to fight it. Why don't they *vote* it? They could *make* it the law in six months by such overwhelming numbers that no one would dare to evade or defy it. They can make any law they want, but they prefer to break such laws as we have. That 'alienates public sympathy,' the newspapers say; but the spectacle of their stupidity and helpless wilfulness is so lamentable that I could almost pity them. If they chose, it would take only a few years to transform our government into the likeness of anything they wanted. But they would rather not have what they want, apparently, if they can only keep themselves from getting it, and they have to work hard to do that!"

"I suppose," I said, "that they are misled by the un-American principles and methods of the socialists among them."

"Why, no," returned the banker, "I shouldn't say that. As far as I understand it, the socialists are the only fellows among them who propose to vote their ideas into laws, and nothing can be more American than that. I don't believe the socialists stir up the strikes — at least, among our workingmen; though the newspapers convict them of it, generally without trying them. The socialists seem to accept the strikes as the inevitable outcome of the situation, and they make use of them as proofs of the industrial discontent. But, luckily for the status, our labor leaders are not socialists, for your socialist, whatever you may say against him, has generally thought himself into a socialist. He knows that until the workingmen stop fighting, and get down to voting — until they consent to be the majority — there is no hope for them. I am not talking of anarchists, mind you, but of socialists, whose philosophy is more law, not less, and who look forward to an order so just that it can't be disturbed."

"And what," the minister faintly said, "do you think will be the outcome of it all?"

"We had that question the other night, didn't we? Our legal friend here seemed to feel that we might rub along indefinitely as we are doing, or work out an Altruria of our own; or go back to the patriarchal stage, and own our workingmen. He seemed not to have so much faith in the logic of events as I have. I doubt if it is altogether a woman's logic. *Parole femmine, fatti maschi,*[9] and the logic of events isn't altogether words; it's full of hard knocks, too. But I'm no prophet. I can't forecast the future; I prefer to take it as it comes. There's a little tract of William Morris's though — I forget just what he calls it — that is full of curious and interesting speculation on this point. He thinks that if we keep the road we are now going, the last state of labor will be like its first, and it will be owned."

"Oh, I don't believe that will ever happen in America," I protested.

"Why not?" asked the banker. "Practically, it *is* owned already in a vastly greater measure than we recognize. And where would the great

[9] Italian: "Words are feminine, deeds masculine."

harm be? The new slavery would not be like the old. There needn't be irresponsible whipping and separation of families, and private buying and selling. The proletariat would probably be owned by the state, as it was at one time in Greece; or by large corporations, which would be much more in keeping with the genius of our free institutions; and an enlightened public opinion would cast safeguards about it in the form of law to guard it from abuse. But it would be strictly policed, localized, and controlled. There would probably be less suffering than there is now, when a man may be cowed into submission to any terms through the suffering of his family; when he may be starved out and turned out if he is unruly. You may be sure that nothing of that kind would happen in the new slavery. We have not had nineteen hundred years of Christianity for nothing."

The banker paused, and as the silence continued he broke it with a laugh, which was a prodigious relief to my feelings, and I suppose to the feelings of all. I perceived that he had been joking, and I was confirmed in this when he turned to the Altrurian and laid his hand upon his shoulder. "You see," he said, "I'm a kind of Altrurian myself. What is the reason why we should not found a new Altruria here on the lines I've drawn? Have you never had philosophers — well, call them philanthropists; I don't mind — of my way of thinking among you?"

"Oh, yes," said the Altrurian. "At one time, just before we emerged from the competitive conditions, there was much serious question whether capital should not own labor instead of labor owning capital. That was many hundred years ago."

"I am proud to find myself such an advanced thinker," said the banker. "And how came you to decide that labor should own capital?"

"We voted it," answered the Altrurian.

"Well," said the banker, "our fellows are still fighting it, and getting beaten."

I found him later in the evening talking with Mrs. Makely. "My dear sir," I said, "I liked your frankness with my Altrurian friend immensely; and it may be well to put the worst foot foremost; but what is the advantage of not leaving us a leg to stand upon?"

He was not in the least offended at my boldness, as I had feared he might be, but he said with that jolly laugh of his, "Capital! Well, perhaps I have worked my candor a little too hard; I suppose there is such a thing. But don't you see that it leaves me in the best possible position to carry the war into Altruria when we get him to open up about his native land?"

"Ah! If you can get him to do it."

"Well, we were just talking about that. Mrs. Makely has a plan."

"Yes," said the lady, turning an empty chair near her own toward me. "Sit down and listen!"

CHAPTER X

I sat down, and Mrs. Makely continued: "I have thought it all out, and I want you to confess that in all practical matters a woman's brain is better than a man's. Mr. Bullion, here, says it is, and I want you to say so too."

"Yes," the banker admitted, "when it comes down to business a woman is worth any two of us."

"And we have just been agreeing," I coincided, "that the only gentlemen among us are women. Mrs. Makely, I admit, without further dispute, that the most unworldly woman is worldlier than the worldliest man; and that in all practical matters we fade into dreamers and doctrinaires beside you. Now, go on!"

But she did not mean to let me off so easily. She began to brag herself up, as women do, whenever you make them the slightest concession.

"Here, you men," she said, "have been trying for a whole week to get something out of Mr. Homos about his country, and you have left it to a poor, weak woman, at last, to think how to manage it. I do believe that you get so much interested in your own talk, when you are with him, that you don't let him get in a word, and that's the reason you haven't found out anything about Altruria yet from him."

In view of the manner in which she had cut in at Mrs. Camp's, and stopped Homos on the very verge of the only full and free confession he had ever been near making about Altruria, I thought this was pretty cool; but, for fear of worse, I said:

"You're quite right, Mrs. Makely. I'm sorry to say that there has been a shameful want of self-control among us, and that, if we learn anything at all from him, it will be because you have taught us how."

She could not resist this bit of taffy. She scarcely gave herself time to gulp it before she said:

"Oh, it's very well to say that now! But where would you have been if I hadn't set my wits to work? Now, listen! It just popped into my mind, like an inspiration, when I was thinking of something altogether different. It flashed upon me in an instant: a good object, and a public occasion."

"Well?" I said, finding this explosive and electrical inspiration rather enigmatical.

"Why, you know, the Union chapel, over in the village, is in a languishing condition, and the ladies have been talking all summer about doing something for it, getting up something — a concert, or theatricals, or a dance, or something — and applying the proceeds to repainting and papering the visible church; it needs it dreadfully. But, of course, those things are not exactly religious, don't you know; and a fair is so much trouble; and *such* a bore, when you get the articles ready, even; and everybody feels swindled; and now people frown on raffles, so there is no use thinking of them. What you want is something striking. We did think of a parlor-reading, or perhaps ventriloquism; but the performers all charge so much that there wouldn't be anything left after paying expenses."

She seemed to expect some sort of prompting at this point; so I said, "Well?"

"Well," she repeated, "that is just where your Mr. Homos comes in."

"Oh! How does he come in there?"

"Why, get him to deliver a Talk on Altruria. As soon as he knows it's for a good object, he will be on fire to do it; and they must live so much in common there that the public occasion will be just the thing that will appeal to him."

It did seem a good plan to me, and I said so. But Mrs. Makely was so much in love with it that she was not satisfied with my modest recognition.

"Good? It's magnificent! It's the very thing! And I have thought it out, down to the last detail — "

"Excuse me!" I interrupted. "Do you think there is sufficient general interest in the subject, outside of the hotel, to get a full house for him? I shouldn't like to see him subjected to the mortification of empty benches."

"What in the world are you thinking of ? Why, there isn't a farm-house, anywhere within ten miles, where they haven't heard of Mr. Homos; and there isn't a servant under this roof, or in any of the boarding-houses, who doesn't know something about Altruria and want to know more. It seems that your friend has been much oftener with the porters and the stable-boys than he has been with us."

I had only too great reason to fear so. In spite of my warnings and entreaties, he had continued to behave toward every human being he met exactly as if they were equals. He apparently could not conceive of that social difference which difference of occupation creates among us. He owned that he saw it, and from the talk of our little group he knew it existed; but when I expostulated with him upon some act in gross violation of society usage, he only answered that he could not imagine that what he saw and knew could actually be. It was quite impossible to keep him from bowing with the greatest deference to our waitress; he shook hands with the head-waiter every morning as well as with me; there

CHAPTER X

was a fearful story current in the house, that he had been seen running
down one of the corridors to relieve a chamber-maid laden with two heavy
waterpails, which she was carrying to the rooms to fill up the pitchers.
This was probably not true; but I myself saw him helping in the hotel
hayfield one afternoon, shirt-sleeved like any of the hired men. He said
that it was the best possible exercise, and that he was ashamed he could
give no better excuse for it than the fact that without something of the
kind he should suffer from indigestion. It was grotesque, and out of all
keeping with a man of his cultivation and breeding. He was a gentleman
and a scholar, there was no denying, and yet he did things in contraven-
tion of good form at every opportunity, and nothing I could say had any
effect with him. I was perplexed beyond measure, the day after I had
reproached him for his labor in the hayfield, to find him in a group of
table-girls, who were listening while the head-waiter read aloud to them
in the shade of the house; there was a corner looking toward the stables
which was given up to them by tacit consent of the guests during a certain
part of the afternoon. I feigned not to see him, but I could not forbear
speaking to him about it afterwards. He took it in good part, but he said
he had been rather disappointed in the kind of literature they liked, and
the comments they made on it; he had expected that with the education
they had received, and with their experience of the seriousness of life,
they would prefer something less trivial. He supposed, however, that a
romantic love-story, where a poor American girl married an English lord,
formed a refuge for them from the real world which promised them so
little and held them so cheap. It was quite useless for one to try to make
him realize his behavior in consorting with servants as a kind of scandal.

The worst of it was that his behavior, as I could see, had already
begun to demoralize the objects of his misplaced politeness. At first,
the servants stared and resented it, as if it were some tasteless joke;
but in an incredibly short time, when they saw that he meant his
courtesy in good faith, they took it as their due. I had always had a
good understanding with the head-waiter, and I thought I could safely
smile with him at the queer conduct of my friend toward himself and
his fellow-servants. To my astonishment he said, "I don't see why he
shouldn't treat them as if they were ladies and gentlemen. Doesn't he
treat you and your friends so?"

It was impossible to answer this, and I could only suffer in silence, and
hope the Altrurian would soon go. I had dreaded the moment when the
landlord should tell me that his room was wanted; now I almost desired
it, but he never did. On the contrary, the Altrurian was in high favor with
him. He said he liked to see a man make himself pleasant with everybody;

and that he did not believe he had ever had a guest in the house who was so popular all round.

"Of course," Mrs. Makely went on, "I don't criticise him — with his peculiar traditions. I presume I should be just so myself if I had been brought up in Altruria, which, thank goodness, I wasn't. But Mr. Homos is a perfect dear, and all the women in the house are in love with him, from the cook's helpers, up and down. No, the only danger is that there won't be room in the hotel parlors for all the people that will want to hear him, and we shall have to make the admission something that will be prohibitive in most cases. We shall have to make it a dollar."

"Well," I said, "I think that will settle the question as far as the farming population is concerned. It's twice as much as they ever pay for a reserved seat in the circus, and four times as much as a simple admission. I'm afraid, Mrs. Makely, you're going to be very few, though fit."

"Well, I've thought it all over, and I'm going to put the tickets at one dollar."

"Very good. Have you caught your hare?"

"No, I haven't, yet. And I want you to help me catch him. What do you think is the best way to go about it?"

The banker said he would leave us to the discussion of that question, but Mrs. Makely could count upon him in everything if she could only get the man to talk. At the end of our conference we decided to interview the Altrurian together.

I shall always be ashamed of the way that woman wheedled the Altrurian, when we found him the next morning, walking up and down the piazza, before breakfast. That is, it was before our breakfast; when we asked him to go in with us, he said he had just had his breakfast, and was waiting for Reuben Camp, who had promised to take him up as he passed with a load of hay for one of the hotels in the village.

"Ah, that reminds me, Mr. Homos," the unscrupulous woman began on him at once. "We want to interest you in a little movement we're getting up for the Union chapel in the village. You know it's the church where all the different sects have their services alternately. Of course, it's rather an original way of doing, but there *is* sense in it where the people are too poor to go into debt for different churches, and — "

"It's admirable!" said the Altrurian. "I have heard about it from the Camps. It is an emblem of the unity which ought to prevail among Christians of all professions. How can I help you, Mrs. Makely?"

"I knew you would approve of it!" she exulted. "Well, it's simply this: The poor little place has got so shabby that *I'm* almost ashamed to be seen going into it, for one; and want to raise money enough to give it a new coat of paint outside and put on some kind of pretty paper, of an ecclesiastical pattern, on the inside. I declare those staring white walls, with the cracks in the plastering zigzagging every *which* way, distract me so that I can't put my mind on the sermon. Don't you think that paper, say of a Gothic design, would be a great improvement? I'm sure it would; and it's Mr. Twelvemough's idea, too."

I learned this fact now for the first time; but, with Mrs. Makely's warning eye upon me, I could not say so, and I made what sounded to me like a Gothic murmur of acquiescence. It sufficed for Mrs. Makely's purpose, at any rate, and she went on, without giving the Altrurian a chance to say what he thought the educational effect of wall paper would be:

"Well, the long and short of it is that we want you to make this money for us, Mr. Homos."

"I?" He started in a kind of horror. "My dear lady, I never made any money in my life! I should think it *wrong* to make money!"

"In Altruria, yes. We all know how it is in your delightful country, and I assure you that no one could respect your conscientious scruples more than I do. But you must remember that you are in America now. In America you have to make money, or else — get left. And then you must consider the object, and all the good you can do, indirectly, by a little Talk on Altruria."

He answered, blandly: "A little Talk on Altruria? How in the world should I get money by that?"

She was only too eager to explain, and she did it with so much volubility and at such great length, that I, who am good for nothing till I have had my cup of coffee in the morning, almost perished of an elucidation which the Altrurian bore with the sweetest patience.

When she gave him a chance to answer, at last, he said: "I shall be very happy to do what you wish, madam."

"*Will* you?" she screamed. "Oh, I'm *so* glad! You *have* been so slippery about Altruria, you know, that I expected nothing but a point-blank refusal. Of course, I knew you would be kind about it. Oh, I can hardly believe my senses! You can't think what a dear you are." I knew she had got that word from some English people who had been in the hotel; and she was working it rather wildly, but it was not my business to check her. "Well, then, all you have got to do is to leave the whole thing to me, and not bother about it a bit till I send and tell you we are ready to listen. There comes Reuben with his ox-team! Thank you *so* much, Mr. Homos. No one need be ashamed to enter the house of God" — she said Gawd, in an access of piety — "after we get that paint and paper on it; and we shall have them on before two Sabbaths have passed over it."

She wrung the Altrurian's hand; I was only afraid she was going to kiss him.

"There is but one stipulation I should like to make," he began.

"Oh, a thousand," she cut in.

"And that is, there shall be no exclusion from my lecture on account of occupation or condition. That is a thing that I can in nowise countenance, even in America; it is far more abhorrent to me even than money-making, though they are each a part and parcel of the other."

"I thought it was that!" she retorted joyously. "And I can assure you, Mr. Homos, there shall be nothing of that kind. Every one — I don't care who it is, or what they do — shall hear you who buys a ticket. Now, will that do?"

"Perfectly," said the Altrurian, and he let her wring his hand again.

She pushed hers through my arm as we started for the dining-room, and leaned over to whisper jubilantly: "That will fix it! He will see how much his precious lower classes care for Altruria if they have to pay a dollar apiece to hear about it. And I shall keep faith with him to the letter."

I could not feel that she would keep it in the spirit; but I could only groan inwardly and chuckle outwardly at the woman's depravity.

It seemed to me, though I could not approve of it, a capital joke, and so it seemed to all the members of the little group whom I had made especially acquainted with the Altrurian. It is true that the minister was somewhat troubled with the moral question, which did not leave me wholly at peace; and the banker affected to find a question of taste involved, which he said he must let me settle, however, as the man's host; if I could stand it, he could. No one said anything against the plan to Mrs. Makely, and this energetic woman made us take two tickets apiece, as soon as she got them printed, over in the village. She got little hand-bills printed, and had them scattered about through the neighborhood, at all the hotels, boarding-houses, and summer cottages, to give notice of the time and place of the Talk on Altruria. She fixed this for the following Saturday afternoon, in our hotel parlor; she had it in the afternoon so as not to interfere with the hop in the evening; she put tickets on sale at the principal houses, and at the village drug-store, and she made me go about with her and help her sell them at some of the cottages in person.

I must say I found this extremely distasteful, especially where the people were not very willing to buy, and she had to urge them. They all admitted the excellence of the object, but they were not so sure about the means. At several places the ladies asked who was this Mr. Homos, anyway; and how did she know he was really from Altruria? He might be an impostor.

Then Mrs. Makely would put me forward, and I would be obliged to give such account of him as I could, and to explain just how and why he came to be my guest; with the cumulative effect of bringing back all the misgivings which I had myself felt at the outset concerning him, and which I had dismissed as too fantastic.

The tickets went off rather slowly, even in our own hotel; people thought them too dear; and some, as soon as they knew the price, said frankly they had heard enough about Altruria already, and were sick of the whole thing.

Mrs. Makely said this was quite what she had expected of those people; that they were horrid and stingy and vulgar; and she should see what face they would have to ask her to take tickets when *they* were trying to get up something. She began to be vexed with herself, she confessed, at the joke she was playing on Mr. Homos, and I noticed that she put herself rather defiantly *en evidence* in his company, whenever she could in the presence of these reluctant ladies. She told me she had not the courage to ask the clerk how many of the tickets he had sold out of those she had left at the desk. One morning, the third or fourth, as I was going in to breakfast with her, the head-waiter stopped her as he opened the door, and asked modestly if she could spare him a few tickets, for he thought he could sell some. To my amazement the unprincipled creature said, "Why, certainly. How many?" and instantly took a package out of her pocket, where she seemed always to have them. He asked, Would twenty be more than she could spare? and she answered, "Not at all! Here are twenty-five," and bestowed the whole package upon him.

That afternoon Reuben Camp came lounging up toward us, where I sat with her on the corner of the piazza, and said that if she would like to let him try his luck with some tickets for the Talk he would see what he could do.

"You can have all you want, Reuben," she said, "and I hope you'll have better luck than I have. I'm perfectly disgusted with people."

She fished several packages out of her pocket this time, and he asked, "Do you mean that I can have them all?"

"Every one, and a band of music into the bargain," she answered recklessly. But she seemed a little daunted when he quietly took them. "You know there are a hundred here?"

"Yes, I should like to see what I can do amongst the natives. Then there is a construction train over at the junction, and I know a lot of the fellows. I guess some of 'em would like to come."

"The tickets are a dollar each, you know," she suggested.

"That's all right," said Camp. "Well, good-afternoon."

Mrs. Makely turned to me with a kind of gasp, as he shambled away. "I don't know about that!"

"About having the whole crew of a construction train at the Talk? I dare say it won't be pleasant to the ladies who have bought tickets."

"*Oh!*" said Mrs. Makely with astonishing contempt, "I don't care what *they* think. But Reuben has got all my tickets, and suppose he keeps them so long that I won't have time to sell any, and then throws them back on my hands? *I* know!" she added, joyously. "I can go around now, and tell people that my tickets are all gone; and I'll go instantly and have the clerk hold all he has left at a premium."

She came back looking rather blank.

"He hasn't got a single one left. He says an old native came in this morning and took every last one of them — he doesn't remember just how many. I believe they're going to speculate on them; and if Reuben Camp serves me a trick like that — Why!" she broke off, "I believe I'll speculate on them myself! I should like to know why I shouldn't! Oh, I should just *like* to make some of those creatures pay double, or treble, for the chances they've refused. Ah, Mrs. Bulkham," she called out to a lady who was coming down the veranda toward us, "you'll be glad to know I've got rid of all my tickets! *Such* a relief!"

"You *have?*" Mrs. Bulkham retorted.

"Every one."

"I thought," said Mrs. Bulkham, "that you understood I wanted one for my daughter and myself, if she came."

"I certainly didn't," said Mrs. Makely, with a wink of concentrated wickedness at me. "But if you do, you will have to say so now, without any ifs or ands about it; and if any of the tickets come back — I let friends have a few on sale — I will give you two."

"Well, I do," said Mrs. Bulkham, after a moment.

"Very well, it will be five dollars for the two. I feel bound to get all I can for the cause. Shall I put your name down?"

"Yes," said Mrs. Bulkham, rather crossly; but Mrs. Makely inscribed her name on her tablets with a radiant amiability, which suffered no eclipse when, within the next fifteen minutes, a dozen other ladies hurried up, and bought in at the same rate.

I could not stand it, and I got up to go away, feeling extremely *particeps criminis.*[10] Mrs. Makely seemed to have a conscience as light as air.

"If Reuben Camp or the head-waiter don't bring back some of those tickets I don't know what I shall do. I shall have to put chairs into the

[10] Latin: "Like a partner in crime."

aisles, and charge five dollars apiece for as many people as I can crowd in there. I never knew anything so perfectly providential."

"I envy you the ability to see it in that light, Mrs. Makely," I said, faint at heart. "Suppose Camp crowds the place full of his train men, how will the ladies that you've sold tickets to at five dollars apiece like it?"

"Pooh! What do I care how they like it! Horrid things! And for repairs on the house of Gawd, it's the same as being in church, where everybody is equal."

The time passed. Mrs. Makely sold chances to all the ladies in the house; on Friday night Reuben Camp brought her a hundred dollars; the head-waiter had already paid in twenty-five. "I didn't dare to ask them if they speculated on them," she confided to me. "Do you suppose they would have the conscience?"

They had secured the large parlor of the hotel, where the young people danced in the evening, and where entertainments were held, of the sort usually given in summer hotels; we had already had a dramatic reading, a time with the phonograph, an exhibition of necromancy, a concert by a college glee club, and I do not know what else. The room would hold perhaps two hundred people, if they were closely seated, and, by her own showing, Mrs. Makely had sold above two hundred and fifty tickets and chances. All Saturday forenoon she consoled herself with the belief that a great many people at the other hotels and cottages had bought seats merely to aid the cause, and would not really come; she estimated that at least fifty would stay away: but if Reuben Camp had sold his tickets among the natives, we might expect every one of them to come and get his money's worth; she did not dare to ask the head-waiter how he had got rid of his twenty-five tickets.

The hour set for the Talk to begin was three o'clock, so that people could have their naps comfortably over, after the one o'clock dinner, and be just in the right frame of mind for listening. But long before the appointed time the people who dine at twelve, and never take an afternoon nap, began to arrive, on foot, in farm-wagons, smart buggies, mud-crusted carry-alls, and all manner of ramshackle vehicles. They arrived as if coming to a circus, old husbands and wives, young couples and their children, pretty girls and their fellows, and hitched their horses to the tails of their wagons, and began to make a picnic lunch in the shadow of the grove lying between the hotel and the station. About two we heard the snorting of a locomotive at a time when no train was due, and a construction train came in view, with the men waving their handkerchiefs from the windows, and apparently ready for all the fun there was to be in the thing. Some of them had a small flag in each hand, the American Stars and Stripes and the white flag of Altruria, in compliment to my guest, I suppose. A good many of the farmers came over to the hotel to buy tickets, which they said they expected to get after they came, and Mrs. Makely was obliged to pacify them with all sorts of lying promises. From moment to moment she was in consultation with the landlord, who decided to throw open the dining-room, which connected with the parlor, so as to allow the help and the neighbors to hear, without incommoding the hotel guests. She said that this took a great burden off her mind, and that now she should feel perfectly easy, for now no one could complain about being mixed up with the servants and the natives, and yet every one could hear perfectly.

She could not rest until she had sent for Homos and told him of this admirable arrangement. I did not know whether to be glad or not when he instantly told her that, if there was to be any such separation of his auditors, in recognition of our class distinctions, he must refuse to speak at all.

"Then what in the world are we to do?" she wailed out, and the tears came into her eyes.

"Have you got the money for all your tickets?" he asked with a sort of disgust for the whole transaction in his tone.

"Yes, and more, too. I don't believe there's a soul, in the hotel or out of it, that hasn't paid at least a dollar to hear you: and that makes it so very embarrassing. Oh, *dear* Mr. Homos! You won't be so implacably high-principled as all that! Think that you are doing it for the house of Gawd."

The woman made me sick.

"Then no one," said the Altrurian, "can feel aggrieved, or unfairly used, if I say what I have to say in the open air, where all can listen equally, without any manner of preference or distinction. We will go up to the edge of the grove overlooking the tennis-court, and hold our meeting there, as the Altrurian meetings are always held, with the sky for a roof, and with no walls but the horizon."

"The very thing!" cried Mrs. Makely. "Who would ever have thought you were so practical, Mr. Homos? I don't believe you're an Altrurian, after all: I believe you are an American in disguise."

The Altrurian turned away, without making any response to this flattering attribution of our nationality to him; but Mrs. Makely had not waited for any. She had flown off, and I next saw her attacking the landlord, with such apparent success, that he slapped himself on the leg and vanished, and immediately the porters and bell-boys and all the men-servants began carrying out chairs to the tennis-court, which was already well set round with benches. In a little while the whole space was covered, and settees were placed well up the ground toward the grove.

By half-past two the guests of the hotel came out and took the best seats, as by right, and the different tallyhoes and mountain wagons began to arrive from the other hotels, with their silly hotel cries, and their gay groups dismounted and dispersed themselves over the tennis court until all the chairs were taken. It was fine to see how the natives and the train-men and the hotel servants, with an instinctive perception of the proprieties, yielded these places to their superiors, and, after the summer folks were all seated, scattered themselves on the grass and the pine-needles about the border of the grove. I should have liked to instance the fact to the Altrurian, as a proof that this sort of subordination was a part of human nature, and that a principle which pervaded our civilization, after the democratic training of our whole national life, must be divinely implanted. But there was no opportunity for me to speak with him after the fact had accomplished itself, for by this time he had taken his place in front of a little clump of low pines and was waiting for the assembly to quiet itself before he began to speak. I do not think there could have been less than five hundred present, and the scene had that accidental pictur-esqueness which results from the grouping of all sorts of faces and costumes. Many of our ladies had pretty hats and brilliant parasols, but I must say that the soberer tone of some of the old farm-wives' brown calicoes and outdated bonnets contributed to enrich the coloring, and there was a certain gayety in the sunny glisten of the men's straw-hats everywhere that was very good.

The sky overhead was absolutely stainless, and the light of the cool afternoon sun streamed upon the slopes of the solemn mountains to the east. The tall pines in the background blackened themselves against the horizon; nearer they showed more and more decidedly their bluish green, and the yellow of the newly-fallen needles painted their aisles deep into the airy shadows.

A little wind stirred their tops, and for a moment, just before the Altrurian began to speak, drew from them an organ-tone that melted delicately away as his powerful voice rose.

CHAPTER XI

"I could not give you a clear account of the present state of things in my country," the Altrurian began, "without first telling you something of our conditions before the time of our Evolution. It seems to be the law of all life, that nothing can come to fruition without dying and seeming to make an end. It must be sown in corruption before it can be raised in incorruption. The truth itself must perish to our senses before it can live to our souls; the Son of Man must suffer upon the cross before we can know the Son of God.

"It was so with His message to the world, which we received in the old time as an ideal realized by the earliest Christians, who loved one another and who had all things in common. The apostle cast away upon our heathen coasts won us with the story of this first Christian republic, and he established a commonwealth of peace and goodwill among us in its likeness. That commonwealth perished, just as its prototype perished, or seemed to perish; and long ages of civic and economic warfare succeeded, when every man's hand was against his neighbor, and might was the rule that got itself called right. Religion ceased to be the hope of this world, and became the vague promise of the next. We descended into the valley of the shadow, and dwelt amid chaos for ages, before we groped again into the light.

"The first glimmerings were few and indistinct, but men formed themselves about the luminous points here and there, and when these broke and dispersed into lesser gleams, still men formed themselves about each of them. There arose a system of things, better, indeed, than that darkness, but full of war and lust and greed, in which the weak rendered homage to the strong, and served them in the field and in the camp, and the strong in turn gave the weak protection against the other strong. It was a juggle in which the weak did not see that their safety was, after all, from themselves; but it was an image of peace, however false and fitful, and it endured for a time. It endured for a limited time, if we measure by the life of the race; it endured for an unlimited time if we measure by the lives of the men who were born and died while it endured.

"But that disorder, cruel and fierce and stupid, which endured because it sometimes masked itself as order, did at last pass away. Here and there one of the strong overpowered the rest; then the strong became fewer and fewer, and in their turn they all yielded to a supreme lord, and throughout the land there was one rule, as it was called then, or one misrule, as we should call it now. This rule, or this misrule, continued for ages more; and again, in the immortality of the race, men toiled and struggled, and died without the hope of better things.

"Then the time came when the long nightmare was burst with the vision of a future in which all men were the law, and not one man, or any less number of men than all.

"The poor dumb beast of humanity rose, and the throne tumbled, and the scepter was broken, and the crown rolled away into that darkness of the past. We thought that heaven had descended to us, and that liberty, equality, and fraternity were ours. We could not see what should again alienate us from one another, or how one brother could again oppress another. With a free field and no favor we believed we should prosper on together, and there would be peace and plenty for all. We had the republic again after so many ages now, and the republic, as we knew it in our dim annals, was brotherhood and universal happiness. All but a very few, who prophesied evil of our lawless freedom, were wrapped in a delirium of hope. Men's minds and men's hands were suddenly released to an activity unheard of before. Invention followed invention; our rivers and seas became the warp of commerce where the steam-sped shuttles carried the woof of enterprise to and fro with tireless celerity. Machines to save labor multiplied themselves as if they had been procreative forces; and wares of every sort were produced with incredible swiftness and cheapness. Money seemed to flow from the ground; vast fortunes 'rose like an exhalation,' as your Milton says.

"At first we did not know that they were the breath of the nethermost pits of hell, and that the love of money, which was becoming universal with us, was filling the earth with the hate of men. It was long before we came to realize that in the depths of our steamships were those who fed the fires with their lives, and that our mines from which we dug our wealth were the graves of those who had died to the free light and air, without finding rest of death. We did not see that the machines for saving labor were monsters that devoured women and children, and wasted men at the bidding of the power which no man must touch.

"That is, we thought we must not touch it, for it called itself prosperity, and wealth, and the public good, and it said that it gave bread, and it impudently bade the toiling myriads consider what would become of them if it took away their means of wearing themselves out in its service. It demanded of the state absolute immunity and absolute impunity, the right to do its will wherever and however it would, without question from the people who were the final law. It had its way, and under its rule we became the richest people under the sun. The Accumulation, as we called this power, because we feared to call it by its true name, rewarded its own with gains of twenty, of a hundred, of a thousand per cent., and to satisfy its need, to produce the labor that operated its machines, there came into existence a hapless race of men who bred their kind for its service, and whose little ones were its prey almost from their cradles. Then the infamy became too great, and the law, the voice of the people, so long guiltily silent, was lifted in behalf of those who had no helper. The Accumulation came under control for the first time, and could no longer work its slaves twenty hours a day amid perils to life and limb from its machinery and in conditions that forbade them decency and morality. The time of a hundred and a thousand per cent. passed; but still the Accumulation demanded immunity and impunity, and, in spite of its conviction of the enormities it had practiced, it declared itself the only means of civilization and progress. It began to give out that it was timid, though its history was full of the boldest frauds and crimes, and it threatened to withdraw itself if it were ruled or even crossed; and again it had its way, and we seemed to prosper more and more. The land was filled with cities where the rich flaunted their splendor in palaces, and the poor swarmed in squalid tenements. The country was drained of its life and force, to feed the centres of commerce and industry. The whole land was bound together with a net-work of iron roads that linked the factories and founderies to the fields and mines, and blasted the landscape with the enterprise that spoiled the lives of men.

"Then, all at once, when its work seemed perfect and its dominion sure, the Accumulation was stricken with consciousness of the lie always at its heart. It had hitherto cried out for a free field and no favor, for unrestricted competition; but, in truth, it had never prospered, except as a monopoly. Whenever and wherever competition had play there had been nothing but disaster to the rival enterprises, till one rose over the rest. Then there was prosperity for that one.

"The Accumulation began to act upon its new consciousness. The iron roads united; the warring industries made peace, each kind under a single leadership. Monopoly, not competition, was seen to be the beneficent means of distributing the favors and blessings of the Accumulation to mankind. But, as before, there was alternately a glut and dearth of things, and it often happened that when starving men went ragged through the streets, the storehouses were piled full of rotting harvests that the farmers toiled from dawn till dusk to grow, and the warehouses fed the moth with the stuffs that the operative had woven his life into at his loom. Then followed, with a blind and mad succession, a time of famine, when money could not buy the superabundance that vanished, none knew how or why.

"The money itself vanished from time to time, and disappeared into the vaults of the Accumulation, for no better reason than that for which it poured itself out at other times. Our theory was that the people, that is to say the government of the people, made the people's money, but, as a matter of fact, the Accumulation made it, and controlled it, and juggled with it; and now you saw it, and now you did not see it. The government made gold coins, but the people had nothing but the paper money that the Accumulation made. But whether there was scarcity or plenty, the failures went on with a continuous ruin that nothing could check, while our larger economic life proceeded in a series of violent shocks, which we called financial panics, followed by long periods of exhaustion and recuperation. There was no law in our economy, but as the Accumulation had never cared for the nature of law, it did not trouble itself for its name in our order of things. It had always bought the law it needed for its own use, first through the voter at the polls in the more primitive days, and then, as civilization advanced, in the legislatures and the courts. But the corruption even of these methods was far surpassed when the era of consolidation came, and the necessity for statutes and verdicts and decisions became more stringent. Then we had such a burlesque of — ”

"Look here!" a sharp nasal voice snarled across the rich, full pipe of the Altrurian, and we all instantly looked there. The voice came from an old farmer, holding himself stiffly up, with his hands in his pockets and his lean frame bent toward the speaker. "When are you goin' to get to Altrury? We know all about Ameriky."

He sat down again, and it was a moment before the crowd caught on. Then a yell of delight and a roar of volleyed laughter went up from the lower classes, in which, I am sorry to say, my friend, the banker, joined, so far as the laughter was concerned. "Good! that's it! first-rate!" came from a hundred vulgar throats.

"Isn't it a perfect shame?" Mrs. Makely demanded. "I think some of you gentlemen ought to say something! What will Mr. Homos think of our civilization if we let such interruptions go unrebuked!"

She was sitting between the banker and myself, and her indignation made him laugh more and more. "Oh, it serves him right," he said. "Don't you see that he is hoist with his own petard? Let him alone. He's in the hands of his friends."

The Altrurian waited for the tumult to die away, and then he said, gently: "I don't understand."

The old farmer jerked himself to his feet again: "It's like this: I paid my dolla' to hear about a country where there wa'n't no co'perations, nor no monop'lies, nor no buyin' up cou'ts; and I ain't agoin' to have no allegory shoved down my throat, instead of a true history, noways. I know all about how it is *here*. Fi'st, run their line through your backya'd, and then kill off your cattle, and keep kerryin' on it up from cou't to cou't, till there ain't hide or hair on 'em left — ”

"Oh, set down, set down! Let the man go on! He'll make it all right with you," one of the construction gang called out; but the farmer stood his ground, and I could hear him through the laughing and shouting keep saying something, from time to time, about not wanting to pay no dolla' for no talk about co'perations and monop'lies that we had right under our own noses the whole while, and you might say, in your very bread troughs; till, at last, I saw Reuben Camp make his way towards him, and, after an energetic expostulation, turn to leave him again.

Then he faltered out, "I guess it's all right," and dropped out of sight in the group he had risen from. I fancied his wife scolding him there, and all but shaking him in public.

"I should be very sorry," the Altrurian proceeded, "to have any one believe that I have not been giving you a bona fide account of conditions in my country before the Evolution, when we first took the name of Altruria in our great, peaceful campaign against the Accumulation. As for offering you any allegory or travesty of your own conditions, I will simply say that I do not know them well enough to do so intelligently. But, whatever they are, God forbid that the likeness which you seem to recognize should ever go so far as the desperate state of things which we finally reached. I will not trouble you with details; in fact, I have been afraid that I had already treated of our affairs too abstractly; but, since your own experience furnishes you the means of seizing my meaning, I will go on as before.

"You will understand me when I explain that the Accumulation had not erected itself into the sovereignty with us unopposed. The workingmen who suffered most from its oppression had early begun to band themselves against it, with the instinct of self-preservation, first trade by trade, and art by art, and then in congresses and federations of the trades and arts, until finally they enrolled themselves in one vast union, which included all the workingmen whom their necessity or their interest did not leave on the side of the Accumulation. This beneficent and generous association of the weak for the sake of the weakest did not accomplish itself fully till the baleful instinct of the Accumulation had reduced the monopolies to one vast monopoly, till the stronger had devoured the weaker among its members, and the supreme agent stood at the head of our affairs, in everything but name, our imperial ruler. We had hugged so long the delusion of each man for himself, that we had suffered all realty to be taken from us. The Accumulation owned the land as well as the mines under it and the shops over it; the Accumulation owned the seas and the ships that sailed the seas, and the fish that swam in their depths; it owned transportation and distribution, and the wares and products that were to be carried to and fro; and by a logic irresistible and inexorable, the Accumulation *was,* and we were *not.*

"But the Accumulation, too, had forgotten something. It had found it so easy to buy legislatures and courts that it did not trouble itself about the polls. It left us the suffrage, and let us amuse ourselves with the periodical election of the political clay images which it manipulated and moulded to any shape and effect at its pleasure. The Accumulation knew that it was the sovereignty, whatever figure-head we called president, or governor, or mayor: we had other names for these officials, but I use their analogues for the sake of clearness, and I hope my good friend over there will not think I am still talking about America."

"No," the old farmer called back, without rising, "we hain't got there quite yit."

"No hurry," said a trainman. "All in good time. Go on!" he called to the Altrurian.

The Altrurian resumed:

"There had been, from the beginning, an almost ceaseless struggle between the Accumulation and the proletariat. The Accumulation always said that it was the best friend of the proletariat, and it denounced, through the press which it controlled, the proletarian leaders who taught that it was the enemy of the proletariat, and who stirred up strikes and tumults of all sorts, for higher wages and fewer hours. But the friend of the proletariat, whenever occasion served, treated the proletariat like a deadly enemy. In seasons of over-production, as it was called, it locked the workmen out, or laid them off, and left their families to starve, or ran light work, and claimed the credit of public benefactors for running at all. It sought every chance to reduce wages; it had laws passed to forbid or cripple the workmen in their strikes; and the judges convicted them of conspiracy, and wrested the statutes to their hurt, in cases where there had been no thought of embarrassing them, even among the legislators. God forbid that you should ever come to such a pass in America; but, if you ever should, God grant that you may find your way out as simply as we did at last, when freedom had perished in everything but name among us, and justice had become a mockery.

"The Accumulation had advanced so smoothly, so lightly, in all its steps to the supreme power, and had at last so thoroughly quelled the uprisings of the proletariat, that it forgot one thing: it forgot the despised and neglected suffrage. The ballot, because it had been so easy to annul its effect, had been left in the people's hands; and when, at last, the leaders of the proletariat ceased to counsel strikes, or any form of resistance to the Accumulation that could be tormented into the likeness of insurrection against the government, and began to urge them to attack it in the political way, the deluge that swept the Accumulation out of existence came trickling and creeping over the land. It appeared first in the country, a spring from the ground; then it gathered head in the villages; then it swelled to a torrent in the cities. I cannot stay to trace its course; but suddenly, one day, when the Accumulation's abuse of a certain power became too gross, it was voted out of that power. You will perhaps be interested to know that it was with the telegraphs that the rebellion against the Accumulation began, and the government was forced, by the overwhelming majority which the proletariat sent to our parliament, to assume a function which the Accumulation had impudently usurped. Then the transportation of smaller and more perishable wares — "

"Yes," a voice called, "express business. Go on."

"Was legislated a function of the post-office," the Altrurian went on. "Then all transportation was taken into the hands of the political government, which had always been accused of great corruption in its administration, but which showed itself immaculately pure compared with the Accumulation. The common ownership of mines necessarily followed, with an allotment of lands to any one who wished to live by tilling the land; but not a foot of the land was remitted to private hands for purposes of selfish pleasure or the exclusion of any other from the landscape. As all businesses had been gathered into the grasp of the Accumulation, and the manufacture of everything they used and the production of everything that they ate was in the control of the Accumulation, its transfer to the government was the work of a single clause in the statute.

"The Accumulation, which had treated the first menaces of resistance with contempt, awoke to its peril too late. When it turned to wrest the suffrage from the proletariat, at the first election where it attempted to make head against them, it was simply snowed under, as your picturesque phrase is. The Accumulation had no voters, except the few men at its head, and the creatures devoted to it by interest and ignorance. It seemed, at one moment, as if it would offer an armed resistance to the popular will, but, happily, that moment of madness passed. Our Evolution was accomplished without a drop of bloodshed, and the first great political brotherhood, the Commonwealth of Altruria, was founded.

"I wish that I had time to go into a study of some of the curious phases of the transformation from a civility in which the people lived *upon* each other to one in which they lived *for* each other. There is a famous passage in the inaugural message of our first Altrurian president, which compares the new civic consciousness with that of a disembodied spirit released to the life beyond this and freed from all the selfish cares and greeds of the flesh. But perhaps I shall give a sufficiently clear notion of the triumph of the change among us, when I say that within half a decade after the fall of the old plutocratic oligarchy one of the chief directors of the Accumulation publicly expressed his gratitude to God that the Accumulation had passed away forever. You will realize the importance of such an expression in recalling the declarations some of your slaveholders have made since the Civil War, that they would not have slavery restored for any earthly consideration.

"But now, after this preamble, which has been so much longer than I meant it to be, how shall I give you a sufficiently just conception of the existing Altruria, the actual state from which I come?"

"Yes," came the nasal of the old farmer again, "that's what we are here fur. I wouldn't give a copper to know all you went through beforehand. It's too dumn like what we have been through ourselves, as fur as heard from."

A shout of laughter went up from most of the crowd, but the Altrurian did not seem to see any fun in it.

"Well," he resumed, "I will tell you, as well as I can, what Altruria is like; but, in the first place, you will have to cast out of your minds all images of civilization with which your experience has filled them. For a time, the shell of the old Accumulation remained for our social habitation, and we dwelt in the old competitive and monopolistic forms after the life had gone out of them — that is, we continued to live in populous cities, and we toiled to heap up riches for the moth to corrupt, and we slaved on in making utterly useless things, merely because we had the habit of making them to sell. For a while we made the old sham things, which pretended to be useful things and were worse than the confessedly useless things. I will give you an illustration from the trades, which you will all understand. The proletariat, in the competitive and monopolistic time, used to make a kind of shoes for the proletariat, or the women of the proletariat, which looked like fine shoes of the best quality. It took just as much work to make these shoes as to make the best fine shoes; but they were shams through and through. They wore out in a week, and the people called them, because they were bought fresh for every Sunday — "

"Sat'd'y night shoes," screamed the old farmer. "I know 'em. My gals buy 'em. Half dolla' a pai', and not wo'th the money."

"Well," said the Altrurian, "they were a cheat and a lie in every way, and under the new system it was not possible, when public attention was called to the fact, to continue the falsehood they embodied. As soon as the Saturday night shoe realized itself to the public conscience an investigation began, and it was found that the principle of the Saturday night shoe underlay half our industries and made half the work that was done. Then an immense reform took place. We renounced, in the most solemn convocation of the whole economy, the principle of the Saturday night shoe, and those who had spent their lives in producing sham shoes — "

"Yes," said the professor, rising from his seat near us, and addressing the speaker, "I shall be very glad to know what became of the worthy and industrious operatives who were thrown out of employment by this explosion of economic virtue."

"Why," the Altrurian replied, "they were set to work making honest shoes; and, as it took no more time to make a pair of honest shoes which lasted a year than it took to make a pair of dishonest shoes that lasted a week, the amount of labor in shoemaking was at once enormously reduced."

"Yes," said the professor, "I understand that. What became of the shoemakers?"

"They joined the vast army of other laborers who had been employed, directly or indirectly, in the fabrication of fraudulent wares. These shoe-makers — lasters, buttonholers, binders, and so on — no longer wore themselves out over their machines. One hour sufficed where twelve hours were needed before, and the operatives were released to the happy labor of the fields, where no one with us toils killingly, from dawn till dusk, but does only as much work as is needed to keep the body in health. We had a continent to refine and beautify; we had climates to change, and seasons to modify, a whole system of meteorology to readjust, and the public works gave employment to the multitudes emancipated from the soul-destroying services of shams. I can scarcely give you a notion of the vastness of the improvements undertaken and carried through, or still in process of accomplishment. But a single one will, perhaps, afford a suffi-cient illustration. Our southeast coast, from its vicinity to the pole, had always suffered from a winter of antarctic rigor; but our first president conceived the plan of cutting off a peninsula, which kept the equatorial current from making in to our shores; and the work was begun in his term, though the entire strip, twenty miles in width and ninety-three in length, was not severed before the end of the first Altrurian decade. Since that time the whole region of our southeastern coast has enjoyed the climate of your Mediterranean countries.

"It was not only the makers of fraudulent things who were released to these useful and wholesome labors, but those who had spent themselves in contriving ugly and stupid and foolish things were set free to the public employments. The multitude of these monstrosities and iniquities was as great as that of the shams — "

Here I lost some words, for the professor leaned over and whispered to me: "He has got *that* out of William Morris. Depend upon it, the man is a humbug. He is not an Altrurian at all."

I confess that my heart misgave me; but I signalled the professor to be silent, and again gave the Altrurian — if he was an Altrurian — my whole attention.

CHAPTER XII

"And so," the Altrurian continued, "when the labor of the community was emancipated from the bondage of the false to the free service of the true, it was also, by an inevitable implication, dedicated to beauty and rescued from the old slavery to the ugly, the stupid, and the trivial. The thing that was honest and useful became, by the operation of a natural law, a beautiful thing. Once he had not time enough to make things beautiful, we were so overworked in making false and hideous things to sell; but now we had all the time there was, and a glad emulation arose among the trades and occupations to the end that everything done should be done finely as well as done honestly. The artist, the man of genius, who worked from the love of his work, became the normal man, and in the measure of his ability and of his calling each wrought in the spirit of the artist. We got back the pleasure of doing a thing beautifully, which was God's primal blessing upon all his working children, but which we had lost in the horrible days of our need and greed. There is not a workingman within the sound of my voice but has known this divine delight, and would gladly know it always if he only had the time. Well, now we had the time, the Evolution had given us the time, and in all Altruria there was not a furrow driven or a swath mown, not a hammer struck on house or on ship, not a stitch sewn or a stone laid, not a line written or a sheet printed, not a temple raised or an engine built, but it was done with an eye to beauty as well as to use.

"As soon as we were freed from the necessity of preying upon one another, we found that *there was no hurry*. The good work would wait to be well done; and one of the earliest effects of the Evolution was the disuse of the swift trains which had traversed the continent, night and day, that one man might overreach another, or make haste to undersell his rival, or seize some advantage of him, or plot some profit to his loss. Nine-tenths of the railroads, which in the old times had ruinously competed, and then in the hands of the Accumulation had been united to impoverish and oppress the people, fell into disuse. The commonwealth operated the few lines that were necessary for the collection of materials and the distribution of manufactures, and for pleasure travel and the affairs of state; but the roads that had been built to invest capital, or parallel other roads, or 'make work,' as it was called, or to develop resources, or boom localities, were suffered to fall into ruin; the rails were stripped from the landscape, which they had bound as with shackles, and the road-beds became highways for the use of kindly neighborhoods, or nature recovered them wholly and hid the memory of their former abuse in grass and flowers and wild vines. The ugly towns that they had forced into being, as Frankenstein was fashioned, from the materials of the charnel, and that had no life in or from the good of the community, soon tumbled into decay. The administration used parts of them in the construction of the villages in which the Altrurians now mostly live; but generally these towns were built of materials so fraudulent, in form so vile, that it was judged best to burn them. In this way their sites were at once purified and obliterated.

"We had, of course, a great many large cities under the old egoistic conditions, which increased and fattened upon the country, and fed their cancerous life with fresh infusions of its blood. We had several cities of half a million, and one of more than a million; we had a score of them with a population of a hundred thousand or more. We were very proud of them, and vaunted them as a proof of our unparalleled prosperity, though really they never were anything but congeries of millionaires and the wretched creatures who served them and supplied them. Of course there was everywhere the appearance of enterprise and activity, but it meant final loss for the great mass of the business men, large and small, and final gain for the millionaires. These and their parasites dwelt together, the rich starving the poor and the poor plundering and misgoverning the rich; and it was the intolerable suffering in the cities that chiefly hastened the fall of the old Accumulation and the rise of the Commonwealth.

"Almost from the moment of the Evolution the competitive and monopolistic centers of population began to decline. In the clear light of the new order it was seen that they were not fit dwelling-places for men, either in the complicated and luxurious palaces where the rich fenced themselves from their kind, or in the vast tenements, towering height upon height, ten and twelve stories up, where the swarming poor festered in vice and sickness and famine. If I were to tell you of the fashion of those cities of our egoistic epoch, how the construction was one error from the first, and every correction of an error bred a new defect, I should make you laugh, I should make you weep. We let them fall to ruin as quickly as they would, and their sites are still so pestilential, after the lapse of centuries, that travelers are publicly guarded against them. Ravening beasts and poisonous reptiles lurk in those abodes of the riches and the poverty that are no longer known to our life. A part of one of the less malarial of the old cities, however, is maintained by the commonwealth in the form of its prosperity, and is studied by antiquarians for the instruction, and by moralists for the admonition it affords. A section of a street is exposed, and you see the foundations of the houses; you see the filthy drains that belched into the common sewers, trapped and retrapped to keep the poison gases down; you see the sewers that rolled their loathsome tides under the streets, amidst a tangle of gas pipes, steam pipes, water pipes, telegraph wires, electric lighting wires, electric motor wires, and grip-cables; all without a plan, but make-shifts, expedients, devices, to repair and evade the fundamental mistake of having any such cities at all.

"There are now no cities in Altruria, in your meaning, but there are capitals, one for each of the Regions of our country, and one for the whole commonwealth. These capitals are for the transaction of public affairs, in which every citizen of Altruria is schooled, and they are the residences of the administrative officials, who are alternated every year, from the highest to the lowest. A public employment with us is of no greater honor or profit than any other, for with our absolute economic equality there can be no ambition, and there is no opportunity for one citizen to outshine another. But as the capitals are the centers of all the arts, which we consider the chief of our public affairs, they are oftenest frequented by poets, actors, painters, sculptors, musicians, and architects. We regard all artists, who are in a sort creators, as the human type which is likest the divine, and we try to conform our whole industrial life to the artistic temperament. Even in the labors of the field and shop, which are obligatory upon all, we study the inspirations of this temperament, and in the voluntary pursuits we allow it full control. Each, in these, follows his fancy as to what he shall do, and when he shall do it, or whether he shall do anything at all. In the capitals are the universities, theaters, galleries, museums, cathedrals, laboratories and conservatories, and the appliances of every art and science, as well as the administration buildings; and beauty as well as use is studied in every edifice. Our capitals are as clean and quiet and healthful as the country, and these advantages are secured simply by the elimination of the horse, an animal which we should be as much surprised to find in the streets of a town as the plesiosaurus or the pterodactyl. All transportation in the capitals, whether for pleasure or business, is by electricity, and swift electrical expresses connect the capital of each region with the villages which radiate from it to the cardinal points. These expresses run at the rate of a hundred and fifty miles an hour, and they enable the artist, the scientist, the literary man, of the remotest hamlet, to visit the capital (when he is not actually resident there in some public use) every day, after the hours of the obligatory industries; or if he likes, he may remain there a whole week or fortnight, giving six hours a day instead of three to the obligatories, until the time is made up. In case of very evident merit, or for the purpose of allowing him to complete some work requiring continuous application, a vote of the local agents may release him from the obligatories indefinitely. Generally, however, our artists prefer not to ask this, but avail themselves of the stated means we have of allowing them to work at the obligatories, and get the needed exercise and variety of occupation in the immediate vicinity of the capital.

"We do not think it well to connect the hamlets on the different lines of radiation from the capital, except by the good country roads which traverse each region in every direction. The villages are mainly inhabited by those who prefer a rural life; they are farming villages; but in Altruria it can hardly be said that one man is more a farmer than another. We do not like to distinguish men by their callings; we do not speak of the poet This or the shoemaker That, for the poet may very likely be a shoemaker in the obligatories, and the shoemaker a poet in the voluntaries. If it can be said that one occupation is honored above another with us, it is that which we all share, and that is the cultivation of the earth. We believe that this, when not followed slavishly, or for gain, brings man into the closest relations to the deity, through a grateful sense of the divine bounty, and that it not only awakens a natural piety in him, but that it endears to the worker that piece of soil which he tills, and so strengthens his love of home. The home is the very heart of the Altrurian system, and we do not think it well that people should be away from their homes very long or very often. In the competitive and monopolistic times men spent half their days in racing back and forth across our continent; families were scattered by the chase for fortune, and there was a perpetual paying and repaying of visits. One-half the income of those railroads which we let fall into disuse came from the ceaseless unrest. Now a man is born and lives and dies among his own kindred, and the sweet sense of neighborhood, of brotherhood, which blessed the golden age of the first Christian republic, is ours again. Every year the people of each Region meet one another on Evolution day, in the Regionic capital; once in four years they all visit the national capital. There is no danger of the decay of patriotism among us; our country is our mother, and we love her as it is impossible to love the stepmother that a competitive or monopolistic nation must be to its citizens.

"I can only touch upon this feature and that of our system as I chance to think of it. If any of you are curious about others, I shall be glad to answer questions as well as I can. We have, of course," the Altrurian proceeded, after a little indefinite pause, to let any speak who liked, "no money in your sense. As the whole people control affairs, no man works for another, and no man pays another. Every one does his share of labor, and receives his share of food, clothing, and shelter, which is neither more nor less than another's. If you can imagine the justice and impartiality of a well-ordered family, you can conceive of the social and economic life of Altruria. We are, properly speaking, a family rather than a nation like yours.

"Of course we are somewhat favored by our insular, or continental position; but I do not know that we are more so than you are. Certainly, however, we are self-sufficing in a degree unknown to most European countries; and we have within our borders the materials of every comfort and the resources of every need. We have no commerce with the egoistic world, as we call that outside, and I believe that I am the first Altrurian to visit foreign countries avowedly in my national character, though we have always had emissaries living abroad incognito. I hope that I may say without offense that they find it a sorrowful exile, and that the reports of the egoistic world, with its wars, its bankruptcies, its civic commotions, and its social unhappiness, do not make us discontented with our own condition. Before the Evolution we had completed the round of your inventions and discoveries, impelled by the force that drives you on; and we have since disused most of them as idle and unfit. But we profit, now and then, by the advances you make in science, for we are passionately devoted to the study of the natural laws, open or occult, under which all men have their being. Occasionally an emissary returns with a sum of money, and explains to the students of the national university the processes by which it is lost and won; and at a certain time there was a movement for its introduction among us, not for its use as you know it, but for a species of counters in games of chance. It was considered, however, to contain an element of danger, and the scheme was discouraged.

"Nothing amuses and puzzles our people more than the accounts our emissaries give of the changes of fashion in the outside world, and of the ruin of soul and body which the love of dress often works. Our own dress, for men and for women, is studied, in one ideal of use and beauty, from the antique; caprice and vagary in it would be thought an effect of vulgar vanity. Nothing is worn that is not simple and honest in texture; we do not know whether a thing is cheap or dear, except as it is easy or hard to come by, and that which is hard to come by is forbidden as wasteful and foolish. The community builds the dwellings of the community, and these, too, are of a classic simplicity, though always beautiful and fit in form; the splendors of the arts are lavished upon the public edifices, which we all enjoy in common."

"Isn't this the greatest rehash of Utopia, New Atlantis, and City of the Sun,[11] that you ever imagined?" the professor whispered across me to the banker. "The man is a fraud, and a very bungling fraud at that."

---

[11] The professor refers to three of the best-known utopian writings of the Renaissance: *Utopia* (1516) by Sir Thomas More, *New Atlantis* (1627) by Francis Bacon, and *City of the Sun* (1627) by Tommaso Campanella.

"Well, you must expose him, when he gets through," the banker whispered back.

But the professor could not wait. He got upon his feet, and called out: "May I ask the gentleman from Altruria a question?"

"Certainly," the Altrurian blandly assented.

"Make it short!" Reuben Camp's voice broke in, impatiently. "We didn't come here to listen to your questions."

The professor contemptuously ignored him. "I suppose you occasionally receive emissaries from, as well as send them to, the world outside?"

"Yes, now and then castaways land on our coasts, and ships out of their reckonings put in at our ports for water or provision."

"And how are they pleased with your system?"

"Why, I cannot better answer than by saying that they mostly refuse to leave us."

"Ah, just as Bacon reports!" cried the professor.

"You mean in the New Atlantis?" returned the Altrurian. "Yes; it is astonishing how well Bacon in that book, and Sir Thomas More in his Utopia, have divined certain phases of our civilization and polity."

"I think he rather *has* you, professor," the banker whispered, with a laugh.

"But all those inspired visionaries," the Altrurian continued, while the professor sat grimly silent, watching for another chance, "who have borne testimony of us in their dreams, conceived of states perfect without the discipline of a previous competitive condition. What I thought, however, might specially interest you Americans in Altruria is the fact that our economy was evolved from one so like that in which you actually have your being. I had even hoped you might feel that, in all these points of resemblance, America prophesies another Altruria. I know that to some of you all that I have told of my country will seem a baseless fabric, with no more foundation, in fact, than More's fairy tale of another land where men dealt kindly and justly by one another, and dwelt, a whole nation, in the unity and equality of a family. But why should not a part of that fable have come true in our polity, as another part of it has come true in yours? When Sir Thomas More wrote that book, he noted with abhorrence the monstrous injustice of the fact that men were hanged for small thefts in England; and in the preliminary conversation between its characters he denounced the killing of men for any sort of thefts. Now you no longer put men to death for theft; you look back upon that cruel code of your mother England with an abhorrence as great as his own. We, for our part, who have realized the Utopian dream of brotherly equality, look back with the same abhorrence upon a state where some were rich and some poor, some taught and some untaught, some high and some low, and the hardest toil often failed to supply a sufficiency of the food which luxury wasted in its riots. That state seems as atrocious to us as the state which hanged a man for stealing a loaf of bread seems to you.

"But we do not regret the experience of competition and monopoly. They taught us some things in the operation of the industries. The labor-saving inventions which the Accumulation perverted to money-making, we have restored to the use intended by their inventors and the Creator of their inventors. After serving the advantage of socializing the industries which the Accumulation effected for its own purposes, we continued the work in large mills and shops, in the interest of the workers, whom we wished to guard against the evil effects of solitude. But our mills and shops are beautiful as well as useful. They look like temples, and they are temples, dedicated to that sympathy between the divine and human which expresses itself in honest and exquisite workmanship. They rise amid leafy boseages beside the streams, which form their only power; for we have disused steam altogether, with all the offenses to the eye and ear which its use brought into the world. Our life is so simple and our needs are so few that the handwork of the primitive toilers could easily supply our wants; but machinery works so much more thoroughly and beautifully that we have in great measure retained it. Only, the machines that were once the workman's enemies and masters are now their friends and servants; and if any man chooses to work alone with his own hands, the state will buy what he makes at the same price that it sells the wares made collectively. This secures every right of individuality.

"The farm work, as well as the mill work and the shop work, is done by companies of workers; and there is nothing of that loneliness in our woods and fields which, I understand, is the cause of so much insanity among you. It is not good for man to be alone, was the first thought of his Creator when he considered him, and we act upon this truth in everything. The privacy of the family is sacredly guarded in essentials, but the social instinct is so highly developed with us that we like to eat together in large refectories, and we meet constantly to argue and dispute on questions of æsthetics and metaphysics. We do not, perhaps, read so many books as you do, for most of our reading, when not for special research, but for culture and entertainment, is done by public readers, to large groups of listeners. We have no social meetings which are not free to all; and we encourage joking and the friendly give and take of witty encounters."

"A little hint from Sparta," suggested the professor.

The banker leaned over to whisper to me, "From what I have seen of your friend when offered a piece of American humor, I should fancy the

Altrurian article was altogether different. Upon the whole, I would rather not be present at one of their witty encounters, if I were obliged to stay it out."

The Altrurian had paused to drink a glass of water, and now he went on: "But we try, in everything that does not inconvenience or injure others, to let every one live the life he likes best. If a man prefers to dwell apart, and have his meals in private for himself alone, or for his family, it is freely permitted; only he must not expect to be served as in public, where service is one of the voluntaries; private service is not permitted; those wishing to live alone must wait upon themselves, cook their own food and care for their own tables. Very few, however, wish to withdraw from the public life, for most of the discussions and debates take place at our midday meal, which falls at the end of the obligatory labors, and is prolonged indefinitely, or as long as people like to chat and joke, or listen to the reading of some pleasant book.

"In Altruria *there is no hurry*, for no one wishes to outstrip another, or in anywise surpass him. We are all assured of enough, and are forbidden any and every sort of superfluity. If any one, after the obligatories, wishes to be entirely idle, he may be so, but I cannot now think of a single person without some voluntary occupation; doubtless there are such persons, but I do not know them. It used to be said, in the old times, that 'it was human nature' to shirk and malinger and loaf, but we have found that it is no such thing. We have found that it is human nature to work cheerfully, willingly, eagerly at the tasks which all share for the supply of the common necessities. In like manner we have found out that it is not human nature to hoard and grudge, but that when the fear, and even the imagination, of want is taken away, it is human nature to give and to help generously. We used to say, 'A man will lie, or a man will cheat in his own interest; that is human nature;' but that is no longer human nature with us, perhaps because no man has any interest to serve; he has only the interests of others to serve, while others serve his. It is in nowise possible for the individual to separate his good from the common good; he is prosperous and happy only as all the rest are so; and therefore it is not human nature with us for any one to lie in wait to betray another or seize an advantage. That would be ungentlemanly, and in Altruria every man is a gentleman, and every woman a lady. If you will excuse me here, for being so frank, I would like to say something by way of illustration, which may be offensive if you take it personally."

He looked at our little group, as if he were addressing himself more especially to us, and the banker called out jollily: "Go on! I guess we can stand it," and "Go ahead!" came from all sides, from all kinds of listeners.

"It is merely this: that as we look back at the old competitive conditions we do not see how any man could be a gentleman in them, since a gentleman must think first of others, and these conditions *compelled* every man to think first of himself."

There was a silence broken by some conscious and hardy laughter, while we each swallowed this pill as we could.

"What are competitive conditions?" Mrs. Makely demanded of me.

"Well, ours are competitive conditions," I said.

"Very well, then" she returned, "I don't think Mr. Homos is much of a gentleman to say such a thing to an American audience. Or, wait a moment! Ask him if the same rule applies to women!"

I rose, strengthened by the resentment I felt, and said, "Do I understand that in your former competitive conditions it was also impossible for a woman to be a lady?"

The professor gave me an applausive nod as I sat down. "I envy you the chance of that little dig," he whispered.

The Altrurian was thoughtful a moment, and then he answered: "No, I should not say it was. From what we know historically of those conditions in our country, it appears that the great mass of women were not directly affected by them. They constituted an altruistic dominion of the egoistic empire, and except as they were tainted by social or worldly ambitions, it was possible for every woman to be a lady, even in competitive conditions. Her instincts were unselfish, and her first thoughts were nearly always of others."

Mrs. Makely jumped to her feet, and clapped violently with her fan on the palm of her left hand. "Three cheers for Mr. Homos!" she shrieked, and all the women took up the cry, supported by all the natives and the construction gang. I fancied these fellows gave their support largely in a spirit of burlesque; but they gave it robustly, and from that time on, Mrs. Makely led the applause, and they roared in after her.

It is impossible to follow closely the course of the Altrurian's account of his country, which grew more and more incredible as he went on, and implied every insulting criticism of ours. Some one asked him about war in Altruria, and he said, "The very name of our country implies the absence of war. At the time of the Evolution our country bore to the rest of our continent the same relative proportion that your country bears to your continent. The egoistic nations to the north and the south of us entered into an offensive and defensive alliance to put down the new altruistic commonwealth, and declared war against us. Their forces were met at the frontier by our entire population in arms, and full of the martial spirit bred of the constant hostilities of the competitive and monopolistic epoch just ended. Negotiations began in the face of the imposing demonstration we made, and we were never afterward molested by our neighbors, who finally yielded to the spectacle of our civilization and united their political and social fate with ours. At present, our whole continent is Altrurian. For a long time we kept up a system of coast defenses, but it is also a long time since we abandoned these; for it is a maxim with us that where every citizen's life is a pledge of the public safety, that country can never be in danger of foreign enemies.

"In this, as in all other things, we believe ourselves the true followers of Christ, whose doctrine we seek to make our life as He made it His. We have several forms of ritual, but no form of creed, and our religious differences may be said to be æsthetic and temperamental rather than theological and essential. We have no denominations, for we fear in this, as in other matters, to give names to things lest we should cling to the names instead of the things. We love the realities, and for this reason we look at the life of a man rather than his profession for proof that he is a religious man.

"I have been several times asked, during my sojourn among you, what are the sources of compassion, of sympathy, of humanity, of charity with us, if we have not only no want, or fear of want, but not even any economic inequality. I suppose this is because you are so constantly struck by the misery arising from economic inequality, and want, or the fear of want, among yourselves, that you instinctively look in that direction. But have you ever seen sweeter compassion, tenderer sympathy, warmer humanity, heavenlier charity than that shown in the family where all are economically equal and no one can want while any other has to give? Altruria, I say again, is a family, and, as we are mortal, we are still subject to those nobler sorrows which God has appointed to men, and which are so different from the squalid accidents that they have made for themselves. Sickness and death call out the most angelic ministeries of love; and those who wish to give themselves to others may do so without hinderance from those cares, and even those duties, resting upon men where each must look out first for himself and for his own. Oh, believe me, believe me, you can know nothing of the divine rapture of self-sacrifice while you must dread the sacrifice of another in it! You are not *free*, as we are, to do everything for others, for it is your *duty* to do rather for those of your own household!

"There is something," he continued, "which I hardly know how to speak of," and here we all began to prick our ears. I prepared myself as well as I could for another affront, though I shuddered when the banker hardily called out: "Don't hesitate to say anything you wish, Mr. Homos. I, for one, should like to hear you express yourself fully."

It was always the unexpected, certainly, that happened from the Altrurian. "It is merely this," he said: "Having come to live rightly upon earth, as we believe, or having at least ceased to deny God in our statutes and customs, the fear of death, as it once weighed upon us, has been lifted from our souls. The mystery of it has so far been taken away that we perceive it as something just and natural. Now that all unkindness has been banished from among us, we can conceive of no such cruelty as death once seemed. If we do not know yet the full meaning of death, we know that the Creator of it and of us meant mercy and blessing by it. When one dies, we grieve, but not as those without hope. We do not say that the dead have gone to a better place, and then selfishly bewail them, for we have the kingdom of heaven upon earth already, and we know that wherever they go they will be homesick for Altruria; and when we think of the years that may pass before we meet them again our hearts ache, as they must. But the presence of the risen Christ in our daily lives is our assurance that no one ceases to be, and that we shall see our dead again. I cannot explain this to you; I can only affirm it."

The Altrurian spoke very solemnly, and a reverent hush fell upon the assembly. It was broken by the voice of a woman wailing out: "Oh, do you suppose, if *we* lived so, we should feel so, too? That I should *know* my little girl was living?"

"Why not?" asked the Altrurian.

To my vast astonishment, the manufacturer, who sat the farthest from me in the same line with Mrs. Makely, the professor, and the banker, rose and asked tremulously: "And have — have you had any direct communication with the other world? Has any disembodied spirit returned to testify of the life beyond the grave?"

The professor nodded significantly across Mrs. Makely to me, and then frowned and shook his head. I asked her if she knew what he meant. "Why, didn't you know that spiritualism was that poor man's foible? He lost his son in a railroad accident, and ever since — "

She stopped and gave her attention to the Altrurian, who was replying to the manufacturer's question.

"We do not need any such testimony. Our life here makes us sure of the life there. At any rate, no externation of the supernatural, no objective miracle, has been wrought in our behalf. We have had faith to do what we prayed for, and the prescience of which I speak has been added unto us."

The manufacturer asked, as the bereaved mother had asked: "And if I lived so, should I feel so?"

Again the Altrurian answered: "Why not?"

The poor woman quavered: "Oh, do believe it! I just *know* it must be true!"

The manufacturer shook his head sorrowfully and sat down, and remained there, looking at the ground.

"I am aware," the Altrurian went on, "that what I have said as to our realizing the kingdom of heaven on the earth must seem boastful and arrogant. That is what you pray for every day, but you do not believe it possible for God's will to be done on earth as it is done in heaven — that is, you do not if you are like the competitive and monopolistic people we once were. We once regarded that petition as a formula vaguely pleasing to the Deity, but we no more expected His kingdom to come than we expected Him to give us each day our daily bread; we knew that if we wanted something to eat we should have to hustle for it, and get there first; I use the slang of that far-off time, which, I confess, had a vulgar vigor.

"But now everything is changed, and the change has taken place chiefly from one cause — namely, the disuse of money. At first, it was thought that some sort of circulating medium *must* be used, that life could not be transacted without it. But life began to go on perfectly well, when each dwelt in the place assigned him, which was no better and no worse than any other; and when, after he had given his three hours a day to the obligatory labors, he had a right to his share of food, light, heat, and raiment; the voluntary labors, to which he gave much time or little, brought him no increase of those necessaries, but only credit and affection. We had always heard it said that the love of money was the root of all evil, but we had taken this for a saying, merely; now we realized it as an active, vital truth. As soon as money was abolished the power to purchase was gone, and even if there had been any means of buying beyond the daily needs, with overwork, the community had no power to sell to the individual. No man owned anything, but every man had the right to anything that he could use; when he could not use it, his right lapsed.

"With the expropriation of the individual the whole vast catalogue of crimes against property shrank to nothing. The thief could only steal from the community; but if he stole, what was he to do with his booty? It was still possible for a depredator to destroy, but few men's hate is so comprehensive as to include all other men, and when the individual could no longer hurt some other individual in his property destruction ceased.

"All the many murders done from love of money, or of what money could buy, were at an end. Where there was no want, men no longer bartered their souls, or women their bodies, for the means to keep themselves alive. The vices vanished with the crimes, and the diseases almost as largely disappeared. People were no longer sickened by sloth and surfeit, or deformed and depleted by overwork and famine. They were wholesomely housed in healthful places, and they were clad fitly for their labor and fitly for their leisure; the caprices of vanity were not suffered to attaint the beauty of the national dress.

"With the stress of superfluous social and business duties, and the perpetual fear of want which all classes felt, more or less; with the tumult of the cities and the solitude of the country, insanity had increased among us till the whole land was dotted with asylums, and the mad were numbered by hundreds of thousands. In every region they were an army, an awful army of anguish and despair. Now they have decreased to a number so small, and are of a type so mild, that we can hardly count insanity among our causes of unhappiness.

"We have totally eliminated chance from our economic life. There is still a chance that a man will be tall or short in Altruria, that he will be strong or weak, well or ill, gay or grave, happy or unhappy in love, but none that he will be rich or poor, busy or idle, live splendidly or meanly. These stupid and vulgar accidents of human contrivance cannot befall us; but I shall not be able to tell you just how or why, or to detail the process of eliminating chance. I may say, however, that it began with the nationalization of telegraphs, expresses, railroads, mines, and all large industries operated by stock companies. This at once struck a fatal blow at the speculation in values, real and unreal, and at the stock exchange, or bourse; we had our own name for that gambler's paradise, or gambler's hell, whose baleful influence penetrated every branch of business.

"There were still business fluctuations as long as we had business, but they were on a smaller and smaller scale, and with the final lapse of business they necessarily vanished; all economic chance vanished. The founders of the commonwealth understood perfectly that business was the sterile activity of the function interposed between the demand and the supply; that it was nothing structural; and they intended its extinction, and expected it from the moment that money was abolished."

"This is all pretty tiresome," said the professor, to our immediate party. "I don't see why we oblige ourselves to listen to that fellow's stuff. As if a civilized state could exist for a day without money or business."

He went on to give his opinion of the Altrurian's pretended description, in a tone so audible that it attracted the notice of the nearest group of railroad hands, who were listening closely to Homos, and one of them sang out to the professor: "Can't you wait and let the first man finish?" and another yelled: "Put him out!" and then they all laughed with a humorous perception of the impossibility of literally executing the suggestion.

By the time all was quiet again I heard the Altrurian saying: "As to our social life, I cannot describe it in detail, but I can give you some notion of its spirit. We make our pleasures civic and public as far as possible, and the ideal is inclusive, and not exclusive. There are, of course, festivities which all cannot share, but our distribution into small communities favors the possibility of all doing so. Our daily life, however, is so largely social that we seldom meet by special invitation or engagement. When we do, it is with the perfect understanding that the assemblage confers with no social distinction, but is for a momentary convenience. In fact, these occasions are rather avoided, recalling as they do the vapid and tedious entertainments of the competitive epoch, the receptions and balls and dinners of a semi-barbaric people striving for social prominence by shutting a certain number in and a certain number out, and overdressing, overfeeding, and overdrinking. Anything premeditated in the way of a pleasure we think stupid and mistaken; we like to meet suddenly, or on the spur of the moment, out of doors, if possible, and arrange a picnic, or a dance, or a play; and let people come and go without ceremony. No one is more host than guest; all are hosts and guests. People consort much according to their tastes — literary, musical, artistic, scientific, or mechanical — but these tastes are made approaches, not barriers; and we find out that we have many more tastes in common than was formerly supposed.

"But, after all, our life is serious, and no one among us is quite happy, in the general esteem, unless he has dedicated himself, in some special way, to the general good. Our ideal is not rights, but duties."

"Mazzini!"[12] whispered the professor.

"The greatest distinction which any one can enjoy with us is to have found out some new and signal way of serving the community; and then it is not good form for him to seek recognition. The doing any fine thing is the purest pleasure it can give; applause flatters, but it hurts, too, and our benefactors, as we call them, have learned to shun it.

"We are still far from thinking our civilization perfect; but we are sure that our civic ideals are perfect. What we have already accomplished is to have given a whole continent perpetual peace; to have founded an economy in which there is no possibility of want; to have killed out political and social ambition; to have disused money and eliminated

---

[12] Giuseppe Mazzini (1805–1872), the Italian patriot, revolutionary, and writer, devoted his entire life to the cause of achieving Italian unity and nationhood.

chance; to have realized the brotherhood of the race, and to have outlived the fear of death."

The Altrurian suddenly stopped with these words, and sat down. He had spoken a long time, and with a fullness which my report gives little notion of; but, though most of his cultivated listeners were weary, and a good many ladies had left their seats and gone back to the hotel, not one of the natives, or the work-people of any sort, had stirred; now they remained a moment motionless and silent before they rose from all parts of the field and shouted: "Go on! Don't stop! Tell us all about it!"

I saw Reuben Camp climb the shoulders of a big fellow near where the Altrurian had stood; he waved the crowd to silence with outspread arms. "He isn't going to say anything more; he's tired. But if any man don't think he's got his dollar's worth, let him walk up to the door and the ticket-agent will refund him his money."

The crowd laughed, and some one shouted: "Good for you, Reub!"

Camp continued: "But our friend here will shake the hand of any man, woman, or child that wants to speak to him; and you needn't wipe it on the grass, first, either. He's a *man!* And I want to say that he's going to spend the next week with us, at my mother's house, and we shall be glad to have you call."

The crowd, the rustic and ruder part of it, cheered and cheered till the mountain echoes answered; then a railroader called for three times three, with a tiger, and got it. The guests of the hotel broke away and went toward the house over the long shadows of the meadow. The lower classes pressed forward, on Camp's invitation.

"Well, did you ever hear a more disgusting rigmarole?" asked Mrs. Makely, as our little group halted indecisively about her.

"With all those imaginary commonwealths to draw upon, from Plato, through More, Bacon, and Campanella, down to Bellamy and Morris, he has constructed the shakiest effigy ever made of old clothes stuffed with straw," said the professor.

The manufacturer was silent. The banker said: "I don't know. He grappled pretty boldly with your insinuations. That frank declaration that Altruria was all these pretty soap-bubble worlds solidified was rather fine."

"It was splendid!" cried Mrs. Makely. The lawyer and the minister came towards us from where they had been sitting together. She called out to them: "Why in the world didn't one of you gentlemen get up and propose a vote of thanks?"

"The difficulty with me is," continued the banker, "that he has rendered Altruria incredible. I have no doubt that he is an Altrurian, but I doubt very much if he comes from anywhere in particular, and I find this quite a blow, for we had got Altruria nicely located on the map, and were beginning to get accounts of it in the newspapers."

"Yes, that is just exactly the way I feel about it," sighed Mrs. Makely. "But still, don't you think there ought to have been a vote of thanks, Mr. Bullion?"

"Why, certainly. The fellow was immensely amusing, and you must have got a lot of money by him. It was an oversight not to make him a formal acknowledgment of some kind. If we offered him money, he would have to leave it all behind him here when he went home to Altruria."

"Just as *we* do when we go to heaven," I suggested; the banker did not answer, and I instantly felt that in the presence of the minister my remark was out of taste.

"Well, then, don't you think," said Mrs. Makely, who had a leathery insensibility to everything but the purpose possessing her, "that we ought at least to go and say something to him personally?"

"Yes, I thing we ought," said the banker, and we all walked up to where the Altrurian stood, still thickly surrounded by the lower classes, who were shaking hands with him, and getting in a word with him now and then.

One of the construction gang said, carelessly: "No all-rail route to Altruria, I suppose?"

"No," answered Homos, "it's a far sea voyage."

"Well, I shouldn't mind working my passage, if you think they'd let me stay after I got there."

"Ah, you mustn't go to Altruria! You must let Altruria come to *you*," returned Homos, with that confounded smile of his that always won my heart.

"Yes," shouted Reuben Camp, whose thin face was red with excitement, "that's the word! Have Altruria right here, and right now!"

The old farmer, who had several times spoken, cackled out: "I didn't know, one while, when you was talk'n' about not havin' no money, but what some on us had had Altrury here for quite a spell, already. I don't pass more'n fifty dolla's through my hands most years."

A laugh went up, and then, at sight of Mrs. Makely heading our little party, the people round Homos civilly made way for us. She rushed upon him, and seized his hand in both of hers; she dropped her fan, parasol, gloves, handkerchief, and vinaigrette in the grass to do so. "Oh, Mr. Homos!" she fluted, and the tears came into her eyes, "it was beautiful, *beautiful*, every word of it! I sat in a perfect trance from beginning to end, and I felt that it was all as true as it was beautiful. People all around me were breathless with interest, and I don't know how I can ever thank you enough."

"Yes, indeed," the professor hastened to say, before the Altrurian could answer, and he beamed malignantly upon him through his spectacles while he spoke; "it was like some strange romance."

"I don't know that I should go so far as that," said the banker, in his turn, "but it certainly seemed too good to be true."

"Yes," the Altrurian responded simply, but a little sadly; "now that I am away from it all, and in conditions so different, I sometimes had to ask myself, as I went on, if my whole life had not hitherto been a dream, and Altruria were not some blessed vision of the night."

"Then you know how to account for a feeling which I must acknowledge, too?" the lawyer asked courteously. "But it was most interesting."

"The kingdom of God upon earth," said the minister, "it ought not to be incredible; but that, more than anything else you told us of, gave me pause."

"You of all men?" returned the Altrurian, gently.

"Yes," said the minister, with a certain dejection, "when I remember what I have seen of men, when I reflect what human nature is, how can I believe that the kingdom of God will ever come upon the earth?"

"But in heaven, where He reigns, who is it does His will? The spirits of men?" pursued the Altrurian.

"Yes, but conditioned as men are here — "

"But if they were conditioned as men are there?"

"Now, I can't let you two good people get into a theological dispute," Mrs. Makely pushed in. "Here is Mr. Twelvemough dying to shake hands with Mr. Homos and compliment his distinguished guest!"

"Ah, Mr. Homos knows what I must have thought of his talk without my telling him," I began, skillfully. "But I am sorry that I am to lose my distinguished guest so soon!"

Reuben Camp broke out: "That was my blunder, Mr. Twelvemough. Mr. Homos and I had talked it over conditionally, and I was not to speak of it till he had told you; but it slipped out in the excitement of the moment."

"Oh, it's all right," I said, and I shook hands cordially with both of them. "It will be the greatest possible advantage for Mr. Homos to see certain phases of American life at close range, and he couldn't possibly see them under better auspices than yours, Camp."

"Yes, I'm going to drive him through the hill country after haying, and then I'm going to take him down and show him one of our big factory towns."

I believe this was done, but finally the Altrurian went on to New York, where he was to pass the winter. We parted friends; I even offered him some introductions; but his acquaintance had become more and more difficult, and I was not sorry to part with him. That taste of his for low company was incurable, and I was glad that I was not to be responsible any longer for whatever strange thing he might do next. I think he remained very popular with the classes he most affected; a throng of natives, construction hands, and table-girls saw him off on his train; and he left large numbers of such admirers in our house and neighborhood, devout in the faith that there was such a commonwealth as Altruria, and that he was really an Altrurian. As for the more cultivated people who had met him, they continued of two minds upon both points.

A Howells Chronology
(1837–1920)

1837: William Dean Howells born in Belmont County, eastern Ohio, March 1.

1840: Family moves to Hamilton, Ohio.

1850: Nathaniel Hawthorne's *The Scarlet Letter*.

1851: Herman Melville's *Moby-Dick*.

1852: Family moves to Jefferson, Ohio. His first publication: a poem in the *Ohio State Journal*. Harriet Beecher Stowe's *Uncle Tom's Cabin*.

1855: Walt Whitman's *Leaves of Grass*.

1856: Works at the *Ohio State Journal* in Columbus until 1861.

1859: John Brown raids Harpers Ferry.

1860: Publishes his first book, *Poems of Two Friends*, with John J. Piatt. Publishes his campaign biography, *Life of Lincoln*.

1861: Appointed American consul in Venice. Civil War begins in April.

1862: Marries Elinor Mead, December 24.

1865: Returns to the United States and goes to work for the *Nation*. Lincoln assassinated. Civil War ends.

1866: Leaves *Nation* to become assistant editor of *Atlantic Monthly* and moves to Cambridge, Massachusetts. Begins lifelong friendship with Henry James.

1869: Begins lifelong friendship with Samuel Clemens (Mark Twain).

1871: Elevated to editor-in-chief of the *Atlantic*.

1872: Publishes *Their Wedding Journey*.

1873: Mark Twain and Charles Dudley Warner's *The Gilded Age*. Depression of the 1870s starts.

1877: Violent strikes on the nation's railroad system.

1879: Publishes *The Lady of Aroostook*. Henry George's *Progress and Poverty*.

1881: Leaves the *Atlantic* after fifteen years.

1882: Publishes *A Modern Instance.*

1885: Publishes *The Rise of Silas Lapham.* Mark Twain's *The Adventures of Huckleberry Finn.*

1886: Begins his long connection with *Harper's Monthly.* Publishes *Indian Summer.* Haymarket riot in Chicago.

1887: Becomes a leader in the fight to save the Chicago anarchists. Publishes *The Minister's Charge.*

1888: Edward Bellamy's *Looking Backward.*

1889: Publishes *Annie Kilburn.*

1890: Publishes *A Hazard of New Fortunes.*

1891: Moves to New York City.

1892: Edits *Cosmopolitan* briefly. Chapters of *A Traveler from Altruria* begin to appear in *Cosmopolitan,* starting in November. Populist party is formed.

1893: Last installment of *Traveler* appears in October. Start of an economic depression that lasts until 1897.

1894: *Traveler* appears in book form in May. Jacob Coxey's "army" of unemployed march on Washington, D.C. Pullman strike in Chicago. Henry Demarest Lloyd's *Wealth against Commonwealth.*

1895: Publishes *My Literary Passions.*

1896: William McKinley defeats William Jennings Bryan in presidential election.

1899: Thorstein Veblen's *The Theory of the Leisure Class.*

1900: Theodore Dreiser's *Sister Carrie.*

1901: Eugene V. Debs founds the Socialist party. McKinley assassinated; Theodore Roosevelt becomes president.

1907: Publishes *Through the Eye of the Needle.*

1910: Elinor Howells dies. Samuel Clemens dies.

1916: Publishes *The Leatherwood God,* his last novel, and also *Years of My Youth.*

1920: Dies in New York City, May 11.

Questions for Consideration

1. The Altrurian advocates a society based on true equality. What does Howells mean by *equality*? Would most Americans define the term the same way as he does?
2. To what extent are Howells's criticisms of American life based on economic considerations and to what extent do they spring from aesthetic or artistic feelings?
3. Howells seems to argue that there is a gulf between the moral principles of traditional Christianity and both the practical and the ideological aspects of modern business. What does he see as the central tensions between these two realms? How would a businessperson who also thought of her- or himself as a Christian answer Howells?
4. Do you think most Americans, either from the nineteenth century or from our own time, would be happy in Altruria? Why or why not?
5. One of Howells's contentions is that the unrestrained freedom of American capitalism has many negative results for the society as a whole. What are some of those negative results and how does Howells propose to correct them?
6. Is it possible to distill from Howells's descriptions of his women characters, and from other remarks he makes about women, a coherent picture of what he believes to be the traits and attitudes of an ideal woman?
7. Americans have always prized and praised individualism. What does Howells think about that national ideal?
8. Is there a view of human nature behind the social, economic, and political arrangements of Altruria? How plausible is Howells's view of human character and motivations? If you think that he has got the picture of what men and women are like all wrong, do you think that "real" men and women could establish a society such as Altruria?
9. What does Howells think about money?
10. What does Howells think about technology?
11. What does Howells think about cities?
12. What is Howells trying to say about law by means of the character of the lawyer? About religion by means of the character of the minister? About modern culture by means of the character of the novelist? About college and university attitudes by means of the character of the professor?
13. Does Howells believe that there are serious incompatibilities between

college and university education and a life in business? How would you evaluate his arguments on this particular matter?

14. What does the Altrurian's description of his own society leave out? If you had been a member of his audience, and if there was a time for questions at the end, what would you have liked to ask him?

Selected Bibliography

The scholarly attention that has been bestowed upon the life and work of William Dean Howells has been enormous — as is fitting for so prolific and prominent a figure in the history of American letters. The titles listed here represent nothing more than likely places for curious readers to start their inquiries. Nearly all of the books and articles suggested below carry their own notes and bibliographies which will assist researchers as they delve deeper and deeper into their work.

The basic listing of Howells's own writings is William M. Gibson and George Arms, *A Bibliography of William Dean Howells* (New York: New York Public Library, 1948). That list is supplemented in Jacob Blanck, "William Dean Howells," in *Bibliography of American Literature* (New Haven: Yale University Press, 1963), 384–88. While not a substitute for actually reading Howells himself, helpful brief plot summaries of his major works can be found in George C. Carrrington, Jr., and Ildiko dePapp Carrington, *Plots and Characters in the Fiction of William Dean Howells* (Hamden, Conn.: Archon, 1976). There have been several published collections of critical responses to Howells. Clayton L. Eichelberger, *Published Comment on William Dean Howells through 1920: A Research Bibliography* (Boston: G. K. Hall, 1976) is a good place to begin studying the reactions to Howells while he was still alive; and Edwin H. and Norma W. Cady, *Critical Essays on W. D. Howells, 1866–1920* (Boston: G. K. Hall, 1983) reprints a generous sampling of that contemporary criticism. Later commentary is surveyed in James Woodress and Stanley P. Anderson, "A Bibliography of Writing about William Dean Howells," *American Literary Realism,* Special Issue (1969): 1–139. Two additional compilations of Howells criticism are also useful: Kenneth E. Eble, ed., *Howells: A Century of Criticism* (Dallas: Southern Methodist University Press, 1962) and Paul A. Eschholz, ed., *Critics on William Dean Howells* (Coral Gables: University of Miami Press, 1975). And for the latest word see two essays by Howells scholar John W. Crowley, "Howells in the Seventies: A Review of Criticism," *ESQ: A Journal of the American Renaissance* 25 (1979), and "Howells in the Eighties: A Review of Criticism," *ESQ: A Journal of the American Renaissance* 32 (1986).

There have been several biographies of Howells, but the two that have emerged as standards are Kenneth S. Lynn, *William Dean Howells: An American Life* (New York: Harcourt Brace Jovanovich, 1971) and the two volumes by Edwin H. Cady, *The Road to Realism: The Early Years, 1837–1885, of William Dean Howells* and *The Realist at War: The Mature Years, 1885–1920, of William Dean Howells* (Syracuse: Syracuse University Press, 1956, 1958). Other worthy biographies have been written by Oscar Firkins (1924), Van Wyck Brooks (1959), and Edward Wagenknecht (1969). Two perceptive and charming older essays on Howells should not be ignored; they are Alfred Kazin, *On Native Grounds: A Study of American Prose Literature from 1890 to the Present* (New York: Harcourt, Brace & Co, 1942), chap. 1; and Daniel Aaron, "William Dean Howells: The Gentleman from Altruria," in his *Men of Good Hope* (New York: Oxford University Press, 1951), chap. 5.

Two particular aspects of Howells's life have received especially interesting treatment. His troubled youth is examined in a pioneering article, Edwin H. Cady, "The Neuroticism of William Dean Howells," *Publication of the Modern Language Association* 61 (1946): 229–38, and in a pair of excellent recent monographs, John W. Crowley, *The Black Heart's Truth: The Early Career of W. D. Howells* (Chapel Hill: University of North Carolina Press, 1985) and Rodney D. Olsen, *Dancing in Chains: The Youth of William Dean Howells* (New York: New York University Press, 1991). Howells's social, political, and economic views, including his steady march toward the democratic socialism espoused in *A Traveler from Altruria*, are traced expertly in Robert Hough, *The Quiet Rebel: William Dean Howells as a Social Commentator* (Lincoln: University of Nebraska Press, 1959); Clara M. Kirk, *W. D. Howells, Traveler from Altruria, 1889–1894* (New Brunswick: Rutgers University Press, 1962); and William R. H. Alexander, *William Dean Howells: The Realist as Humanist* (New York: B. Franklin, 1981).

The cultural environment Howells helped to define and in which he labored is explored superbly in David E. Shi, *Facing Facts: Realism in American Thought and Culture, 1850–1920* (New York: Oxford University Press, 1995) and in H. Wayne Morgan, *Unity and Culture: The United States, 1877–1900* (London: The Penguin Press, 1971). Within that cultural setting, literature is examined in Jay Martin, *Harvests of Change: American Literature, 1865–1914* (Englewood Cliffs, N. J.: Prentice-Hall, 1967); Warner Berthoff, *The Ferment of Realism: American Literature, 1884–1919* (New York: Free Press, 1965); Daniel H. Borus, *Writing Realism: Howells, James, and Norris in the Mass Market* (Chapel Hill: University of North Carolina Press, 1989); Eric Sundquist, ed., *American Realism: New Essays* (Baltimore: Johns Hopkins University Press, 1982); and Amy Kaplan, *The Social Construction of American Realism* (Chicago: University of Chicago Press, 1988). For the vogue of utopian fiction during this period, see Robert L. Shurter, *The Utopian Novel in America, 1865–1900* (New York: AMS Press, 1973); Jean Pfaelzer, *The Utopian Novel in America, 1886–1896: The Politics of Form* (Pittsburgh: University of Pittsburgh Press, 1984); or Kenneth M. Roemer, *The Obsolete Necessity: America in Utopian Writings, 1888–1900* (Kent, Ohio: Kent State University Press, 1976). The defining work on the mysterious-stranger story is Roy R. Male, *Enter, Mysterious Stranger: American Cloistral Fiction* (Norman: University of Oklahoma Press, 1979).

The economic and social conditions that caused Howells and others such profound concern have also been treated in numerous first-rate scholarly studies. Two older but still quite serviceable general surveys of the period are Samuel Hays, *The Response to Industrialism, 1885–1914* (Chicago: University of Chicago Press, 1957) and Robert H. Wiebe, *The Search for Order, 1877–1920* (New York: Hill and Wang, 1967). Also valuable are two volumes from the New American Nation Series: John Garraty, *The New Commonwealth, 1877–1890* (New York: Harper and Row, 1968) and Harold U. Faulkner, *Politics, Reform, and Expansion, 1890–1900* (New York: Harper and Row, 1959). Alan Trachtenberg, *The Incorporation of America: Culture and Society in the Gilded Age* (New York: Hill and Wang, 1982) is filled with provocative insights. For American business and industry in this period, a fine place to start is Alfred D. Chandler, *Visible Hand: The Managerial Revolution in American Business* (Cambridge, Mass.: Belknap Press, 1977). Also helpful on this topic is Glenn Porter, *The Rise of Big Business, 1860–1910* (New York: Crowell, 1973); Thomas Cochran and William Miller, *The Age of Enterprise: A Social History of Industrial America* (New York: Macmillan, 1942); and Edward C. Kirkland, *Industry Comes of Age: Business, Labor, and Public Policy, 1860–1897* (New York: Holt, Rinehart and Winston, 1961).

Those displaced and cast aside by the growth of business and industry have also been studied extensively by historians. For American workers, see David Montgomery, *The Fall of the House of Labor: The Workplace, the State, and American Labor Activism, 1865–1925* (New York: Cambridge University Press, 1987) and Herbert Gutman, *Work, Culture, and Society in Industrializing America: Essays in American Working-Class and Social History* (New York: Knopf, 1976). Interesting accounts of the traumatic labor strife of the late nineteenth century can be found in Robert V. Bruce, *1877: The Year of Violence* (Chicago: Quadrangle Books, 1970); Paul Avrich, *The Haymarket Tragedy* (Princeton: Princeton University Press, 1984); or two excellent accounts of a particularly important strike that occurred just before Howells began to write *A Traveler from Altruria*: Paul Krause, *The Battle for Homestead, 1880–1892: Politics, Culture and Steel* (Pittsburgh: University of Pittsburgh Press, 1992) and David P. Demarest, *"The River Ran Red": Homestead 1892* (Pittsburgh: University of Pittsburgh Press, 1992). The special problems of women workers are addressed in Alice Kessler-Harris, *Out to Work: A History of Wage-Earning Women in the United States* (New York: Oxford University Press, 1982) and Susan E. Kennedy, *If All We Did Was To Weep at Home: A History of White Working-Class Women in America* (Bloomington: Indiana University Press, 1979). Balanced and competent histories of American socialism include Howard Quint, *The Forging of American Socialism* (Columbia: University of South Carolina Press, 1953); David Shannon, *The Socialist Party of America: A History* (Chicago: Quadrangle Books, 1976); and Paul Buhle, *Marxism in the United States: Remapping the History of the American Left* (London: Verso, 1987).

On farmers, see the pioneering work by Fred A. Shannon, *The Farmer's Last Frontier: Agriculture, 1860–1897* (New York: Farrar and Rinehart, 1945) or Lawrence Goodwyn, *Democratic Promise: The Populist Movement in America* (New York: Oxford University Press, 1976). For the plight of African Americans, see John Hope Franklin and Alfred A. Moss, Jr., *From Slavery to Freedom: A History of African Americans* (New York: Knopf, 1994), chaps. 12–15; Leon Litwack, *Been in the Storm So Long: The Aftermath of Slavery* (New York: Knopf, 1979); or Rayford W. Logan, *The Betrayal of the Negro: From Rutherford B. Hayes to Woodrow Wilson* (New York: Collier, 1965). For the situation of urban blacks, see the early chapters of the pioneering study, Gilbert Osofsky, *Harlem: The Making of a Ghetto: Negro New York, 1890–1930* (New York: Harper and Row, 1966). August Meier, *Negro Thought in America: Racial Ideologies in the Age of Booker T. Washington* (Ann Arbor: University of Michigan Press, 1963) is a pathbreaking attempt to examine the response of black leaders and intellectuals to the pervasive racism of American society. For a first-hand look at the urban poor, see the classic journalistic account by Jacob Riis, *How the Other Half Lives: Studies Among the Tenements of New York* (Boston: Bedford Books of St. Martin's Press, 1996 edition). See also Paul Boyer, *Urban Masses and Moral Order in America, 1820–1920* (Cambridge, Mass.: Harvard University Press, 1978) and Robert Bremner, *The Discovery of Poverty in the United States* (New Brunswick: Transaction Publishers, 1992 edition). On immigrants, see Thomas J. Archdeacon, *Becoming American: An Ethnic History* (New York: Free Press, 1983) or Alan M. Kraut, *The Huddled Masses: The Immigrant in American Society, 1880–1921* (Arlington Heights, Ill.: Harlan Davidson, 1982).

That the economic developments and social dislocations of the late nineteenth century had repercussions on American social thought should go without saying. It is possible to list only a few of the most suggestive and original of the dozens of important studies of American intellectual life during this period. R. Jackson Wilson, *In Quest of Community: Social Philosophy in the United States, 1860–1920* (New York: Wiley, 1968) shows how many intellectuals in various fields sought for some alternative to the rampant individualism they saw threatening the nation's stability and morality. John L. Thomas, *Alternative America: Henry George, Edward Bellamy, Henry Demarest Lloyd, and the Adversary Tradition* (Cambridge, Mass.: Harvard University Press, 1983) discusses the attempts of those three early reformers to invent a better social system than the one that so offended their sensibilities. Sidney Fine, *Laissez-Faire and the General-Welfare State: A Study of Conflict in American Thought* (Ann Arbor: University of Michigan Press, 1956) still holds up very well as an introduction to conflict in economic, social, and religious thought. The literature on the social effects of Darwin's theory of evolution is vast, but a good beginning can be made with Cynthia Eagle Russett, *Darwin in America: The Intellectual Response, 1865–1912* (San Francisco: Freeman, 1976) or with Robert Bannister, *Social Darwinism: Science and Myth in Anglo-American Social Thought* (Philadelphia: Temple University Press, 1979).

An exciting but difficult study of social thought in both America and Europe is James T. Kloppenberg, *Uncertain Victory: Social Democracy and*

Progressivism in European and American Thought, 1870–1920 (New York: Oxford University Press, 1986). R. Jeffrey Lustig, *Corporate Liberalism: The Origins of Modern American Political Theory, 1890–1920* (Berkeley: University of California Press, 1982) is an important interpretation of the evolution of modern liberalism. T. J. Jackson Lears, *No Place of Grace: Antimodernism and the Transformation of American Culture, 1880–1920* (New York: Pantheon, 1981) is a stimulating account of those intellectuals who recoiled from the new America of the Gilded Age. Finally, one should not ignore two illuminating essays by Dorothy Ross: "Liberalism," in Jack P. Greene, ed., *Encyclopedia of American Political History: Studies of the Principal Movements and Ideas* (New York: Scribner, 1984), 750–63, and "Socialism and American Liberalism: Academic Social Thought in the 1880s," *Perspectives in American History* 11 (1977–78): 5–80.

The upsetting impact of social, economic, and intellectual developments on American religion is explored in Paul A. Carter, *The Spiritual Crisis of the Gilded Age* (DeKalb: Northern Illinois University Press, 1971); George W. Marsden, *Fundamentalism and American Culture: The Shaping of Twentieth-Century Evangelicalism, 1870–1925* (New York: Oxford University Press, 1980); and Ferenc M. Szasz, *The Divided Mind of Protestant America, 1880–1930* (University, Ala.: University of Alabama Press, 1982). An excellent essay is Donald H. Meyer, "American Intellectuals and the Victorian Crisis of Faith," in Daniel W. Howe, ed., *Victorian America* (Philadelphia: University of Pennsylvania Press, 1976). For the story of American skepticism and atheism, consult James Turner, *Without God, Without Creed: The Origins of Unbelief in America* (Baltimore: Johns Hopkins University Press, 1985).

Index

Boldface entries indicate characters in the novel.